AF529483

INFORMATION ACCESS, MANAGEMENT AND EXCHANGE IN THE TECHNOLOGICAL AGE

INFORMATION ACCESS, MANAGEMENT AND EXCHANGE IN THE TECHNOLOGICAL AGE

Editors

Dr. M Bavakutty

M C K Veeran

T K Muhammed Salih

Ess Ess Publications

4837/24, Ansari Road, Darya Ganj,
New Delhi-110002
✆ : 3260807, 3201533
Fax : 3274173
E-mail: essess@del3.vsnl.net.in
url:http://www.essessbooks.com

First Published 2003

ISBN : 81-7000-354-7

Price : Rs. 875/-

Published by :

Ess Ess Publications

4837/24, Ansari Road, Darya Ganj,
New Delhi - 110 002
Phone : 3260807
Fax : 3274173
E-mail : essess@del3.vsnl.net.in
url:http://www.essessbooks.com

Laser Typesetting:

Mukesh Graphics

L-2/8, DDA Market,
Mangolepuri, New Delhi
Ph. : 7924405

Printed at :

Print Line

List of Authors

1. Prof. C. A. Augustine
Library and Information Science Consultant
Nancheriyil Garden,
Ozhukupara,
Vattappara,
Trivandrum – 695 028.

2. K C Abdul Majeed,
Lecturer,
Dept. of Library & Inf. Science,
Farook College,
Calicut – 673 632.

3. S. Ally Sornam
Head,
Department of Library and Information Science,
Bishop Heber College,
Tiruchy – 620 017, Tamilnadu.

4. Arifa. k.,
Junior Research Fellow,
Department of Library and Information Science,
University of Calicut – 673 635

5. Prof. (Dr.) M. Bavakutty,
Professor & Head,
Dept. of Library & Inf. Science,
University of Calicut.

6. R. Biju,
Library and Information Center,
Indian Institute of Management,
Kozhikode – 673 601

7. Dinesan. K.
Junior Librarian,
Dept. of Anthropology,
Kannur University,
Thalassery Campus, Palayad P.O.,
Kannur Dt.

8. R. Dhanapal,
Head, Department of Computer Science,
Bishop Heber College,
Tiruchirappalli-620 017, Tamil Nadu.

9. G. Dhanasegaran,
Deputy Librarian,
Dr.T.P.M Library,
M.K. University,
Madurai-625021, Tamilnadu.

10. J. Dominic,
Assistant Librarian,
Karunya Institute of Technology,
Coimbatore-641 114.

11. A.C. Ganesh
Chief Web Writer,
Express Network Private Limited,
Express Internet Division,
Chennai-600002, Tamilnadu

12. K.H. Hussain,
Documentation Officer,
Kerala Forest Research Institute,Peechi,
Kerala 68056.

13. Jyoti Misra,
Assistant Librarian,
Tagore Library,
Lucknow University,
Lucknow – 226 007 (UP).

14. Manjunatha. K.
Librarian,
T.A. Pai Management Institute,
Manipal – 576 119, Karnataka.

15. P. Mounissamy,
Library, Assistant
Regional Engineering College,
Thiruchirapalli-15.

16. Mohamed Haneefa. K.,
Research Scholar,
Dept. of Library & Inf. Science,
University of Calicut.

17. Musthafa. K.M.,
Department of Library and Information Science,
Aligarh Muslim University,
Aligarh—202 002.

18. Noushad Ali P.M.,
Lecturer, Department of Library and Information Science,
Aligarh Muslim University,
Aligarh—202002.

19. T.P.O. Nasirudheen,
Lecturer & Head,
Dept. of Library & Inf. Science,
Farook College,
Calicut – 673 632.

20. Dr. M. Nagarajan
Reader,
Department of Library and Information Science,
Annamalai University,
Annamalai Nagar-608002, Tamilnadu.

21. M. Natarajan
Scientist,
INSDOC Regional Centre,
CSIR Madras Complex,
Taramani, Chennai – 600 113.

22. K. Nithiakalyani
Student,
PG Department of Library and Information Science,
Bishop Heber College,
Tiruchy – 620 017, Tamilnadu.

23. P.J. Nirmala,
Librarian,
Karunya Institute of Technology,
Coimbatore-641 114.

24. P.P. Noufal,
Research Associate,
Library and Information Center,
Indian Institute of Management,
Kozhikode – 673 601

25. Prof. A. Neelameghan,
216, 4th Main Road,
16th Cross Road,
Bangalore-560 055.

26. K. Prasanna,
Library and Information Center,
Indian Institute of Management,
Kozhikode – 673 601

27. Dr. Rabinarayan Mishra,
Workshop Instructor,
P.G. Dept. of Lib. & Inf. Science,
Sambalpur University,
Jyoti Vihar –768 019, Orissa.

28. Ramesha,
Assistant Librarian,
University Library,
Karnatak University,
Dharwad - 580 003.

29. C.P. Ramasesh
Deputy Librarian,
Mysore University Library,
Manasagangotri, Mysore – 570 006.

30. P. Rajendran,
Librarian,
S.R.M. Engineering College,
S.R.M. Nagar, Kattankulathur – 603 203.

31. Dr. K. S. Raghavan
Professor and Head,
Department of Library and Information Science,
Madras University,
Chepauk Building, Chennai - 600005.

32. R. Raman Nair,
Librarian,
Govt. Brennen College,
Thalassery.

33. K. Raveendran Asari,
Head,
Department of Medical Documentation,
Mahatma Gandhi University,
Kottayam – 68600.

34. Dr. S. Surianarayanan,
Librarian,
Sri Paramakalyani College,
Alwarkurichi- 627412, Tamilnadu.

35. M.G. Sreekumar,
Librarian,
Indian Institute of Management Kozhikode (IIMK),
REC P.O.,
Calicut – 673 601.

36. Dr. R. Samyuktha,
Deputy Librarian,
Dr. A.L.M. PGIBMS,
University of Madras,
Chennai.

37. Dr. D. Shivalingaiah,
Reader,
Dept. of Library & Inf. Science,
Mangalore University,
Mangalagangotri –574 199, Karnataka.

38. Prof. S. Seetharama,
17, Varadarajulu Street,
Chennai - 600 008.

39. Prof. N.R. Satyanarayana,
Professor and Head, Dept of Library and Information Science,
Lucknow University,
Lucknow-226 007.

40. T. Sunitha,
Library and Information Center,
Indian Institute of Management,
Kozhikode – 673 601

41. P. Sreejaya,
Library and Information Center,
Indian Institute of Management,
Kozhikode – 673 601

42. M. Tamizhchelvan
Librarian,
The New Indian Express,
Mount Road,
Chennai – 600 002, Tamilnadu,

43. R. M. Vatnal,
Asst. Librarian, University Library,
Karnatak University,
Dharwad - 580 003.

44. Y. Venkatesh
Lecturer,
Department of Studies in Library and Information Science,
University of Mysore,
Manasagangotri,
Mysore – 570 006.

45. P. Yesudoss,
Assistant Librarian,
S.R.M. Engineering College,
S.R.M. Nagar,
Kattankulathur – 603 203.

Contents

Preface

Library and Information Science profession has recognized the importance of the application of Information Technology as well as the need for developing new methods and techniques for the management of information in a technological environment. It is in this context, the CHMK Library and Department of Library and Information Science, University of Calicut jointly organized a National Seminar on "**Information Access, Management and Exchange in the Technological Age**" during 28th – 29th May 2002. This is the fourth of the series of annual seminars organized in this University. The Seminar was sponsored by the Library Endowment, University of Calicut.

The following are the facets of the theme of the Seminar: Electronic publishing; Intellectual property rights in the digital era; Social implications of wireless technology; Equitable access for the disadvantaged and the disabled; Information security and privacy; Misuse of Information Communication Technology; Implication of Information and Communication; Technology on Distance education; Exchange of electronic bibliographic data; Cross-cultural networking partnerships; Research in a global environment and Preservation of the past for the future. It is expected that the papers presented on the theme in the Seminar will help to reduce the gap between theory and practice in library field.

The fourth **P.Kunhammed Memorial Lecture** was delivered by the eminent Information Scientist and UN Consultant Prof. A. Neelameghan. The theme of the lecture was "Development Information Communication and ICTs".

There are 31 papers contributed by 45 authors, who are practicing Librarians, Library and Information Science Teachers and Research Scholars. Of these, 13 papers are single authored and 18 papers are co-authored. Most of the papers are based on practical experiences, problems, surveys or case studies. This volume is a very useful contribution carrying modern ideas and experiences on the theme of the Seminar. We hope that the papers included in this volume would stimulate interest among Library and Information Science professionals in the technological age.

We are grateful to all who have helped us in the efforts of organizing this Seminar in a befitting manner and to bring out this volume. Our sincere gratitude is due to our former Vice Chancellor Prof. (Dr.) K K N Kurup for his whole hearted support, encouragement, advice and guidance; Dr. T A V Murthy, Director, INFLIBNET, Ahamedabad for his presence and enlightening keynote address in the inaugural session of the Seminar; the teachers and students of the Department of Library and Information Science the staff of the CHMK Library, University of Calicut for their active participation and full involvements in the Seminar, Smt. Leela. K., CHMK Library for undertaking all the typing work and all the members of the Organising Committee of the Seminar.

We are particularly thankful to Sri. Sumit Sethi, Managing Director, Ess Ess Publications, New Delhi who has taken lots of pain to bring out this volume within a minimum time as in the case of previous volumes.

C.U. Campus,
01-11-2002.

Dr. M. Bavakutty
M.C.K. Veeran
T.K. Muhammed Salih

1

Digital Imaging Of Location Bound Knowledge And Information For Conservation And Access

Prof. C. A. Augustine,
Library & Information Science Consultant,
Alancheril Gardens,
Vattappara, Thiruvananthapuram.

ABSTRACT

Digital imaging of all printed materials is now universally the primary concern of the information profession. But, there is an almost 'marginalized' area of knowledge deserving to be specially taken care of in our efforts towards digitization. This pertains to certain unique, rare, and indigenous items of information resource. They may be either in the form of archives, and manuscripts or the various indigenous knowledge systems, folklore, folk arts and crafts, artifacts and museum pieces that indicate and illustrate the historical, socio-cultural, economic and even technological evolution specific cultural/geographic groups. Further, there are the unrecorded parts of public knowledge available in specific geographical areas or cultural groups, like all indigenous and traditional knowledge maintained and transmitted to generations through the oral tradition. All the above mentioned items could be generally characterized as 'location bound knowledge resources'. In this category, unlike in the case of the printed materials, each item is a unique entity identified with a particular situation, institution or individual. The digitization of these location bound knowledge resources will not only enhance their use through wider accessibility but also will lead to their proper conservation and preservation. Digitization of printed materials can be undertaken and accomplished anywhere in the world, and even on a shared basis. But work in respect of these location bound knowledge resources have to be done only locally and with local initiative. This paper examines the special features of these species of knowledge and highlights the various aspects in the planning, policies, strategies, priorities and programmes relating to the digitization of location bound knowledge resources. In this respect the respective responsibilities and functions of international organizations, national and state governments, institutions, and library and information profession are generally indicated.

INTRODUCTION

The most outstanding phenomenon of the present age is the Internet. It has totally revolutionized the intellectual habits of people. It is being used very extensively for communication, education, research, entertainment and for what not. Scholarly communications are now more often through the Internet than through the scientific journal. The quantum of information that is available for accessing through Internet is extremely large. According to the National Public Radio's estimation 'At a recent count, it had over a billion pages and it continues to grow at the rate of at least a million pages a day' (2001).

Accessing, managing and exchanging all sorts of information through Internet has become the order of the day. In this new order, the end-user is finding more pleasure in accessing online every document and information that he comes to need than through libraries and reading. Many of the Internet users even believe that Internet can give them much more information than what libraries and library-based services can do. It is true that Internet contains a vast ocean of information to which it provides easier, speedier, inexpensive and more convenient access. It is equally true that only a small part of the knowledge preserved in our libraries (in various physical formats like printed materials, manuscripts and archives) is now available in the Internet. The technological capability of the Internet is almost beyond doubt. But the practical reality is far from satisfactory. The 'virtual library' situation ("for example, the ability to browse around a library system without actually having to physically go to it", Barker, 1997,P.95) that a serious Internet user is expecting on the Net will turn out to be a mirage, because what Internet can give now is only an incomplete and very poor picture of the knowledge existing in his/her subject of search. This happens because not all the available documents are now digitized and entered into the Net. The exclusive Internet user must therefore be duly warned about what Internet is presently incapable of giving and what they are missing without having recourse to libraries and reading materials.

INTERNET AND THE GLOBAL LIBRARY

Taking full advantage of the technological developments in harnessing information world attention should be directed towards making Internet as comprehensive as possible in respect of our already available knowledge and information resources. Considering the amount of materials still remaining to be transferred to a digital medium, like all printed materials, manuscripts, archives and other graphic and processed documents, a total digitization of the knowledge resources is a practical impossibility. Even if we restrict the scope of this work to printed materials only, it is going to be a Herculean task. Nevertheless, there are many enthusiasts like Natalia Grygierczyk of the Netherlands who worked out the Utrecht Electronic Library Project. This project was for establishing a scientific electronic library for the staff and students of Utrecht University. It had a budget of Dfl. 2,100,00 (approx. 700,00 British pounds) and a duration of three years with a project staff of about 60 people. Inspired by the success of this project he dreams about the establishment of the Global Library on the Internet. The following optimistic words from him cannot be just ignored:

> "Let us make a mental voyage into the year 2050. Optical-fibre cables and quantum-leap processors constitute the structure of the Global Library, a repository comprising a colossal digital collection amounting to the volume of at least 25,000,000 complete *Britannica*s. The Global Library literally encompasses the entire world and has no main entrance. At any given moment it provides any person with unimpeded access to its contents. Wherever you are, whatever you wish to read in whatever language, it is all available to you. All this is available, it is at your finger tips, accessible within a blink of an eye. Without having to browse through dreary catalogues, without being afraid of missing a crucial information because of an erroneous code, a wrong signature, because of not properly entered data or of not knowing the author's name." (1997).

THE OLD AND THE NEW ON INTERNET

Internet users must realize that in spite of the technical possibility the practical reality of the Global Library is going to be too far away. At present, the digitized information and knowledge resources accessible through Internet are of two categories. One consists of the various electronic information originally communicated online. In the second category are materials originally brought out in printed or any other analog mode but later transferred into the digital mode. While resources in the first category will be a fast growing phenomenon, those in the second category will be relatively small in size and slow growing. The idea of the Global Library can be realized only if digitization of all the old documents is completed. This involves comprehensive planning, proper strategies, programmes and activities on a global level with national, regional and local initiatives. Resources have to be mobilized, priorities have to be decided, and agencies have to be named before proceeding with the work. So far, digitizing retrospective collections is attempted by libraries and organizations on ad hoc basis and often as research or experimental projects.

BEYOND PRINTED MATERIALS

Digitization of all printed materials available in the world will be normally taking the first priority. This sector is comparatively small by number of individual titles since our libraries altogether are now holding numerous copies of one and the same item. Each of these items need be digitized and brought into the full text database only once. Work in this connection can be undertaken and accomplished anywhere in the world and on a widely shared basis, avoiding duplication of efforts and unnecessary wastage. Digital conversion of the printed materials is now universally the primary concern of information profession. But, there are other knowledge resources that are crucially important and worth capturing into the digital medium. At present these remain as a 'marginalised section' of knowledge resources. It is about digitization of this special category of knowledge resources that this paper has been written.

LOCATION-BOUND RESOURCES

The expression 'location bound knowledge and information resources' has been used to mean all knowledge resources that are identified with particular places, cultures, institutions or individuals, each one being either unique, rare, unrecorded or invisible, which could be collected, handled or used presently only in their local situations. The following species can be identified in this category:

- Archives
- Manuscripts
- Inscriptions
- Art works like pictures, paintings and photographs,
- Craft works,
- Museum pieces
- Indigenous and traditional knowledge systems and their recorded resources
- Oral traditions of various knowledge systems including the unrecorded Folklore.

Manuscripts and archives are largely concentrated in different manuscript libraries and national, state or institutional archives. They are unique collections in the sense that items found in one library or archive will not be there in another library or archive. Besides these, there are similar materials in individual possessions. These collections may include even family records and personal diaries that throw light on important events and persons. They lie scattered in different parts of the state or country, and therefore have to be systematically surveyed and searched out. For every society, culture or locality, there will be its own traditional knowledge resources and indigenous systems. A part of them may have been brought to printing while another significant part still remains as manuscripts, most of them being in individual or family possessions. Typical examples, in the context of Kerala particularly, are the knowledge resources in Ayurveda and Siddha medical systems. It is a custom that practitioners who are often hereditary custodians of these knowledge systems impart them to new generations most often orally. To capture all these widely scattered knowledge into the digital medium will be a great task. Building up of multimedia digital databases of all the various artifacts of the past, like the museum pieces, art and craft works, etc. that may indicate and illustrate the historical, socio-cultural, economic and even technological evolution of specific cultural/geographic groups will be another significant task. Lastly, but not in any way of the least importance, must be mentioned the unrecorded part of public knowledge existing in specific geographic areas or cultural groups, like all indigenous and traditional knowledge, maintained and transmitted through the oral tradition, like the folklore, folk arts and crafts, etc.

DIGITAL IMAGING

The term 'digital imaging' is used in this paper to mean the process of capturing a digitized image from a printed, graphic or processed material and even a three-dimensional object. Alternative terms like 'digitization', 'digital capturing', and 'digital conversion' are also found used by writers on the subject to mean almost one and the same thing. According to Stuart D. Lee, "Digitization is the conversion of analog signal or code into a digital signal or code. Most of our everyday life is spent in the analog world, receiving natural signals. Our eyes take in colours, our ears pitch the tone, delivered to them in waveforms. The digital world cannot deal with these continually changing patterns and needs to get the information into a medium which computers can handle. It does this by sampling the analog patterns and converting them to simple numerical values, in this case ones and zeros, or *bits* as they are often called. It is for this reason that people often use terms like 'conversion' or 'capture' as synonymous with digitization – i.e. the analog signal is *converted* to a digital one, or the analog is *captured* into digital form." (2000).

Some people have used the words "scanning" and "digitization" almost synonymously. But, strictly speaking, they are different. Scanning is a method used for conversion of the image-based analog material into digital form. Digitization, on the other hand, means the conversion of any analog material into digital form, including sound and video. " In other words, all scanning is digitization, but not all digitization is scanning′.(2000).

INCREASING ACCESS THROUGH DIGITIZATION

At this point it is necessary to understand why we want to digitize the location bound knowledge resources. The two obvious reasons are:

- to increase access, and
- to preserve the original.

The location bound materials generally have only limited access. Firstly, because one has to go to the place where the original item is kept for viewing, reading or listening to which is not possible for all. Secondly, because physical access to the original will be often curtailed for reasons of safety, risk of corruption or damage. Digitization can increase access to the material as an accurate facsimile of the original in digital form can be made available to any number of users simultaneously. Further, they can also make copies of the same without affecting the life and quality of the original. Once put on the Web it will be possible for many to come across these materials and use them, almost ensuring a global access and use.

BETTER PRESERVATION THROUGH DIGITIZATION

Many precious items coming under the category of location bound materials are either already in a bad physical condition or prone to faster deterioration. This is also the major reason why their use is often severely restricted, including photocopying. One significant advantage of digitization is that high quality digital copies of the original can be made for using as preservation copies. But the problem is about the longevity of the digital file, which cannot be predicted now correctly. It may be only less than 20 years or so, whereas in the case with a microfilm master, under correct conditions, it will be readable in hundreds of years (Lee, 2001, P. 6). But, in another way, digitization will certainly promote preservation of the original. It will deflect away the demand for handling the original as many users will be fully satisfied with the high quality digital copy accessible in the Web site. The original need not be exposed to photocopier or microfilm camera, as copying from a digital file will take only some seconds. Such a rescuing of the original from frequent handling and consequent deterioration and damage is known as "rescue digitization".

CONSERVATION OF UNRECORDED TRADITIONAL KNOWLEDGE

More than preserving the already recorded knowledge what digitization promises today is conservation of the unrecorded part of knowledge. This is particularly important when we consider the large amount of traditional knowledge that exists in specific communities, cultures and countries. In the context of Kerala there are many such knowledge systems and resources. Knowledge of indigenous medical systems like Ayurveda and Siddha were referred to earlier. Although there are many well-known printed books and manuscripts in these subject areas much of the knowledge still remains unrecorded. In traditional medicines it is usual that the practitioners belong to different hereditary lines of *vaidya* families and the knowledge and experiences of the elders are passed on to their own younger generations, only orally. Another rich area of traditional knowledge is Tribal Medicines. Traditional knowledge systems are also prevailing in Kerala pertaining to different arts, crafts, occupations, etc. like metallurgy, smithy, carpentry, boat building, architecture (Vasthu silpa), etc. Effective measures have not been taken so far to collect and record all these traditional knowledge. Digitization can be used as a very effective tool in recording the unrecorded.

SPECIAL PROBLEMS INVOLVED

From the point of view of problems involved, the location bound knowledge resources can be broadly categorized into two:

- The unrecorded knowledge/items where an original first time recording by digital capturing is involved, and
- The recorded knowledge items in various analog formats that are to be converted to digital format.

The problems in respect of each category are different. In the first case, because the resources are lying widely scattered, and very often in undeveloped areas, identification of the knowledge sources and collection of the knowledge proper become the most difficult part of the mission. Very often there will be diffidence, mistrust, resistance, and antagonism from the side of the individuals and groups who are the committed guardians of this knowledge lore. Proper planning and strategic programmes incorporating proven methods of social survey, social education, and consciousness raising of the folk about the benefits of conserving their knowledge can produce good results.

The special problems even in respect of the recorded knowledge resources will vary from species to species. In the case of the archives, the physical material will be paper with either handwritten or typewritten, or mimeographed texts. In one and the same archive bundle there can be different types, qualities, shades and sizes of paper. The physical condition of the sheets may be different from one another, some being very fragile, brittle or soiled and some others being wrinkled, folded or torn. The text may be of uneven brightness. These are problems for scanning and capturing their digital images. Almost similar problems are there in the case of manuscripts also. In addition, the size, shape and material of the manuscripts are crucial factors in deciding equipment and process of digital imaging. Manuscripts of Kerala are mostly on palm leaves and they are of different sizes and shapes. Too long but very narrow size of palm leaves can cause problems while scanning or photographing. Some of the visual art works like mural and oil paintings are likely to be affected if exposed to powerful light and warmth. Museum pieces particularly glassware and brassware can cause reflections or glares while exposed to photoflashes and lights. On the whole, most of the materials in this category are unique, rare or singular items that cannot be replaced if lost. Therefore, security against the risk of loss or damage to the original is of paramount concern in their digital imaging. In such cases digital imaging can be done from microfilm masters of the original. But, digital imaging of microfilms, microfiche, slides and transparencies also involve special problems.

DIGITIZATION PROCESS

A digitization process must include the following phases of work:

- Project idea instigation
- Selection and assessment of materials
- Preparation of the materials
- Digital imaging or capturing
- Editing the digital file
- Delivering the digital file
- Developing support services

Once the project is accepted, the materials for digital imaging should be assessed by a variety of experts. A good digitization project will have to ensure the involvement of different types of expertise and manpower as listed below at its different stages:

- Subject experts
- Conservation experts
- Digital and film photographers
- Cataloguers
- I T Specialists
- Management
- Administration

Digital imaging process involves three basic elements:

(a) the source item/ the original,

(b) a capturing device, like a scanner or a digital camera, and

(c) a computer installed with a software for interfacing with the scanner, and a storage device, like a Hard Disk, for recording the digitized image.

The source items emphasized in this paper are of a wide variety. Their special features were indicated already. Selecting, assessing and preparing the materials for digitization are jobs to be entrusted to subject experts and conservation experts. Curative concerns often dominate digitization projects. For library and information personnel who happen to initiate such projects it is necessary to have a deeper understanding on various aspects of digital imaging process. Three broad aspects of this knowledge are:

(i) the anatomy of the digital image,

(ii) the formats of the digital files, both for storage and delivery,

(iii)the hardware and software.

ANATOMY OF THE DIGITAL IMAGE

The anatomy deals with how the digital image of a source document or item can be divided into 'dots' or 'pixels' (picture elements). This decides the resolution which is measured in terms of 'dpi' (dots per inch). The more the dpi the higher is the quality of the image. Each pixel or dot can capture a number of variations of black, white, gray and colours, as coded and programmed by the software. This capacity is referred to as 'bit-depth'. If in a 1-bit coding only 2 variables (say, black and white) could be recorded, in an 8-bit coding 256 shades of gray and colours could be captured. If the bit depth is raised to 24 the different patterns of colours that could be captured will be 16,777,216 (more than 16 million). The bit-depth and dpi are the most decisive factors in image quality. But any unimaginative increase in dpi and bit-depth will seriously affect the resulting file size and the required storage space. A standard formula for calculating the file size is given below (Lee, 2000, P.42-3):

Resulting file size = (dpi × dpi × bit-depth × dimension of original item in inches (height × width))/8

Illustration: (100 dpi × 100 dpi × 1 bit-depth × (1"×1")) /8
= 10,000/8
= 1250 bytes or 1.25 Kb.

While the above is in 1-bit depth for bi-tone recording (in black and white) another example for colour recording with 600 dpi and 24 bit-depth and for the same 1 sq. in. source item will need a disk space as follows:

(600 × 600 × 24 × 1) /8 = 1,080,000 bytes = 10.8 Mb.

The nature of the source materials discussed in this paper will necessitate sound decisions in respect of quality of images on a cost-effective basis.

DIGITAL FILE FORMATS

The choice of the digital file formats is another crucial question arising in digital imaging. This has to be addressed at two levels. One is as the format to be chosen for capturing and archiving images. The other is as the format to be chosen for delivery of the files to end-users in different forms, like a fax message, a CD-ROM copy or on the Web. A number of digital image file formats are now available. But, without having direct reference to any particular product in the market, some qualities of a good digital file format can be mentioned:

- The format chosen must enable cross-platform use.
- It should not be tied to any particular scanner or display.
- It must allow for high quality images that can be saved without any loss from the original capture.
- Conversion from this used format to other formats must be
- Straightforward and loss less.
- It must enable creation of master files from which file formats suited to
- delivery including the Web delivery must be possible.
- Finally, it must allow a high ratio of compression which is absolutely
- lossless and without affecting the quality of the images.

HARDWARE AND SOFTWARE

The most decisive part of any digital imaging project is the choice and utilization of the hardware and software. Without going into the technological differences of the hardware it can be noted that there are now different products in the market with different capacities and in different price ranges. They are classed as Flatbed Scanners. Sheet-feeders, Drum Scanners, Slide Scanners, Microfilm Scanners, Digital Cameras, etc. Each of this hardware has merits and demerits in relation to specific requirements. The final choice must depend upon many considerations, like the content, material, format, physical constituency and dimensions of the sources. The contents may be in black and white or in different shades of gray, or multi-coloured. The physical material may be different like, paper, parchment, papyrus, palm leaves, tree barks, plaques / sheets of metals, etc. Some of the soft materials may be fragile and brittle, or in loose leaves of varying sizes and even oversized, or as rolls or codices. Other relevant points for consideration here are the quality, quantum, and speed of execution, the skill involved, ease of handling, connectivity to computers, etc. The quality of work is assessed in terms of the bit-depth and resolution, reduction of optical noise, and the file format obtainable. The location bound materials in question may represent all the different properties and problems listed above. Hence all the different types of hardware will become necessary for a complete digital imaging lab.

The software needs of digital imaging are for three purposes: image capturing, image processing and image delivering. Image capturing needs a software that can interface the computer with the scanner/ camera and receive and store the images as files. This software must enable one to control the scanning settings like resolution, bit-depth, etc. and allow to previewing the images. The processing software makes possible editing of the captured images after necessary cropping, fine-tuning and colour balancing. The third type of software is required for formatting the files as suited to storing and final display or delivery.

CATALOGUING AND METADATA

The most important professional job for librarians in a digitization project is cataloguing the digital images. Without proper cataloguing the data files cannot be systematically stored and accessed. Unlike in the case of a library catalogue the fields or descriptive elements to be entered in the catalogue record of a digitized object will be numerous and they will vary according to the source objects. These descriptions are known as "metadata" (in the IT jargon) which simply means 'data about data'. "Metadata describes content, structure, context and other aspects of a digital object and is critical to resource discovery (documents and images) in digital libraries" (Griffin, 1997, P.138). A comprehensive metadata system suitable to all types of source objects/ materials will have to be developed or adopted for use in the digitization project. In this regard, the JISC Image Digitization Initiative (JIDI) in the UK higher education sector has brought out a lengthy set of field definitions for metadata of digital images. The fields are identified at five levels of catalogue description, namely of the *collection*, the *work*, the *visual document*, the *person* and the *organization*. JIDI has listed the fields coming under each of these levels, almost exhaustively (Lee, 2000 P. 112-15). Traditional library cataloguing systems or their formats, like MARC, CCF, AACR and ISBD are not found directly suited to the description requirements of the special materials we have discussed in this paper. At present, the most widely used solution to the problem of digital image cataloguing is reported to be the Standard Generalized Mark-up Language (SGML) or 'its most recent descendant, the Extensible Mark-up Language (XML)'. XML is led and promoted by the World Wide Web Consortium (W3C). The HyperText Mark-up Language (HTML) used by the Web for hyper linking is also an application of the SGML. SGML has several merits. It is non-proprietary, platform and software independent, and allowing highly sophisticated level of mark –up. SGML documents are easily convertible to other formats. SGML controls the marking up of documents. This is done by its Document Type Definition (DTD) which is almost a set of rules for defining the type of mark-up to be used, what it contains, where it can occur, etc. The DTD also checks whether the document conforms to its rules and understands what the mark-up is meant to indicate.

For digitization of the various location bound knowledge and information resources a more detailed type of cataloguing and description will become necessary. Two separate sets of descriptions have to be provided in each case, namely, the description of the original source and the description of the digital image. Each type of sources will need its own special descriptive fields and in addition the technical details of the digital copy. This is a challenging area for library and information professionals to develop a better and simpler system of metadata elements that can describe a wide range of digitized special materials for delivery on the Web. Whereas the use of SGML/XML can be continued as it is now for extensive linking of the marked-up documents.

DIGITIZATION AGENCY

Another important issue to be addressed is the arrangement for getting the digital imaging work done. The two possibilities are (i) developing an in-house digitization lab, and (ii) outsourcing under contractual arrangement with an external agency. These alternatives have relative advantages and disadvantages.

In-house arrangement can enable complete curatorial control over the work as internal conservators will observe the process throughout, ensure quality images being produced after previewing and satisfying, establish in due course better standards of performance and procedure, and acquire better staff skill through training and experience. There is no security risk, as the material will not have to be taken out of the institution for digital imaging. Above all, the institution would be benefited by developing an own lab with all equipment and competent staff for taking up further projects. The only disadvantages worth noting are the high cost involved in equipping the lab, the time taken for training the staff and in attaining the optimum level of productivity and hence the higher unit cost of production incurred in the initial period of the project. Compared to in-house digitization outsourcing has some obvious benefits. The established expertise and state-of-the-art technology (hardware and software) of commercial companies are almost not achievable to institutions. The latter will be as far as possible continuing with the old equipment and technologies. Commercial agencies can execute works at competitive rates and in target times. But a very serious disadvantage is that the material has to be left in the custody of the contractor for some time at least and some degree of safety risk is always inherent. This becomes crucial in the case of rare and precious but fragile items. Another great risk involved is about copyright infringement on the digital image file by the contractor. The final solution may lie in any Government department or quasi - government body establishing a full fledged digital imaging centre and taking up digitization projects of individual institutions. Such a centre can have also necessary mobile labs to be sent to institutions

PROGRESS IN DIGITIZATION

The subject of digitization of libraries has attracted the attention of many countries and organizations. The 1990s for librarians were a decade of digitization. 'Countless millions of pounds, dollars, francs and marks have been ploughed into digital projects that have involved the conversion of library, museum and archive collections. It is no coincidence that this has gone hand in hand with the development of the world wide web, the final piece of the jigsaw needed to solve the problem of increasing access to cultural resources' (2001). Lee has listed about 50 important library digitization projects in his book. Although many of these pioneering projects were for digitizing printed materials some at least have either partly or wholly dealt with the types of resources we have emphasized in this paper. (A list of some relevant projects is given as an appendix). For instance, two pioneering projects in digitization of manuscripts are worth mentioning, viz. the digitization of the Beowulf Manuscripts by the British Library and the Celtic and Medieval Manuscripts Collection in the University of Oxford. As regards the museum objects, it is worth noting that for the last several years Britain's museums have been offering their collections either online or via CD-ROM. One notable work among them was of the Ashmolean Museum in Oxford, and the British Museum, the Natural History Museum and the Imperial War Museum in London. The Bibliotheque Nationale de France converted over 100,000 visual images and about 20 million pages of text. In the case of fine arts particularly, the Art Museum Image Consortium (AMICO) founded by the Association of Art Museum Directors' Educational Foundation, Inc. has taken up the digitization of 50,000 images in fine arts. Similarly, the Bridgeman Art Library is a virtual gallery and image service bringing together a collection drawn from 800 museums and art galleries. The Bodleian Broadside Ballads Project and the photographs digitization project of Shetland Museum are also representative examples. Then, coming to archives, the National Archives and Records Administration's Electronic Access Project is a worthy example to cite. Although these pioneering efforts were mainly in Europe they could solve many a problems of digitization and for beginners like us they are dependable sources of first hand information and practical guidance in all matters connected with digitizing projects.

INDIAN PROSPECTS

In India there is a great scope for digitization work in respect of the traditional knowledge contained in the various indigenous medical systems, like Ayurveda, Unani, Sidhha, Yoga, Naturopathy and even Folklore Medicine. The Department of Indian System of Medicine and Homeopathy is reported to have taken up the issues relating to digitization of indigenous medical knowledge systems very seriously. The Department constituted an inter-disciplinary task force for preparing a report on establishing a Traditional Knowledge Digital Library (TKDL) in the year 1999. Although the main objective of this Digital Library is to prevent the patenting of all non-original inventions based on our traditional systems and medicines, the final outcome will be the conservation of this part of our knowledge and making them accessible in the digital form. The Task Force had submitted its detailed report with many valuable findings and recommendations. According to them, creating a more or less comprehensive database of our medicinal plants will be less than the cost of travel and stay and legal charges we are right now incurring in a year for defending our cases against outside patent claims. (2001).

In Kerala things are too slow as the situation stands at present. As regards indigenous medical knowledge systems the Kottakkal Aryavaidyasala in Malappuram has initiated the work of a digital database of medical compositions. Although this is at present intended only to serve their production and marketing needs, eventually it is possible develop this as a comprehensive database of Ayurveda medicines and their compositions. The Department of State Archives has initiated a comprehensive project proposal for digitizing its collection with the technical collaboration of the C-DIT. Some such instigation for digital imaging projects is already under consideration of the State Department of Archaeology and the Sanskrit College, Pattampi. The C-DIT has successfully completed an experimental project in digitization of manuscripts in Malayalam script. It has made a multimedia CD-ROM of the classic *Saraswatee Kantabharanam* of Nilakanta Sastri. The Oriental Manuscript Library and Research Institute in the Kerala University, during the last few years, has been working on a microfilming project and many manuscripts have been done already. The State Archives Department also has done some such microfilming work. For them prospective digitization project will involve scanning of the microfilm masters besides their other manuscripts and archives in the original form.

CONCLUSION

The main emphasis of this paper has been on digitization of a category of resources referred to as location bound knowledge and information resources for the purpose of their better preservation and increased access. These resources are special in many respects: by their variety, rarity and uniqueness, their unorganized and mostly inaccessible condition at present, and lack of organized efforts in conserving this part of knowledge especially the traditional knowledge systems and more particularly the unrecorded part of this knowledge. Interests in respect of digitizing archives and manuscripts have already begun to appear in our country although much could not be accomplished in this direction. In the case of many of the other resources no serious effort has been so far made. What is lacking at present is a definite will on the part of the Government of India and the State Governments to get these things done as priority matter. Digitization projects generally are very expensive, and digitization of non-print materials will cost several times more. Individuals and institutions have severe limitations in respect of time, money and expertise required for these projects. Firstly, financial resources have to be mobilized and allocations to be made on a purposive basis. Secondly, there should be proper leadership with necessary expertise to map out the locations of these knowledge resources, to oversee, control and guide specific projects. Both these are in the realm of the governments. Library and information profession must be able to prevail upon the concerned ministries and departments. Policy decisions have to be taken, strategies have to be evolved, and action programmes have to be identified and executed. This is an area where international co-operation can be sought from bodies like UNESCO, UNDP and FID.

BIBLIOGRAPHY AND REFERENCES:

Grygierczyk, Natalia (1997): 'The Infinite Library: putting strategic policy into practice' *in* Raitt, David *Ed. Libraries for the New Millenium,* London, Library Association P. 65-88.

Dreyfus, Hubert L (2001): *On the Internet*, New York, Routledge.

Gould, S and Ebdon, R (1999): *IFLA/UNESCO. Survey on digitization and preservation,* IFLA.

Griffin, Stephen M (1997): 'Digital Libraries and NSF/DARPA/NASA Digital Libraries Initiative' *in* Raitt, David, *Ed. Libraries for the New Millenium*, London, Library Association, P. 114-47.

Gupta, V K (2001). 'Report of the Task Force on Traditional Knowledge Digital Library: a gist' *Journal of Intellectual Property Rights* Vol. 6, March 2001. P.121-33.

Kenney, A and Chapman, S (1996): *Digital imaging for libraries and archives.* Cornell University Library.

Kenney, A R and Rieger, O Y (1998): *Managing digital imaging projects: an RLG workshop.* RLG.

Kenney, A R and Rieger, O Y, *Eds.* (2000): *Moving theory into practice: digital imaging for libraries and archives.* RLG.

Klijn, E and de Ludenet, Y (2000): *In the picture: preservation and digitization of European photographic collections.* European Commission.

Lee, Stuart D (2000): *Digital imaging; a practical handbook.* London, Library Association.

Raitt, David, *Ed.* (1997): *Libraries for the new millenium; implications for Managers.* London, Library Association.

RLG/NPO (1999): *Guidelines for digital imaging.* NPO.

APPENDIX

Some Relevant Digitization Projects Abroad

AMICO Art Museum Image Consortium (*http://www.amico.org/home.html*)

Asmolean Museum (*http://www.ashmol.ox.ac.uk/*)

Beazley Archive (*http://www.beasley.ox.ac.uk/*)

Bibliotheque Nationale de France (*http://www.bnf.fr/*)

Bodleian Broadside Ballads Project (*http://www.bodley.ox.ac.uk/mh/ballads/*)

Bridgeman Art Library (*http://www.bridgeman.co.uk*)

British Library's *Directory of Digitized Collections* (*http://thoth.bl.uk/*)

Burney Collection at the British Library (*http://minos.bl.uk/diglib/access/microfilm-digitization.html*)

Celtic and Medieval Manuscripts (*http://image.ox.ac.uk/*)

CORBIS (*http://www.corbis.com/*)

Harvard University (*http://via.harvard.edu:748/VIA.html*)

National Archives and Records Administration's Electronic Access Project (*http://www.nara.gov/nara/*)

National Portrait Gallery (*http://www.npg.org.uk/*)

The Shetland Museum (*http://www.shetland-museum.org.uk/museum/*)

2

Development Communication And ICTs

Prof. A. Neelameghan
Hon. Visiting Professor,
Documentation Research & Training Centre,
ISI,Mysore Road
8th Mile,
Bangalore 560 059.

ABSTRACT

Discusses issues relating to Development Communication in developing and rural societies and presents some case histories to illustrate. It is difficult to talk about developing environment independently and separated from the rest of local, urban, state, national, and global environments and the developments thereof. With the wide reach and spread of Information and Communication Technologies (ICT), which have enhanced considerably the interactions among all sections of the society and also make them interdependent, consideration of the rural areas insolated from other sections of the society is even more difficult. Explains the possibilities and effects of e-governance, resources management, distance learning and outreach services using ICT. Briefly consider ICT support to research and study, management and e-governance and ICT impacts on the economics of wealth production; shift in power foci, work culture; politics; legal and ethical aspects, psychology and the digital divide.

At the outset let me express my gratitude to the organizers of the Kunhammed Memorial Lectures for inviting me to present this year's lectures. In the past years the lectures in this series have been delivered by distinguished library and information professionals. I would also like to pay my respects to Shri Kunhammed, who, I learnt, had rendered distinguished service to the University and has endeared himself to his colleagues and users of the Calicut University library.

BACKGROUND AND PREMISES

The principal landmarks in the progress of human civilization and development have been around two inter-related axes, namely, the capacity to

1) Explore, produce, store, transfer and use energy.

For example, Heat, fire (sun, lightning, friction); Wheel; Explosives; Steam energy, engine; Electricity; Natural gas, coal, oil; Nuclear energy; Solar battery; biogas, wind, tide.

2) Recording and communication of messages.

For example, oral communication and gestures; Marks on cave walls and rocks;

Hieroglyphics; Block printing; Papyrus; Printing from moveable metallic types; Paper; Celluloid film; Photography; Telegraph, telephone; Xerography; Electronic valve; Transistor; Microchip; Convergent technologies.

Thanks to ICTs and extended and fast travel facilities, people are now better connected and hence there are more interactions among them locally nationally and globally. By the end of 2001 more number of people were connected via the Internet. Half a billion people around the world had access to Internet from their homes. Of these nearly 500 million could surf the web (an increase of 5.1 % on the July-Sept. 2001 figure). People from Asia continued to connect faster than anywhere else (home access grew by 5.6 percent during the last quarter of the year) [Source: — Nielsen/ NetRatings, Hong Kong]

During the present decade, as compared to the preceding decades, in many countries of the world, there is:

§ Much larger financial investment in the ICT sector – production, services, and in research and development (R&D).

§ There is a significant increase in the range of applications of ICTs:

§ A larger proportion of the workforce in the developed countries and many of

§ The developing countries too is involved in information generation, storing, organizing, retrieving, preparation of information products, dissemination and other related services;

§ There is a growing inter-dependence of the developing and developed countries in and through the ICT sector; and

§ Globalization in almost all sectors (science, technology, the arts, and social sciences).

The trend is that during the next decade, 20-25 % of conventional publications and audio, video records will be produced and stored in digital form. Convergent technologies – text, audio, video, TV – will facilitate extension of communication to rural areas, virtual team work, global access to experts, video conferencing, etc., saving travel and multiple conferènces cost. Some of these trends are likely to continue for another couple of decades at least.

ICT IMPACT ON EDUCATION, RESEARCH AND SCHOLARLY COMMUNICATION

Economic, social, political and technological changes and developments interact and mutually influence one another. National developments impact on the functioning of local institutions; and national events and institutions are impacted upon by global developments. Such impacts have become more frequent and almost inevitable due to the emerging and converging ICT and facilities for domestic and international travel. The teacher, the researcher, the student, and the practising professional must keep themselves updated with the rapidly changing environment, at the local, national and global levels, lest they become obsolescent and outdated.

The impact of ICTs on scholarly publication and communication will have significant impact and affect the way libraries, more particularly digital libraries, may function in the future. In the next decade, over 20 percent of conventional publications and audio, video records will be produced and stored in digital form.

The material will always be copied from the original master work in the digital form, which means that the mechanical aspects of printing and publishing a list of works, etc. may more be necessary. With electronic publishing and distribution, the material can be accessed on the network as soon as the author has keyed in the data / text, or created graphs and images. Mechanical aspects of printing and publishing and of resources directories can be bypassed A person can be an author, editor, and publisher as well.

Students, teachers, researchers and others need not personally visit the library. They can browse online the library catalogues and other resource directories; and electronic methods can deliver the required texts, images and even voice recordings in their workplace, dormitory, home or wherever they are. Distance learning and delivery of education to remote areas could become a reality.

Information seekers will have almost seamless global access to a wide range of information resources, including peer groups and experts, whole texts, voice recording, multimedia, etc. via satellites and networks of networks such as the Internet, without the intervening services of editors, indexers, publishers, and perhaps librarians too.

Three key roles of libraries in learning are: sharing of expensive resources, preserving and organizing artifacts (cultural role) and bringing together people and ideas (social role. Lectures, demos, and hands-on training in the classroom or lab can be organized with the instructors and experts operating at global distance. This, in turn, will permit more integration of different types of learning through sharing of resources, and expertise and conserving time, energy and expenses). Libraries can support provision of various types information and learning materials, including audio and video, .to remote areas via satellite, cable networks and TV.

ICT IN MANAGEMENT

ICTs are now providing support to almost all areas of management – in decision making, resources mobilization and deployment, programme implementation and monitoring, marketing, budgeting, office management, etc. in different types of enterprises, in the public and private sectors. A few examples are:

- § Resources management
- § Health care delivery
- § Disaster management
- § Crime detection; forensic work
- § E-governance; telecentres, Inter-departmental linking: information access, cooperation, coordination

Sub-national level (State, District, Taluq, Village) linkages. Within each domain and with other larger units and nationally. Telecentres.

FLATTER HIERARCHIES; BETTER ACCESS TO DECISION / POLICY MAKING CENTRES AND INDIVIDUALS.

- § Environment protection and management
- § Fast global reach of messages and instant response.

IMPACT OF ICT ON ECONOMICS OF WEALTH

- **Agrarian Economy :** In an agrarian economy, the possession of land and control over labour was the basis of production and of the national economy
- **Industrial Economy :** In an industrial economy, capital, technology and labour are the basis of production and wealth. Industrial economy also gave rise to the managerial class as distinct from the owners, share holders and the labour.
- **Information> Knowledge economy:** In the post-industrial economy, the possession of useful information and knowledge becomes the base of the economy.

Corresponding to the change in the economic base, there is a shift in the power foci. In the agrarian economy possession and/ or control over land and labour is the base of power. In an industrial economy, possession of capital, technology and mass action (e.g. mass strikes) are the basis of power. In a Knowledge economy the power shifts to the individuals who possess expertise and knowledge. In most developing countries an agrarian economy and industrial economy coexist in various proportions. In some of them there is an emergence of a knowledge economy.

IMPACT OF ICT ON WORK CULTURE

An impact of ICTs is the change in work culture of people. Such changes include:

- **Telecommuting:** With intranet and Internet facilities and increasing use of microcomputers and laptops at home, enable people to work at home (or away from the office / work place) .especially much of the information handling work, software development, etc. and send the results across to the their respective work place or employers. This facility is perceived as saving on travel time from home to work place and related problems, reduce pollution from exhaust fumes of vehicles, etc.
- Working at home as mentioned above, may enable, especially women, to take of
- Children, the sick, the elderly at home, and thus it could foster closer family ties.
- **Multiple employment possibilities:** Taking advantage of ICT's capabilities,
- Telecommuting and working away from the workplace also opens up opportunities for a person to take up multiple jobs for different enterprises, within and outside the country the worker is located..
- **Virtual team work :** Collaborative work on a project with researchers / workers · involved located not only in different

parts within a country but also globally. This applies also to consultancy work, outsourcing of expertise, etc.

Psychological aspects of the use of ICT include the overabundance of information and unchecked and unfiltered information creating information overload, which in turn can cause information anxiety. The generation gap problems between those who are growing up in and with ICT and those of an earlier generation are well known.

We shall now consider some characteristics of rural communities in developing countries, their role in national development, and the problems and barriers to communication of development information to such communities and between them and others involved in development activities. I shall briefly describe some of the development communication situations and experiences that I have encountered and take note of the role of information and communication technologies in development communication. It will be helpful to define a few select terms.

WORKING DEFINITIONS

Development

'Development' is the bridge between the hopes and dreams of people on the one hand and the realities of the world they live in on the other. Information is an essential support to and also the traffic on, that bridge.

COMMUNICATION AND COMMUNICATIVE ACTION

The term 'Communication', is derived from the term 'to commune', meaning 'to share'. Information communication' is the sharing of information, essentially among people, as differentiated, for example, between computers.

Communication is more than the action of announcing or exchange of information. Communication is a form of action in giving advice, making an argument, assertion, command, demand, inquiry, judgment, request, report, warning, alerting, and similar *interpersonal statements.* Through communicative action, in a special sense, the participants seek to enhance mutual understanding so as to facilitate cooperative and coordinated action and mutual support and to recognize the roles and functions of the participants in the programme, project, community, group etc. Validity conditions for and the effectiveness of, communicative action depends on the respective orientations of the communicator and the communicate toward the material world, social world, subjective world influenced by culture, and linguistic world and their knowledge and understanding of the context.

DEVELOPMENT COMMUNICATION

Development communication is the communication of information that enhances the capacity of recipient individuals and groups to select and integrate appropriate exogenous knowledge with indigenous knowledge systems to support their socio-economic development within the respective development contexts and to preserve their cultural and spiritual value systems in the process. This should be achieved through a judicious blending of traditional and modern communication media facilitating the exchange of messages among local communities on the one hand and between them and communities of other locales in the country and in other nations on the other.

RURAL COMMUNITY

Features of the Community

Rural or village community - In most of the developing countries over 70 percent of the population are partly semi-literate and partly illiterate. They live in a vast number of rural villages, often spread out, into small communities. However, they constitute a vital base of the national economy as they produce the raw materials of food, clothing, and shelter that are converted into consumable products used and enjoyed by a much larger population nationally and even internationally. They also constitute a large base of a democratic socio-political system Further, they live close to nature and have the knowledge of and stake in, the nurture and preservation of natures offerings. Rural people possess a fund of valuable native knowledge relating to food, health and medicine, plants and animals, social and cultural value systems, ethno-music and the arts. This knowledge needs to be recorded, processed, disseminated and utilized. A good portion of such knowledge may not have been written down, but transmitted by word of mouth. Equity and justice requires that development planning should cover all sections of the society; and the benefits of development should be shared in appropriate measures by all in the society.

People at the grass roots suffer from various societal handicaps. Being barely literate they are susceptible to economic, social, political and technological exploitation by others. This together with other factors has resulted in their failure to receive appropriate basic education facilities, health care delivery, employment and other economic and social benefits. These factors individually and collectively increase the vulnerability of these people and widen the gap – economic, social and technological – between them and others, for, example the urban communities.

Reaching out to barely literate people in the remote rural areas implies that conventional printed materials are of little use to them. Studies indicate that people in rural areas do seek survival information - relating to their work, business or trade, on matters relating to health, sanitation, family and child welfare, and on government programmes, regulations, and other development messages.

Much of such information they get from the visiting government officials and extension workers, the village elders, the local doctor, teacher, non-governmental organizations involved in rural development, and through radio and television where available and accessible.

PARTIES INVOLVED IN DEVELOPMENT EFFORTS

In a rural development programme / project there may be several parties involved at different levels, depending partly on the structure of the programme / project and on whether it is sponsored / supported by governmental or non-governmental agencies or a mix of the two, and on the sources of funding, and expertise. For example, interested and involved parties may include the end-beneficiaries of the output of development (tangible and intangible); the programme implementers (technical and managerial); the donor agencies and individuals; the legislators, policy makers, financial controllers, tax agencies, etc. Obviously, all of the parties need to be informed about the programme, may be on different aspects. In this context the type of information and nature of flow of information are important considerations.

RURAL DEVELOPMENT PROGRAMMES

Information Utilization

The pattern of flow of information has been studied, among other things, by Hall and De in respect of over 250 international agency supported rural development projects. Menou 's study noted a correlation between the measure of the capacity to utilize information and economic development – greater the utilization capacity higher the level of economic development.

Information needs of the rural community and how they seek information, and where do they get information from, if at all, need to be understood. Upadhya and Rao have reviewed the related literature. McChombu has studied the information needs and sources used by the rural community in four different countries of Africa. Bhatnagar and Schware present case studies from India including the application of information and communication technology (ICT) in community development programmes.

The use of folk arts for disseminating information on social issues to rural folks has been used in many developing countries, such as, India, for centuries. In recent times, innovative folk performing arts and media forms are used by such organizations as CDL (Communication for Development and Learning), CREA of Delhi and other NGOs, for dissemination of information and building advocacy among rural people and women in particular e.g. Tumhari Amrita and 'Women can't wait', a solo play by Sara Jones, all as part of a mission to take IT to poor children. Ian Witten has briefly described several initiatives in developing countries to communicate with and disseminate information to, rural folks and to bridge the digital divide

Ashoka, a global non-profit organization founded in1981, is involved in 'social entrepreneurship'; it has been trying to extend ICT enabled education to rural and urban under-priviledged children. In the first week of December 2001 Ashoka-Innovators for the Public, Infosys, Azim Premji Foundation, and other IT giants jointly organized a four-day workshop - 'Building Blocks for Technology Enabled Learning'. The workshop was aimed at making under-priviledged children in the slums of Bangalore city and rural schools familiar with IT and its use in education. The discussions centred around such issues as, IT-enabled learning in rural and urban environments, feasibility and role of IT in the learning process, and content, resources, and infrastructure required for an IT-enabled curriculum. Abhijit Lahiri, in his Curzon Seshachalam Endowment Lectures described briefly many initiatives in India to make information available to enhance the efficiency and effectiveness of rural people and the progress in e-governance in India. TARAhaat programme of Development Alternative, New Delhi, the experiences with telecentres in Africa and India, and the work of the M.S. Swaminathan Research Foundation, Chennai, especially in Pondicherry area are noteworthy

A special issue of *International Development* devoted to the theme "Equity, growth and participation: the information age," carries papers on communicating with rural folks and the problems thereof, the potential of folk arts, radio and television in this context, and present profiles of selected programmes to reach the masses. Increasingly the State and Central governments, and NGOs are involved in rural community development and information exchange is an integral part of these exercises.

The *InfoDev exchange Newsletter* carries information on

ongoing projects and other news items on information for development including the application of ICTs to reach rural communities. Reports and news bulletins of the International Development Research Centre (Canada) and of NGOs involved in development programmes are good sources of information on ongoing projects on information communication and outreach services to rural communities especially in developing countries.

Nobel Laureate anthropologist Margaret Mead, in her analysis of the impact of technology on various communities and groups, has reported on many instances of the failure of introduction of new ideas and innovations among South Pacific communities by international expert missions, there being several barriers to the communication to and acceptance of the ideas by, those communities. Erich Fromm (quoted by Benge) has also reported such instances of failures from Africa.

Upadhya notes: "The fact that nations have come to attach value and importance to the information sector is evident from such activities of governments and inter-governmental and non-governmental agencies as those related to the formulation of national information policies, development of information infrastructures, application of ICTs to development information systems and services, etc. Several developing countries are in the process of designing, developing and implementing mechanisms that could facilitate access to and enhancement of the use and application of data and information… There is an increasing flood of information generated all over the world; at the same time scientific and technical information is becoming increasingly more expensive and less affordable to developing countries. The dominant form in which information is made available, transmitted and exchange is changing from print to electronic media; and in communities that cannot afford or access information there is an 'information draught' situation. The situation appears to be particularly critical in the developing countries." Mchombu addresses some of the basic issues of accessing, processing and using development information in Sub-Saharan Africa. From these and other case histories we may summarize the barriers to development communication in the rural environment in particular into various categories as given in the succeeding sections.

OBSTACLES TO DEVELOPMENT COMMUNICATION

In most developing environments one encounters low literacy level, poor information communication facilities in terms of number and quality of newspapers in local languages / dialects, telephones, radio receivers, television sets etc. say per hundred persons due to historical, economic and political reasons, poor resources and / or resource mobilization and management capacity, and absence of an information use culture. The major barriers to effective communication can be grouped as follows:

- Language-related
- Culture-related
- Media-related; technology-related
- Relation between communicator and communicatee
- Level of communication competence of communicator and of communicatee
- Level of subject competence / knowledge of communicator and communicatee
- Presentation of information
- Legal, administrative and political factors
- Physical handicaps of communicator and communicartee
- Information system-related

LANGUAGE-RELATED FACTORS

- Multiplicity of languages and dialects (common to most developing regions of the world)
- Use of jargon – technical and other lingo
- Neologisms
- Use of codes in communication, including in man-machine interface.

- Synonyms, homonyms, and homographs, leading to misinterpretation of messages

CULTURE-RELATED FACTORS

- Diversity of cultures and traditions
- Apprehensions about technology
- Alienness to reality – differences in role perception, needs and experiences
- Difficulties in comprehending and accepting other cultural practices
- Inadequate or wrong understanding of local culture
- Misinterpretation of local practices

MEDIA-RELATED FACTORS

- Tradition, e.g. oral tradition |
- Visual perception | User-related
- Comprehension problems | factors
- Distortion introduced by media
- Voice distortion | Loss of
- Image distortion | information
- Environmental noise |
- Use of inappropriate or inadequate technology facilities

COMMUNICATOR-COMMUNICATEE RELATION

- Nature of relation – employer-employee; family relationship
- Standing in the subject
- Level, length and experience of previous interactions

COMPETENCE LEVELS OF COMMUNICATOR AND COMMUNICATEE

- Education
- Field of specialization
- Communication ability

PRESENTATION OF INFORMATION-RELATED FACTORS

- Standard vis-à-vis audience
- Clarity and organization of ideas
- Repetition, redundancy, and precision
- Style and elegance

LEGAL, ADMINISTRATIVE AND POLITICAL FACTORS

- Misinformation and disinformation – unintended; deliberate
- Propaganda
- Withholding and / or restrictions in the use, of information
- Economic reasons
- Confidentiality reasons –individual and corporate
- Security reasons – individual and corporate
- Administrative reasons.
- Use of the power of information and ICT for improving the welface of society, especially the disadvantaged sections, providing them information on their rights, privileges and responsibilities as citizens, women, children, and the socially, physically and mentally challenged; empowerment of citizen, especially women and those in rural areas. On the other hand, they may also be used by the State or social groups for exercising control over the dissemination, accessibility and availability of such information through selective filtration or complete blackout; controlling the media, file transfers, etc.; indulging in deliberate misinformation and disinformation activities;
- Cyber terrorism; data manipulation and the like.

Transborder data flow, patent information, copyright, personal and corporate privacy are related issues.

Physical and Mental Handicaps of Communicator and Communicatee

More particularly impaired vision and / or hearing, and mental, psychological and behavioural factors that affect communication.

INFORMATION SYSTEM-RELATED FACTORS

Some or all of the factors mentioned above may affect the information systems and services and interface between communicator and communicatee. In addition, the following system-related factors can affect efficiency and effectiveness of information delivery.

- Adequacy of information sources
- Adequacy of access to information sources, including location of information sources.
- Adequacy of information services
- Competence of information service personnel
- Level of user-friendliness of system
- Adequacy of user-sensitization, user orientation, user education
- Cost of information system and service
- Delay in information access and delivery
- Difficulties in obtaining pertinent information at the right time, in a form convenient to information seeker, user

CONTEXTUAL FRAMEWORK

In general, development communication has an organizational structure, that of the institution or development programme and also a symbolic structure, that is the meanings and values attached to the messages by the generators, the communicators and the recipients of the information. The three may not be co-terminus. Hence, effective development communication has to be achieved through a judicious blend of traditional and modern communication media and methods so as to facilitate the exchange of information among local communities on the one hand and between them and people of different categories elsewhere at the local, national, regional and international levels, on the other.

Within this framework the information communicated shoule

- be relevant to the development concerns of the people at the grass roots, that is, agriculture, literacy, food, water, health and sanitation, women, family and child welfare, conservation of natural and other resources, fuel and energy, environment protection, etc.;
- help prevent exploitation of people and/or deny them their rights to development, by others, whether the latter be locals, nationals or of other nations;
- build and enhance indigenous capacity to access, retrieve and use effectively development messages; and
- guide people in the positive, beneficial use of knowledge and prevent its use in ways that are harmful to people, material, and environment.

The method of presentation of development messages and the media used should enable overcoming barriers to communication. In this context it is important to consider such factors as:

- the information content, that is what messages are being disseminated and made accessible;
- accessibility to all at an affordable cost; and
- building / enhancing the capacity of people and institutions to select and use appropriate technology in information communication.

Development communication entails not merely providing access to data and information but also ensuring that the information is properly and effectively used and that it leads to an improvement in some aspect of the lives of the people. The latter need not necessarily be the users of the information.

Multimedia, videocassette, and CD-Rom have been used In developing countries for dissemination of information to and for use as learning tools by rural people. Such devices, prepared in local languages could be used in a large measure in the Indian context. But the contents should be carefully selected and planned and should relate to the needs of the target audience. In the past the medium of folk arts have been used in various campaigns with some success. These could be converted to multimedia and ported on to CD-ROMs, video-cassettes, etc. and more widely broadcast via TV and cable networks. Here collaborative efforts by different expert groups, financial support, and the assistance of TV and cable networks need to be mobilized.

It is also desirable to prepare a machine-readable well indexed inventory of materials already available in the country and kept updated. When the networks are established such inventories can be consulted online to facilitate inter-library and inter-institutional lending and also in preparing new materials.

Libraries, especially public libraries and community information centres can play useful roles. Libraries have information resources; information professionals have experience and expertise to organize and present information to meet specific user needs. Trained in media technology and communication skills, they can, in collaboration with extension workers, government organizations, and NGOs, play decisive roles. Local libraries can also collect and record information about specific local resources, practices, and innovations for wider dissemination.

Public and community libraries in some developing countries are using satellite communication to transmit information to and about, rural areas. Schools in rural areas could also benefit from such services

India has a strong IT manpower, especially in software development, and networking Networks such as DISNIC (NIC) are useful in collecting, recording and transmitting data required for planning, plan implementation monitoring, etc. at national and sub-national levels (state, district, taluq, village level).

India has made progress in extending and improving the telecom infrastructure in the recent past, but the pace is slow for a vast and populous country. Some of the developing countries of Asia (China, Korea, Thailand, Malaysia, Indonesia) are ahead of

India in this regard. There have, however, some welcome changes in recent months. Yet, the priorities have to be reviewed, policies revised and new strategies adopted to create a level playing field for the public, the private sector, academic institutions and NGOs, to enable them contribute substantially to development indifferent ways

CASE STUDIES

Case studies in E-Governance

The last two decades saw citizens all over the world demand better governance The tremendous growth in ICTs holds sufficient promise to fulfill these aspirations In the well researched book *E-Gov – E-Business Strategies for Government / Douglas Holmes and Nicholas Brealey*, (London, 2002) gives many examples from different parts of the world, from both developing and developed countries, how e-government can deliver public services in a consumer-friendly manner with better transparency and accountability.

In the beginning, of course, there was fear, mistrust and turf protection in many laces; however IT and an integrated online service have survived and come to stay. Thus:

- The entire Dhar village of Madhya Pradesh is now wired-up and connected to a network of cyber cafes for the benefit of farmers.
- Land records are accessible online in several Asian countries and banks aceept this for sanction of loans.
- Grain merchants are able to check product prices across India, at a cost that is less than five percent of a telephone call.
- Multimedia mobile units drive around Costa Rica providing Internet access, e-mail, and computer training to rural citizens.
- Estonia today is among the top 20 most connected countries of the world; two decades ago the country had no privately owned computers.

- One billion annual health insurance claims are sumitted electronically in France.
- It takes just 25 seconds for police in Scandinavia to transmit a fingerprint image to another force.

Thanks to uniformization of customs procedures and application of ICTs travel and financial transactions across the thirteen countries of the European Union has become almost seamless.

I an H. Witten, in his invited presentation 'Visions of the Digital Library", at ICADL-4, Bangalore, 10-12 December 2001, several examples from developing environments: The Kataayi Cooperative in Uganda; disseminating humanitarian information in Africa; in disaster relief situations; in preserving indigenous culture; and capture and dissemination of locally produced information. He relates these cases to the fulfillment of Dr Ranganathan's Five Laws.

Bhatnagar and Schware, ed., (2000) present interesting case reports from India under the following headings:

- Improving Services to Citizens and Bringing in Transparency.
- Decision Support to Public Administration for Improving Planning and Monitoring of Development Programmes.
- Empowering Citizens through Access to Information and Knowledge.
- Use of ICT for Training in Rural Areas.

IMPROVEMENT IN HEALTH CARE DELIVERY

One of the main reasons for the poor health care delivery in rural areas and areas remote from the metropolis and towns in developing countries is that the services of qualified and experienced doctors and other auxiliary health personnel are not easily and quickly accessible. One among several reasons why doctors and health personnel may not opt to work in these remote areas is that access to information about developments in their fields of interest is found to be inadequate and they feel isolated in this sense.

In the early 1950s, while doing graduate studies in the USA, I had made an analysis of the coverage of some 4500 medical periodicals by ten indexing and abstracting services (mostly English language). The report was partly published subsequently (Neelameghan, 1954). One of the findings of the work was that out of over 900 medical periodicals published in the Latin American countries fewer than ten were indexed by the ten abstracting and indexing services taken together. The probable reasons for this poor coverage were thought to be that several of the so-called periodicals were newsletters issued by individual clinics and hospitals reporting on cases; these cases, mostly reported in Spanish and Portuguese languages were deemed to be more of local interest; and many of the publications were irregular. However local news and case reports are of interest to the local medical practitioners and health workers.

Before the spread of national communications networks and the Internet, BIREME (the western wing of WHO), planned a project (LILACS), which brought together for cooperative work medical libraries in the Latin American countries. Selected medical libraries in each country were assigned the task of indexing certain medical journals in the country according to an agreed upon bibliographical format and using CDS/ISIS. The list of entries was sent to a national centre. The latter would then collate the entries and pass them on to the BIREME centre in Brazil. The centre then put the material on a CD and distributed copies periodically to medical practitioners. The CD also held UNEP's environment databases, international health legislation databases, medical subject headings, and union catalogue of medical periodicals in Brazil. Doctors willing to work in remote areas were also provided with microcomputers to use the CD. An item published in a medical journal could be located in the libraries through the union catalogue and photocopies obtained. Over a period of time the service caught on and health personnel were not averse to working in areas far removed from the cities. The remote areas thus began to receive better health care delivery.

These days BIREME provides access and connectivity via the Internet to several other medical information services, including full text translations of papers into Spanish / Portuguese of current journals and people to people contact.

INFORMATION PRESENTATION

I had occasion to visit a government department of agriculture in a developing country in Africa. We were discussing technology transfer and the problems of communicating research findings to the field level workers, such as, farmers. My host narrated the following instance.

A paper published in a scientific journal had reported that laboratory research and pilot field studies had shown that when seedlings (of a particular cereal) were planted 5 cm apart there was optimal use of water and better growth of the young plants. The department wished to spread the information among the farmers so they would adopt the technique in practice.

Of course no farmer could read and understand the English language research paper. The practical but technical information had to be translated and presented in a manner acceptable to and easily grasped by the farmers. Help from a known specialist in mass communication in anotherAfrican country was sought. One cannot expect farmers to use a scale to measure out the 5 cm in the field! He 'translated' the 5 cm to be roughly equivalent to the width of a closed fist. A large picture of farmers bending in the field with one fist closed and placed near the ground and the other hand planting seedlings on both sides was drawn up and shown to farmers. They interpreted the message of the picture correctly, and the picture was multi-copied for wider distribution. Later a video of the picture was made to show dynamic movement, adding greater realism to the message and being able to disseminate information to a larger audience at the same time.

POLICY – NOT TO USE A SOPHISTICATED TECHNIQUE

During one of my early visits to China (PR) on behalf UNESCO, in the 1980s, I was assigned, among other tasks, to survey the use of information in projects and practices relating to alternative energy sources (e.g. biogas, solar, wind, hydro-pump, etc.) and to collect information on such projects. By arrangement I visited biogas units, solar energy centres, etc. in different towns, had discussions and collected information, all through interpreters. Before arriving China I had read some papers in journals, mostly from Europe and USA, on the use of alternative energy sources in China, especially biogas and hydro-pumps.

Regarding hydro-pumps most of the articles appreciated their widespread use in agriculture / irrigation; but they also noted that the efficiency of the pumps was only about 75 percent whereas the then available technology could deliver up to 95 percent efficiency. Toward the end of my tour I had a meeting with one of the directors in the government department concerned with energy matters. During the course of the dialogue I told him what I read about the lower efficiency of the hydro-pumps used in the fields, whether this was due to non-availability of information on the current technology, or inaccessibility to the technology, or whether the farmers were not made aware of the current technological developments. The director said they knew about the technological development (in fact there are Chinese translations of foreign language papers), and has tested the new more sophisticated technology. However, as a matter of policy, they have not advised the farmers the use of the sophisticated technology for the following reasons: (1) The hydro-pumps that the farmers were then using were locally made and relatively cheaper, within the budget resources of the farmers; to raise the efficiency of the pump from, say 75 to 85 percent, the cost of the pump would almost double and go beyond the financial resources of the farmer. That would considerably reduce the number of users of the pump for irrigation, which will result in overall reduction in the yields of the farms; and (2) if anything goes wrong with the sophisticated / hitech pump, immediate local repair may not be possible; the farmer may have to wait for a expert technician to come from elsewhere and that will cost more and take time; meanwhile the farmers will be idle. Presently the local smithy, if not the farmer himself/herself could repair the indigenous pumps.

This is considerably cheaper and there is less idle time. Therefore, taking all these factors into consideration, as a matter of policy the high tech pumps have not then been introduced in field irrigation..

DIFFERENCES IN THE PERCEPTION OF DEVELOPMENT PRIORITIES

While on a development information assistance mission in Thailand, I happened to travel with the Vice-President (VP) of a development bank located in one of the South Pacific island countries. As we chatted about our respective work areas, I asked the VP as to how they go about evaluating development support requests, what types of information and data are required for the purpose, how the bank obtains such information from the rural areas, etc. He explained what they normally do – their own files on earlier grants, information from other similar countries, and people, especially locals, in the field, are used. But, he said, sometimes much depends upon the perception of the local people as to what they consider as their priority, which may be quite different from the perception of the bank. He narrated the following instance.

The development bank noted that the mosquito menace and other health hazards of a small town in one of the Pacific islands could be greatly mitigated by improving the local drainage and sewerage system. The bank was prepared to provide substantial financial support if the town authorities (council) would take up the work on a priority basis. However, from consultations with the local councilors and discussions with other elders of the town it became evident that the local top priority was to have a 'town band' more than anything else! Because the neighbouring town had such a town band and they made 'much noise' flaunting their possession during festivities! The priority perception of the locals could not be changed in spite of much discussion and persuasion attempts. Finally, a compromise was arrived at: the town council would have a band but it should also take up work for the improving the sewerage system. In such instances an outsider's (even donor's) perception of priority may not be imposed on that of the locals.

MISSING DETAIL MAKES MUCH DIFFERENCE

A town in a South Pacific island wishing to install biogas generator using the local night-soil, obtained the know-how from another developing country in the region. Financial assistance was available. Operations were started without much of a hitch. After preliminary tests and trials full-scale operations were begun. At the end of a year's operation yield of biogas was quite small. Information was exchanged with the institutions from where the know-how was obtained. Some changes were tried out; and yet after more than three years' of operation and effort and much additional expenditure the yield had not improved. A thorough examination by an outside expert showed that the locals had followed the instructions correctly, but he remembered a similar situation in another developing country – due to the difference in the acidity of the night soil of the user locale and that of the place from where the know-how was obtained. A missing apparently minor detail makes a great difference.

CONNECTING PEOPLE – PEACESAT

In 1983 I had occasion to participate in a demonstration of the information exchange process in the PEACESAT programme during a seminar in Manila using a simple foldable antenna. Some ten years later the facility was used to setup a discussion among and approval of some six librarians of the national libraries of as many islands in the Pacific on a project for developing an information network for the region prepared by an international group meeting in Papua New Guinea.

The Pan-Pacific Education and Communication Experiment by Satellite (PEACESAT), currently based within the Social Research Institute of the University of Hawaii, is a public service telecommunications network that links educational institutions, regional organizations, and governments in the Pacific Islands region. In partnership with the Telecommunications and Information Policy Group encourages development and public service telecommunications. PEACESAT is funded, in part, by the National

Telecommunications and Information Administration of the U.S. Department of Commerce and other programme partners. Currently there are 52 PEACESAT sites in 22 Pacific Island jurisdiction. Each site is able to use either voice of data capabilities. Some of the sites will be able to use the new digital capabilities. The facility provides the means for international cooperation in public service telecommunications and the sharing of knowledge, information, culture, and resources, thereby partially overcoming the barriers of distance among the Pacific Islands and between them and other centres around the globe.

There are very many programmes for which PEACESAT is used for information exchange among the persons, institutions and agencies involved in development activities. Some are regular periodical programmes (daily, weekly, monthly, etc.) and others are one-time programmes for a specific purpose. Teleconferencing, voice exchange, information and data exchange take place regularly within the framework of some 60 programmes. These cover health, nutrition, women, youth, aids, drug addiction, cerebral palsy and other disabilities in children, animal (livestock) health, fisheries, specific problems in agriculture, environment, distance education, etc. Organization for Community Network, Community Network System On Line, Emergency Weather Information Network, Pacific Island Internet Resources, are associated programmes serving the very dispersed communities.

REFERENCES

Benge, Ronald C. (1972). Communication and identity. London: Clive Bingley.

Bhatnagar, Subash; Schware, Robert, *eds.* (2000). *Information and communication technology in development: cases from India.* New Delhi: Sage Publications.

Crandall, Robert W. (2001). The digital divide: bridging the divide naturally. *Brookings Review.* Winter 2001; 38-41.

Emerging information and communication technologies and developing countries: a global agenda for collaborative research, Cairo Workshop report (1993). *Information Studies*, 2(3); 152-160.

Florina, Carly (2001). Crossing the digital divide. *Executive Excellence.* 4 January 2001; 2-3

Equity, growth and participation: the information age (1993). *Development, Journal of the Society for International Development*, 3(3) (whole issue)

Hall, E. T. (1973). *The silent language*. New Delhi: Affiliated East-West Press.

Hammond, Allen, L. (2001). Digitally empowered development: the growing gap. *Foreign Affairs*, 80(2); 96-102,

Holt, Glen E. (1995). Pathways to tomorrow's service: the future of rural libraries. *Library Trends*, 44(1);190-215.

Lahiri, Abhijit. (2001). The widening digital divide: community information services, the state-of-the-art in India. *CurzonCo Seshachalam Endowment Lecture, Bangalore, 5-7 December 2001*. Bangalore: Sarada Ranganathan Endowment for Library Science; 2001.

Levy-Strauss, C. (1966). *The savage mind*. Chicago: University of Chicago Press.

Mchombu, K.J. (1993). *Information needs and seeking patterns for rural people's development in Africa. Report on phase I of the INFORD Research Project.* Gabaronne, Botswana: Department of Libraryand Information Studies, University of Botswana.

Menou, Michel J. *ed.* (1994). *Measuring the impact of information on development* Ottawa, CA., International Development Research Centre.

A mission to take IT to poor children (2001) *The Hindu*, 2001-12-05.

Morino, Mario (1994). Assessment and evolution of community networking. Paper given at the *Apple Conference on Building Community Networks, Cupertino, California, May 3, 1994.*

Neelameghan, A. (1955). Abstracting services in the medical sciences. *Annals of Library Science*, 2(3); 89-96

Neelameghan, A. (1981). Information transfer: a third world perspective. *IFLA Journal* 7(1); 8-18.

PEACESAT. *http://www.peacesat.hawaii.edu*

Rose, John (2000). Multipurpose community Telecentres in support of people-centered development. *Information Studies*, 6(1); 5-28.

Upadhya, Padma V.; Ravichandra Rao, I.K. (2001). Rural community development information service and related aspects: a literature review. *Information Studies*, 7(3-4); 191-250

White, W. D. (1994). Outreach program for the information highway: designing programs for all. Paper prepared for *NIT (New Information Technology) '94, 7th International Conference, Planning the Global Information Infrastructure, Alexandria, Virginia, November 18-20, 1994.*

Witten, Ian (2001). Vision of digital library. *Digital libraries: dynamic landscape for knowledge access and management. The 4th International Conference of Asian Digital Libraries, 10-12 December 2001.*

3

Access Of Information For The Socially Excluded In Developing Countries With Special Reference To India

Arifa. K.,
Junior Research Fellow,
Department of Library and Information Science,
University of Calicut.

ABSTRACT

A greater penetration of ICT through the Internet, electronic mail, Group Ware, bulletin boards, newsgroups, video conferencing etc. has the capacity to decrease marginalisation. The pace of development in e-technology, e-commerce and e-government is increasing at an ever-greater rate internationally. Increasing public points of internet access through libraries, schools, hostels, hospitals, prisons, setting up community based ICT learning centres in disadvantaged areas, empowering communities through connectivity-all facilities quick economic, social and political transformation. The setting up of computer gyms and kiosks along British lines helps access information. The Indian economic situation, characterized by poverty, unemployment and poor health conditions, creates the socially excluded group, which needs to be 'wired' quickly. Initiative should be taken to combat the lack of telecommunication infrastructure and lack of computing literacy skills. A strong National Information Infrastructure is to be built and Strategic Information Systems covering wider sectors of economy is to be developed besides careful planning of community networks.

INTRODUCTION

The new century and millennium have opened with the world experiencing serious divides – demographic, economic, gender, genetic and digital. Reports on the ever-widening rich-poor divide have been published by organisations like the World Bank and the United Nations Development Programme. In the new digital divide, while the rich countries, and the rich in all nations, are benefiting economically and socially from the 'new economy' based on technology, knowledge, information and innovation, the poor nations and the poor in all countries are being further marginalized in their economic status and standard of life. Information Communication Technology (ICT) itself is an effective tool in combating this social exclusion. This paper aims to explore and discuss the issues and implications of Information and Communications Technology within the context of social exclusion for developing countries with special reference to India.

HERALDING ICT BASED KNOWLEDGE SOCIETIES –THE WAY OUT FOR DEVELOPING COUNTRIES

Knowledge is empowering. The growth of knowledge societies is becoming pivotal for the creation of resilient economies. The human brain is a valued resource in developed countries as is evident by the trends of brain drain from developing to developed countries. Knowledge when combined with capital labours, existing knowledge and other inputs produce goods and services and is thus a factor of productivity. In the developed countries, ICT have been the drivers of the knowledge society. They are providing new and faster ways of delivering and accessing information, innovative ways for real-time communication, and new ways to do business and create livelihood opportunities. ICT breaks all the natural, social, cultural and hierarchical barriers to knowledge sharing in an unprecedented manner

The transformation potential of ICT is not circumscribed to the developed countries. The potential is immense for developing countries but depends on what the perspective is. More than 850 million people in developing countries are excluded from a wide range of information and knowledge. The opportunities arising out of the info-tech revolution are immense and in convergence with a visionary approach and political-stimulant we have a powerful tool to transform the existing societal framework into a more just and equitable one.

The World Bank (1998) organised forum called "Voices of Poor" which got feedback from 60,000 people in 60 countries concluded that people wanted access to knowledge and opportunities instead of charity to fight conditions leading to poverty. And knowledge is not a scarce resource - it is infinitely expansible and proliferates with its use. Knowledge and information is therefore quintessence to initiate the development change process. In a knowledge society, there is not only an efficient transfer of knowledge but also a greater likelihood that such knowledge will be used effectively for empowerment and reducing inequality and poverty. The problem with many developing countries so far has been their inability to recognize the knowledge they possess, put a value to it and use the power of knowledge to their growth. Ironically, the value of the vernacular knowledge gets noticed in developing countries only after its value is recognized and put to use in the developed nations. India is an example, which witnessed a boom in the Internet technology sector because the government stayed out of it, and there were little hindrances to its growth. But moving towards a growth enabling policy framework can create more entrepreneurs within the country.

Developing countries need to recognize and value its human resources capital and capitalize on it to the task of amassing wealth of knowledge, which works for the poor and promotes social equality. The wealth of knowledge, in turn will create opportunities for developing countries to emerge from dependence of low-cost labour as a source of comparative advantage, increasing productivity and incomes. Avenues therefore need to be created for knowledge incubation to be supplemented by capacity-building support and enabling policy frameworks, which provide opportunities to people to use the power of knowledge for propelling their growth.

DIGITAL DIVIDE AND SOCIAL EXCLUSION

Digital divide is now used by politicians worldwide as shorthand to express fears that many people will miss out in a world where access to information, and the skills to handle it, will be increasingly important. There is no sole digital divide but lots of overlapping ones: between old and young, men and women, rich and poor, blacks and whites, northern hemisphere and southern hemisphere and, above all, between developed and developing nations. In the new digital divide, poor countries face the prospect of being further marginalised in an increasingly knowledge-based global economy. The Internet is still being dominated by the west, so being connected to the web is becoming a new dividing line between the rich and the poor. Most of the new business opportunities in the next few decades will be the creation of digital goods or the application of digital and Internet techniques to old economy products. All this will doubly hit those developing countries that the Internet has passed by. Thus Internet could bridge knowledge gap or lead to even greater divide between developing and developed countries.

Barely 2% of the world's population of more than six billion are linked to the Internet. Most people on the planet have never made a telephone call. In the US, Internet access costs a user only 1% of average monthly income, whereas in Uganda it costs more than a month's average (per capita) income. (Literacy Trust.UK.online, 2001). By the mid-1990s, the three more computerized countries in the world (USA, Australia, and Canada) had an average of 23 computers per 100 people, while three of the main developing countries (Brazil, China, and India) had an average of only 0.38 computers per 100 people. In 1995 more than 90 percent of all data networks, 95 percent of all Internet hosts, and 98 percent of ali ISDN networks were in developed nations. (World

Telecommunications Development Report, 1995). If nothing is done the divide between developed and underdeveloped countries will become far more enormous. The developing nations should strive to narrow the digital divide using ICT as a tool to tackle the various aspects of social exclusion.

Social exclusion has become the key concept in the international debate on social disadvantages. This signals the increasing awareness of social risks related to the current socio-economic transformation process. The U K Government's Social Exclusion Unit (1998) defines Social Exclusion as follows:

"Social Exclusion is a shorthand term for what can happen when people or areas suffer from a combination of linked problems such as unemployment, poor skills, low incomes, poor housing, high crime environments, bad health and family breakdown". This area is very wide ranging and can cover topics such as homelessness, ageism, racism, unemployment, poverty, poor educational attainment, sexuality etc. Many people who are socially excluded are on a low-income level and experience the poorest levels of health. The various problems experienced by people who are socially excluded often have a cumulative and reinforcing effect.

HOW THE NEW TECHNOLOGY CAN HELP THE SOCIALLY EXCLUDED- THE POTENTIALS OF ICT

The Internet, electronic mail, groupware, bulletin boards, newsgroups, video-conferencing; these are all examples of ICTs that have the capacity to decrease marginalisation and empower people to participate more fully by giving greater access to information and enabling them to build new or stronger connections to sources of support and assistance. What is required is basic literacy and numeracy, a little technical understanding, a lot of communication skills, and information handling skills. Many of these attributes can be gained, or significantly enhanced, most effectively in a community context, and that context brings with it all sorts of spin-off benefits.

ICTs can bring four major benefits to any socially excluded group:

a) Opening up new communication links or building on those already existing, both amongst excluded groups or agencies and between them.

b) Easier location of, and access to, information resources and support agencies.

c) Improving the range, focus and delivery of services and advice on offer.

d) More opportunities to increase skill levels through education and training.

These benefits can have a profound and far-reaching impact on all types of social exclusion, in part because of the features of ICTs themselves, namely:

a) Location independence.

b) Asynchronous use – senders and receivers do not have to be connected at the same time.

c) Signifiers of social status and identity are hidden (apart from video-conferencing).

d) Fast, cheap and easy to use means of communicating with others.

e) Multiple simultaneous accesses to Web resources.

f) Ability to link Web pages together.

g) Cheap and relatively easy self-publishing.

h) Use both encourages and enables the development of marketable computing skills.

i) Encourages collaboration and networking on a local, national and international level.

The location independence of ICTs is a major factor in their importance to combating social exclusion. Location can be a marginalizing constraint on people whose mobility is restricted, be they elderly, chronically ill, disabled, carriers, without their own transport in rural areas with little public provision or those who simply do not have enough money to travel. E-mail, groupware, video-conferencing and the Internet can all provide access to information and sources of help, as well as opening up the possibility of distance learning or working from the home.

In addition, ICTs provide otherwise isolated individuals the opportunity to make contact with others in similar position, via notice boards, web sites or e-mail, regardless of their location. This can help to build new relationships that might otherwise be unsustainable. Combined with the asynchronous nature of ICTs (other than video-conferencing), it is possible for people to make use of these resources where and when is most convenient for them. Video-conferencing apart, ICTs also provide an element of anonymity, which acts to strip away many of the signifiers of social status and identity that can contribute to the exclusion of certain groups. Ethnic background, gender, age, disability and appearance are all examples of differences that can limit or bias interaction and access to services.

Education, training and employment opportunities are all increased by the use of ICTs as a wide range of online advice agencies give advice and information about where and how to find services. Although the use of ICTs in itself helps to increase computing skills and boost employability, online education and training via distance learning or electronic tutorials can support learning even more. In addition, virtual employment agencies detail job vacancies and enable online applications. Teleworking may also increase the chances of finding employment for those in rural areas or lacking mobility.

ACCESS TO TECHNOLOGY

Access to Information and Communications Technology is a critical determinant of participation or non-participation in the Knowledge Society. Currently, around 50% of the Internet users are in the US; about 25% are in the Europe; and only 12-13% are in the Asia(World Development Report,1998/99)..The UN Human

Development Report (1999) shows the following facts regarding the international access to ICT:

a) There are more computers in America than all the rest of the world put together.

b) South Asia contains 23% of the world's population but has less than 1% of the world's Internet users.

c) In Africa, there are seven Internet hosts for every 1million people.

d) 40% of people in developing countries have never made a telephone call.

e) In 1995, adult literacy was less than 40% in 16 countries.

BARRIERS TO ACCESS

Information and communication technologies play an increasingly important role in reduction of social exclusion and have significant potential to assist with community development, by re-engaging communities and building community identity. However, ICTs can also reinforce social exclusion through inequality of access to the necessary equipment or a lack of the skills necessary to utilise them.

The current ownership of ICTs seems to be a symptom of social exclusion itself in its restriction to relatively well off urban professionals. Even where access to ICT equipment is not a problem, there are other exclusionary factors to consider. Many people lack even basic computing knowledge and skills, a situation that can be compounded by an absence of training or education opportunities. For some e.g. ethic minorities or refugees, language can also be a barrier to effective participation. Certain disabilities or physical impairments may also preclude ICT use without additional adaptive devices. 90% of new jobs demand some level of computing skill but, without training or education, many of those in socially excluded groups will be unable to take advantage of them. Lack of computing knowledge and skills may contribute to the growing divide between the IT literate and those who describe their skills as being "nonexistent". The information superhighway is not the case of a perfect information system as the information available on it is largely North-centric and what needs to be shared among the people in the Southern countries is simply not available on yet. Relevant and locally specific content constitutes the most critical element in growth of knowledge societies after connectivity.

ACCESS INITIATIVES

In order to increase IT access and usage nationwide and to target socially excluded groups, a strategy is to be developed for community based access to IT. It is necessary to create a network of clearly recognisable IT Access centres at local level. Sites for providing public Internet accesses include libraries, schools, government offices, post offices, community and voluntary sector, business sector and hospitals. Limited information can be accessed through kiosks. In order to attain computing skills, ICT learning centers has to be opened in disadvantaged areas.

Older workers and unemployed people should be encouraged to use computers. New College in Nottingham, UK has a mobile centre using satellite technology to bring learning to those like lone parents who cannot get to college. A Computer gym, which works with Peabody Trust in London and other groups is a mobile learning centre that provides informal training for children, teenagers and adults, ranging from basic computer skills to web page design. They find that for many people the cost of a bus fare or the lack of confidence in using schools, libraries or other formal environments prevents take up of free ICT training. Their truck, complete with eight networked computers, printers, scanners, digital cameras and staff, brings technology to people rather than the other way around. Through providing a friendly, relaxed environment they can capture people's imaginations and increase their self-confidence.

The government, the private sector, financial institutions and the aid agencies have an important role to play in improving ICT access by functioning as technology demonstrator, facilitator or propagator. Each country should establish a national ICT strategy that is responsive to sustainable development goals and separate funds need to be leveraged for achievement of these goals. The government has to invest heavily in boosting ICT access through online initiatives. Programmes such as the Sustainable Development Networking Programme of the UNDP and Electronic Networking for Rural Asia Pacific of IDRC/IFAD are providing valuable support in this area in many developing countries around the world. At the last G8 summit in Okinawa, the latest UNDP initiative, the Digital Opportunities Task Force (known as dot force) was endorsed by the world's major economic powers.Dot.force is designed to empower developing countries to start narrowing the digital divide but also to prevent the West's technology elite from extending its lead.

Further, there is a need to increase the penetration of computers among the developing nations by bringing down their costs and setting up community based computer centres in places where it would be impossible to provide individual access to computers. Mechanisms for donation of lower-version computers in places where they could still be put to use also needs to be explored. E-technology can transform essential services for instance through distance learning or distance diagnostic health care. E-government presents a tremendous opportunity for the use of information and communications technology in the provision of government services. If consumers are not educated and equipped to do business electronically then this could represent a serious impediment to the growth of e-commerce there.

COMMUNITY NETWORKING

Empowering communities through each individual is an unprecedented potential offered by the ICT. Community networking is an efficient way to create empowered individuals through increased access to information. Today networks can offer a range of technical facilities and specialist content, usually operating as nonprofit bodies with universities, colleges, libraries and other civic institutions acting as supporters.

US community networker Terry Grunwald, in her book

'Making the Net Work', suggests there are four main areas of benefit for community groups (and others):

a) **Information:** e.g. search engines, receiving newsletters, lurking in forums

b) **Communication:** e.g. one to one and one to many emails

c) **Collaboration:** e.g. working in virtual teams

d) **Visibility:** producing a Web site, publishing your own newsletter

PLANNING A NETWORK

Once the centre, local authority and other agencies decided to promote use of ICTs in a deprived area through a community network, the first step in this direction is to plan a network. Planning requires the following initiatives:

I. Think about the purpose:

1. Is the main aim to promote personal learning and enable people to develop work related skills?
2. Is it to improve the effectiveness of local community organisations?
3. Is it to create some common information service and enhance networking between community interests?

II. Start a process which:

a) Identifies needs in greater detail (whether personal, group, neighbourhood)

b) Audits existing skills and resources

c) Develops ideas for projects to address the needs, and fill the gaps.

   a) Then appoint project champions, recruit small teams to take them forward, gather agency support and resources.

III. Evolve an organisation:

a) How will the initiative be sustained beyond initial funding?

b) Is it necessary to form a new organisation, or could an existing organisation act as banker?

Building an effective community network in the future will depend on the following principles:

a) Joined up strategy and action
b) Joined up working
c) A strong infrastructure
d) Frameworks for performance measurement, regulation and audit broad enough to allow local autonomy.
e) Communities themselves given the power and responsibility to take action.
f) Engaging communities in decision-making
g) A long-term perspective
h) A strong and unequivocal message from central government

POLICY IMPLICATIONS AND NATIONAL INFORMATION INFRASTRUCTURE DEVELOPMENT

The developing countries should be able to efficiently acquire, organize, retrieve and disseminate information to support policy making and development process. They need to both anticipate and accommodate rapidly changing advances in telecommunications, computing power and multi-media and at the same time invest in infrastructure essential to their propagation. The government regulatory frameworks should be "de-bottlenecked" and instead let market forces develop and provide impetus to growth of the sector. In its role as a policy maker, the government needs to set up an information technology vision for the country to spearhead the knowledge revolution. There are four key areas to be pursued to build a national information infrastructure that fosters development in all sectors under its current socioeconomic situations:

i. Capacity Building in Electronic Communications
ii. Strategic Information Systems Development
iii. Immediate Connection to a Full Internet (TCP/IP)
iv. Sensitizing the Governments

ICT DEVELOPMENT—THE INDIAN SCENE

India has witnessed an impressive growth in the IT industry in the last decade. The IT industry in India was valued at $8.5 billion in 1999. A large portion of this can be attributed to export of software services such as customized software development, and software maintenance. The Ministry of Information Technology (MIT) is developed on the vision to make India an IT super power by 2008. Through the MIT the Indian government has undertaken several initiatives to attain this goal.

A country like India, with it's 1 billion population, over 500 districts, nearly 5,000 villages and sprawling metropolis' having population equivalent to that of many countries needs an extensive infrastructure to serve such a large mass of humanity. Currently only every 3 out of 100 people have access to a telephone line, computer penetration per family is fairly low as well.(MoGIT Report,2000). Overall, India's data communication infrastructure is expensive and limited. Teledensity in India is mere 1.5% and narrow bandwidth in most places does not support the use of Internet yet. The typical Indian consumer is not computer "savvy". The hardware and software are still prohibitively expensive and thus not available to the common man. As such, due to the low level of Internet access, e-commerce potential is very limited. The domestic market overall is fairly weak and the country does not have a strong home country customer base. The past and current Indian education system is set in a way that it does not promote creativity among students. Creativity is the key driver for innovation and entreprenuership.

IMPLICATIONS ON THE SOCIALLY EXCLUDED IN INDIA

All the developments in the IT industry in India have their implications on the socially excluded classes also. Efforts to make digitalisation available on public domain and to be linked to the to the information superhighway to enrich local content availability and in promoting its use proves to be of much use to the communities. For example in Dhar district in Madhya Pradesh, the farmers check rates at different agriculture market yards and choose the days when they get a better price. They have learned to access veterinarian advice on the email. In Tumkur district in Karnataka, the computerization of land ownership records has set farmers free from the entangles of the local revenue officials. Efforts from the part of the government to function as an ICT based model has been successfully carried out by the state of Andhra Pradesh by setting Andhra Pradesh State Wide Area Network (APSWAN). APSWAN, which presently connects each district node to the state capital over an optical fibre, would shortly link to 1170 smaller towns and offices. The government now intends to open information kiosks off the APSWAN so that citizen can transact business with the government paving the way ahead for the creation of knowledge societies.

There have been initiatives in the private sector also. Dr Sugata Mitra, vice-president of the Centre for Research in Cognitive Systems at NIIT, put up his first kiosk, containing a personal computer with an Internet connection, in the middle of Delhi in 1999. Street children immediately took to the machines and through their own curiosity and intelligence, learnt to become proficient. Since then he has put up more kiosks in various locations around India with the support of NIIT and other funding agencies. This effort will not only help in teaching computer basics but also other forms of education that will benefit the world's poorest people who have so far been left on the wrong side of the digital divide.

SIMPUTER, short for simple computer, is an invention of a group of Indian scientists, which enables the poor and the illiterate to surf Internet. It is a handheld device, a fraction of the cost of a PC running on three AAA batteries, which will give online access. It uses text-to-speech software called Information Markup Language that allows the Simputer to translate English text into a variety of Indian languages, then read the information aloud to the user. India, with almost 50% of population unable to read or write the Simputer provides access to information superhighway.

The most effective pathway by which technological and information empowerment can reach the unreached, is the one Mahatma Gandhi described over 60 years ago as 'attention to the poorest person'. He said that 'antyodaya' would help to promote a 'sarvodaya' society, characterized by high social synergy, where one individual's economic advancement is not at the cost of another's opportunity. To bridge the digital divide, Computer-aided and Internet-connected knowledge centres were started in rural Pondicherry in South India in 1997 as a part of the bio-village movement launched by the M. S. Swaminathan Research Foundation. All members of the rural population derive benefit from them, regardless of age, gender or social status. The knowledge centres have effectively empowered rural communities with information on the environment, health, sustainable agriculture and aquaculture, meteorology, markets and prices. Generic information is converted into information specific to each location. Providing this kind of life-saving information at the right time and place has generated a hunger for knowledge and a great faith in new technologies among the rural poor.

CONCLUSION

As things stand, access to new technology is distributed very unevenly throughout society. The ability to use new technology is rapidly becoming a skill as fundamental as the established literacies of reading, writing and numeracy. The drive to provide public access to new technology must also be coupled with awareness campaigns, training programmes, initiatives for people with special needs, lower user-costs and more user-friendly interfaces. Nevertheless, it needs to be realized that the formation of global knowledge society is under no single control as information available in the public domain is free to flow everywhere and all people have equal rights to it.

REFERENCES

1. Jayaweera, Wijayananda. "Including the Excluded: for Common Good of All", Tasknet Conference, New Delhi: 23-24 November 1999.
2. Social Exclusion Unit (Ed.): Bringing Britain together: a national strategy

for neighbourhood renewal. Report presented to Parliament by the Prime Minister by Command of Her Majesty, September 1998.

3. Human Development Report 1998/99, UNDP.
4. World Development Report, 1998/99,World Bank, Washington DC.
5. World Telecommunications Development Report, 1995. International
6. Telecommunications Union. Geneva: ITU.
7. Heralding ICT enabled Knowledge Societies
8. http://sdnp.delhi.nic.in/resources/internetinfo/articles/heralding.htm
9. Information and Communication Technology and Social Exclusion
10. http://www.student.city.ac.uk/~dt758/PrIssuesGroupCoursework
11. Information Society Commission Publications
12. http://www.isc.ie/cgi-local/publications.cgi?f=exec&id=34
13. Literacytrust.UK .Who has access to ICT?
14. http://www.literacytrust.uk/Database/ICTaccess.html
15. MoGIT Report. Page.2
16. http://www.american.edu/carmel/ph0616a/Page2.html

4

Information Access in Libraries: Methods and Problems

Manjunatha. K.
Librarian,
T.A. Pai Management Institute,
Manipal.

Dr. D. Shivalingaiah
Reader,
Dept. of Library & Inf. Science,
Mangalore University,
Mangalagangotri.

ABSTRACT

The explosive growth of IT has paved way to unprecedented phenomenon of access to information. The current information landscape is experiencing tremendous growth in the quantity of information, multiple and overlapping types and formats of information, redundancy in the information produced, and the ambiguity about the future of traditional text-based publishing. Open access for global information from a remote place is present day's fashion or necessity. Developing countries are faced with many technological inadequacies. Libraries need to understand the dynamics of service delivery in IT driven world and need balance between print and electronic resources. In this article the authors discuss about information formats and types, methods of information access, information access Process, problems of information access in developing countries. The authors also proposed an Information Access Model integrating print and electronic resources.

INTRODUCTION

The present day world is witnessing technology's edge in storing, processing and disseminating global information through open channels. Open access appears to be a permanent unanticipated feature of the Internet. It offers unparalleled riches to researchers to find out about new discoveries faster than ever before and they want that information delivered electronically to their desktops. Now, with the advent of information technology and digital information system, information is available in various forms and formats, which requires new dimensions while planning and organizing. The present day is characterised by death of distance, death of time zone, digitised storing and manipulation, services not tied to any specific delivery system, and an increased role played by software. Web access has become essential in mediating a digital world.

Cairncross (1997:xi) in her study on "*communications Revolution*" forecasts that the distance will no longer determine the cost of communicating electronically and death of distance will be the single most economic force shaping all of society over the next half century. Further, She (1997:xii) stress that the users anywhere around the corner or around the world and the new ways of communicating will wipe out distance as cost factor. A study by Hukill, Ono and Vallath (2000: 14) also reinforces Cairncross's predictions and further highlight the strength of digital technology, easier network technology, importance of software in scholarly communication.

Libraries play an important role in the academic world by providing access to world-class information resources and services and help to stimulate research among scientists and researchers community. Until 1980s, the libraries virtually had a monopoly on the provision of information through print resources and the users were completely dependant on them for the publications they needed to have. Now, the scene has changed with the emergence of information technologies producing voluminous research information electronic format accessible by anyone online. Today's Users are more knowledgeable with more technical skills and empowered with wider choices for seeking information. The information has become merchandisable asset and as a result many commercial vendors are providing packaged information on payment.

Thus, libraries are facing severe competition from commercial service providers and networking technology in particular Internet and www. Academicians, researchers and business executives are increasingly depending on electronic resources for timely/instant access to the right information. A library's survival depends on its capability to understanding customer* needs and responding fast to satisfy their needs effectively and efficiently. Coogan (1998: 1) also emphasises that "Obtaining information quickly is the main concern of users who want their library to be state-of- the-art and responsive to their needs. Knowledgeable staff provides seamless access to information regardless of format, whether the user is in the library or at a remote location". Considering the information access in information age the authors attempt to address the following questions in this article in special reference to library and information services.

- What is information access?
- What are the methods of information access?
- What is the information Access Process? And
- What are the problems associated with information access?

INFORMATION ACCESS

The late British Prime Minister Benjamin Disraeli once remarked: "As a general rule the most successful man in life is the man with best information" (Satyanarayana, 1986:56). 'Information access' refers to the means or modes through which information is made available, or to an entire range of possibilities for making information and information services available to the users. Campbell et al (1994) define information access as the "ability to quickly and easily find what you want and need in a pool of information".

A person seeks information keeping one or more goals in

mind and the goals may range from trivial information to a sensitive research area. The purpose of information access could be i) to monitor development of a well-known topic over the period of time; or ii) carryout stereotyped series of searches to achieve a particular goal; or iii) to explore/ understand the new subject of interest. Seibert, Kraimer and Liden (2001: 224) argue that a person seeks information to enhance his competency and skills and greater access to Information and information resources leads to his higher level of motivation, career success and organizational performance Further, they (2001:224) postulate that "access to Information and information resources are positively related to career success and satisfaction".

Information access is not a new phenomenon and it exists through ages. Though the concept of information access remains unchanged from the tradition of oral to online, the methods and tools used to access it keep changing over the period. While printing technology led information access primarily through print resources, the Information and communication technologies led it through digital resources accessible on-line. The transformation is illustrated pictorially in Fig.1

Library, the treasure house of information is no exception to this transformation. We can trace similar transformation from historical museum to traditional library to digital library. The transformation is depicted in Fig.2

METHODS OF INFORMATION ACCESS

The personal needs and requirements motivate a person to seek relevant information to satisfy that need. Traditionally, the information professionals have developed a wide variety of techniques to analyse, consolidate, organize and provide access to information. There are many methods through which an individual seek the required information. Broadly speaking there are three methods through which an individual seek information. The three methods are mentioned below.

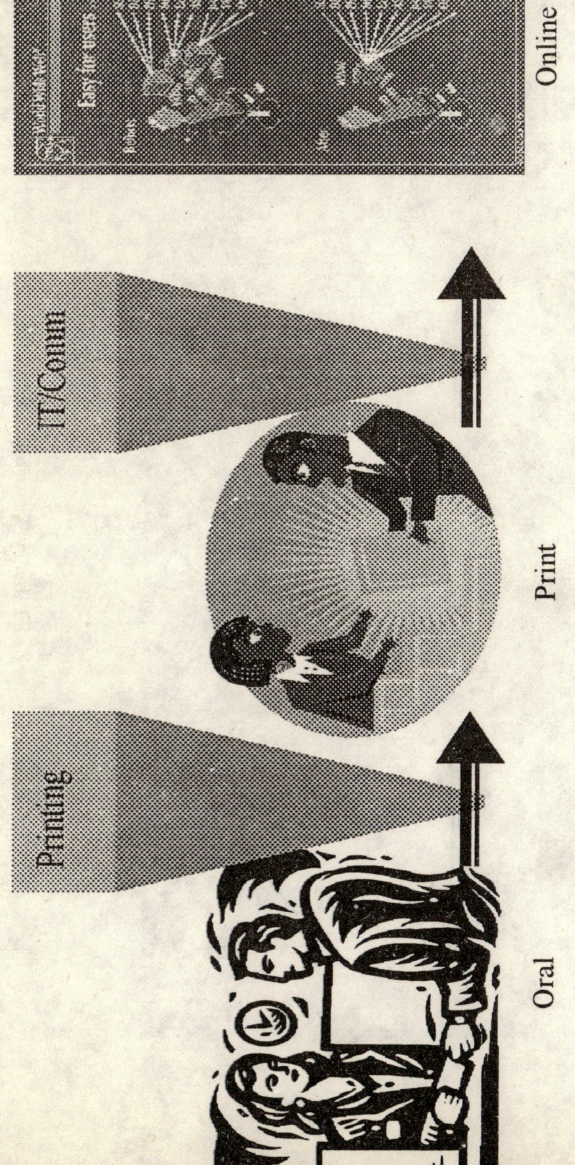

Fig. 1. Transformation of Information Access

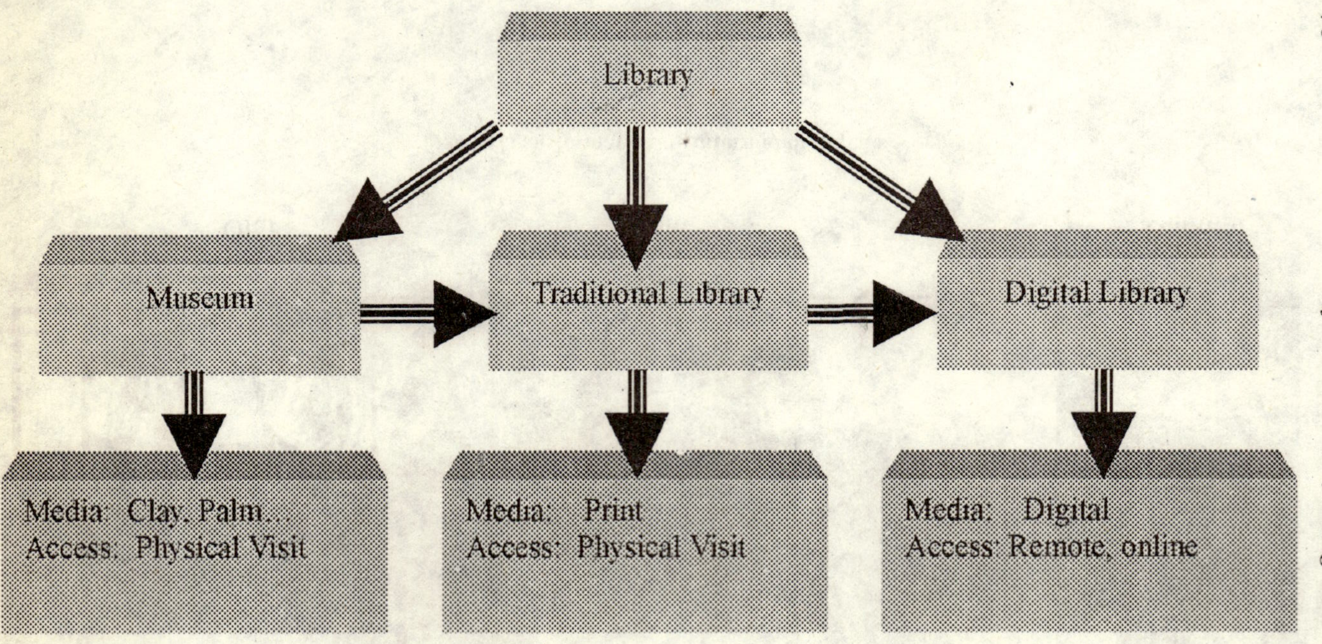

Fig.2. History of Library Transformation

3.1 Personal Contacts,

3.2 Computer Networks or

3.3 Visit to the Library

3.1 Personal Contacts

Personal contacts are often an extremely valuable method of information access. Personal contacts with appropriate individuals and organizations often provide unique perspectives or special information. Interviewing/discussing with experts or conducting own research study are sure ways of accessing information. The main sources of information could be friends, colleagues, teachers, relatives, and experts,

3.2 Computer Networks

Computer networks offer a new potential to satisfy information needs from home, office, or, with a laptop computer, from virtually anywhere. To a great extent, technical issues determine the quality of users' experiences with computer networks. Network technology plays a major role within the information setting by providing more options, more power, more speed, more complexity, and more requirements for technical expertise and competence. The Internet and web's quick and interactive access to large amount of dynamic information of customer queries facilitates improved customer relations (Lederer, Mirchandani and Sims, 1999:121). The power of online access lies in its capability of allowing user for concept searching through natural language. The access to electronic information and resources is done normally through two main channels namely "open access" and "restricted access".

Open Access : Through open access, the user gets free access to information for browsing through net. A few web search engines (yahoo.com; lycos.com; infoseek.com google.com etc.) allow users to the access the information free of cost and simultaneously it generates the revenue from advertisements and sponsorships.

Restricted Access: Information from many professional

associations and full text databases of research journals are not available free to browsers. They would be made available against Use-Based Payment and/or subscriptions. Today, subscriptions are the most popular method of payment for accessing research information on the web.

3.3 Visiting Library

Libraries are the repositories of results of thousands of research studies conducted by scientists and research scholars. They provide access to information, ideas and works of imagination and serve as gateways to knowledge. The users access the information available in print, non-print, micro or electronic format resources. The current information landscape offers a plethora of options for accessing the various formats and types of information as summarised in Table 1.

Table 1

Information Formats and Types

Information Formats	Information Types
Print/Paper: • Magazines/Journals • Books • Newspapers Non-print/ Electronic: • Videocassettes • Online databases • CD-ROMs • Magnetic tapes • Internet files Micro: • Microfilms • Microfiches • Microcards	• Textual • Numeric • Bibliographic/Citation • Graphical (pictures, maps, diagrams, charts etc.) • Audio and visual • Multimedia

Users may interact with any or all the formats in the library while seeking information. They may also encounter with library contact perscnnel to satisfy their information requirements. The mode of accessing information varies from format to format and type to type ranging from general browsing to use of special equipments. The exponential growth of IT and communication technologies have greatly influenced the methods, media and formats of information. As the present article intends to focus on information access in libraries, the personal contacts and computer networks in general are taken for granted and are not discussed. Further, it considers computers networks as an integral element in the domain of library services provided to their customers.

INFORMATION ACCESS IN LIBRARIES

In an academic environment, the users consider the library as their prime source of information. As mentioned earlier library is reservoir of both print and non-print knowledge resources. The library provides information access to its users through:

i) Conventional print resources indexed and catalogued (Print Resources);

ii) Micro documents with reader/printer facility (micro resources);

iii) Collection of networked CD-ROMs, both bibliographic and full text; tape-loaded databases available on a computer (Electronic Resources);

iv) Subscriptions to online services and own website;

v) Staff 's direct interaction (Ref. Services)

vi) Sharing of databases and other resources with neighbouring institutions (resource sharing); and

vii) Interlibrary loan and document delivery services (ILL)

People frustrate when they know that a potentially useful resource or service exists, but they are not able to use it in the timeframe in which it is needed. The conventional library with its massive weight of paper gathering dust and restricting efficient searches is another paper-based institute that sets fingers at the keyboard. The sense that information is "there" somewhere, but cannot be found can drive anyone to digitise (Brown and Duguid, 2000: 179). IT applications are erupting and moving faster than one's imagination resulting in information explosion and the libraries are forced to meet the challenges of users' increasing need for electronic resources. While providing access to electronic resources through campus-wide networks, it is desirable and necessary for library professionals to be knowledgeable about the open access sources and restricted access resources and streamline their efforts to optimise the use of resources.

INFORMATION ACCESS PROCESS

In the "olden days" (i.e. few decades back) Information seeking was relatively a simple process of locating print resources and extracting the required information. A visit to the library or bookstore was generally sufficient. Access points provide users different ways to search for information. The major points of access are keyword, subject, author and title. These may vary depending on whether the user uses a print or electronic resource. In a paper world the tolls to access the information were via catalogue, table of contents and the index. Now, the picture has changed. One must know which source- print or electronic, how to access and manipulate it. Keyword is a very popular way of locating information in print on online resources. The hierarchical metaphors used in print resources are redundant in digital world.

Information access process assumes an interaction cycle consisting of query specification, receipt and examination of retrieved results, and then either stopping or reformulating the query until a desired result is obtained (Baeza-Yates and Ribeiro-Neto, 1999). They also highlight that the user's information need is static and the information seeking process is one of successively refining a query until it retrieves the documents relevant to the original information need. Further, they described a simple interaction model (used by web search engines) as shown in Fig.3 that most information seekers use today

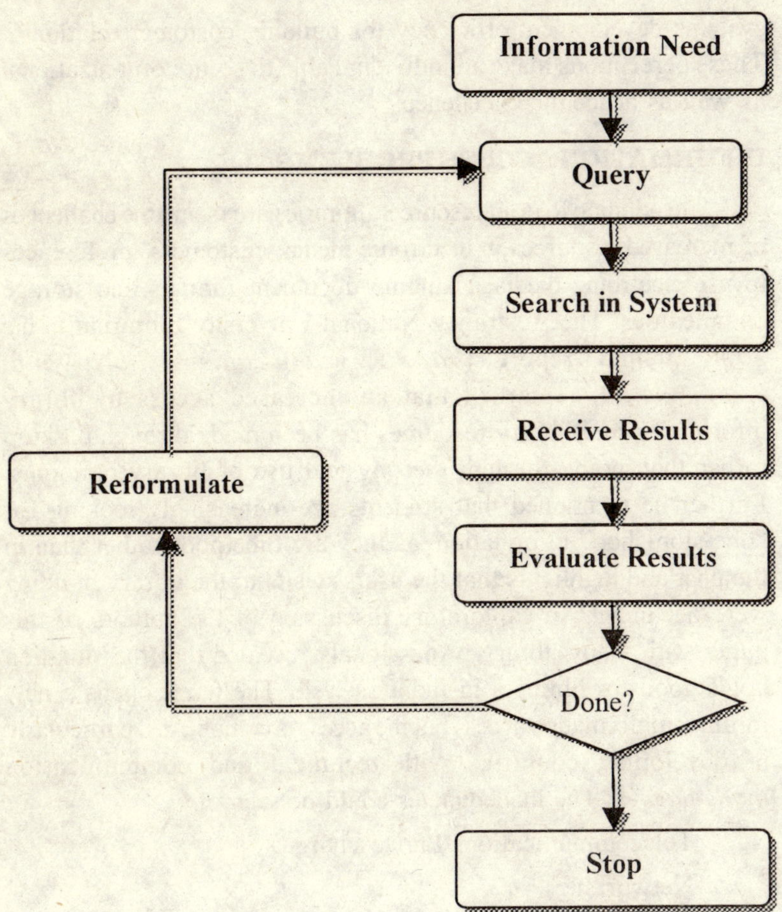

Fig 3. Model of Information Access Processes

O'Day, and Jeffries (1993) noticed that Information searching is only a part of the complete work process. "In addition to" or "in between" the users may engage in reading, annotating and/or analyzing the retrieved information. Further, they divide the information access process into two main components namely "Information search/retrieval and "information Analysis/ synthesis of results". A study by Lederer, Mirchandani and Sims (2001: 117) highlights the "importance of information access, information flexibility, information quality, communications efficiency and systems development efficiency for building customer relations". These perceptions make an individual able to secure organizational as well as academic excellence.

INFORMATION ACCESS PROBLEMS

In addition to print resources, libraries are facing the challenges of increased resources in electronic media; customers' preferences to use electronic media, changing document formats and storage complexities. The Australian National University Librarian in his 2000 annual report (*http://www.anu.edu.au; library.info @anu.edu.au*) remarked that an increased access to library information and library resources has been made through desktop rather than going through the physical use of library buildings. Further he mentioned that students are increasingly looking for "one-stop-shop" information, as they are time poor rather than in the past and highlights that the users' visits to the library building were declining. An exploratory discussion of the authors of this paper with many library professionals revealed that the situation holds good for libraries in India as well. The www opens a new forum for information access but the access is complicated particularly in developing countries with technical and communication *inadequacies*. The inadequacies could be seen in:

- Telecommunications/Phone charges
- Networking
- Computer Hardware and Software.
- Infrastructure
- Web Design
- Fund Allocation
- Professional /Technical skills
- Management's Support
- Speed response to customers
- Campus-wide/Remote access

Wresch's Study (1998: 295) on information access problems

in Africa looks at the many barriers to information access in Africa: - limited budget, restricted access, limited television production, high production costs, miniscule databases and complicated web access. A report on Remote Access Management Programme (RAMP98) submitted to University of California, Davis, reveals the following features, which to be considered while attempting to provide remote access to information.

- Campus-wide remote access
- Cost of campus remote access
- Accessibility
- Speed
- Low Cost of maintenance
- Equal access to all segments
- Accessibility beyond campus area
- Security.
- Cooperation from constituent colleges
- Support of applications that are used through remote access services

India is fast moving towards technological excellence and adoption of its applications. But still there is long way to go. The above-cited issues need to be considered by Govt. and private organizations and policy makers while providing open/remote access to people. Improved infrastructure facilities beyond cities, continuous flow of fund; high-class computers and its accessories at low price and internationally compatible software standards are much desirable to overcome the barriers.

INFORMATION ACCESS MODEL FOR LIBRARIES

Generally, the user interacts with resources, services and staff while searching for information. The encounter between the four elements is shown in Fig.4.

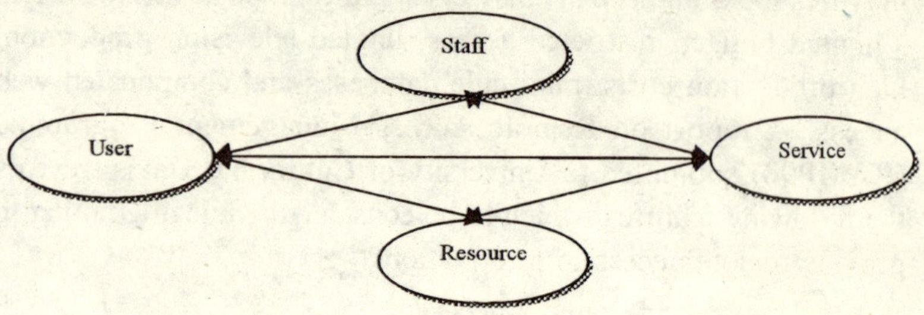

Fig. 4. Interaction Between User and Library

The ultimate goal of a library is to service its customers. Customers or users are the principal beneficiaries and the other elements are equally important to meet the customer needs and improve the customer relationship. Though technological developments and electronic resources are sweeping the world of scholarly communication, the print media cannot be ignored as print media is still considered as a prestige issue among the scientists and researchers' community. Some technical issues are beyond the control of library professionals. We propose the following "Information Access Model" as shown in Fig.5 integrating print and electronic resources.

The proposed model is the amalgamation of print and electronic resources. It also integrates technology adoption, Intra / Inter organizational networking and staff elements. The issues, which need to be considered under each element in the model, are described below.

1 Core Print Collection:

- Develop core book collection with latest editions and new titles.
- Increase research journal collection in core subject area.
- Increase the variety in newspaper in subject area.

2 Electronic Resources:

- Develop In-house databases of print collection in library
- Develop local databases for example union catalog

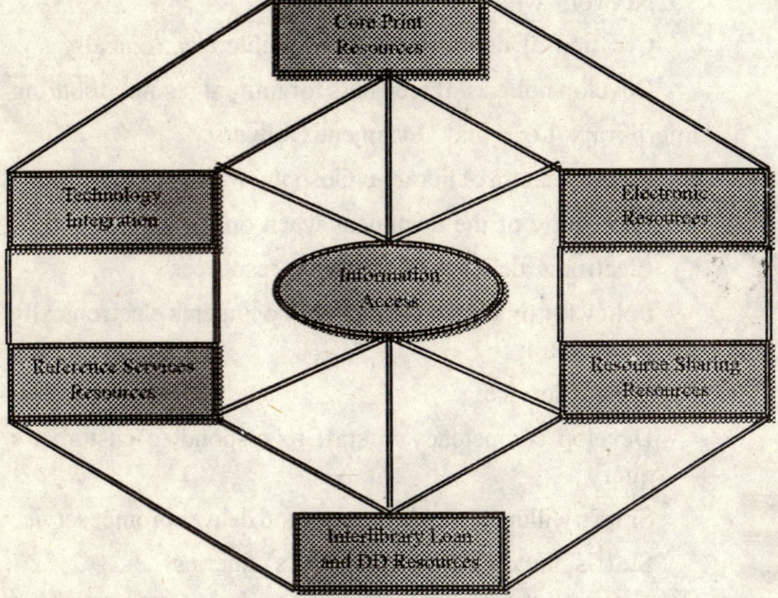

Fig. 5. Information Access Model

- Subscribe to online services or commercial databases
- Providing links to other open web resources.
- Periodic information Alerts

3 Technology Integration:

- Provide access through campus-wide network (Remote Access)/Intranet access
- High-Performance hardware
- Software compatible with international standards
- Standard packaged software from reputed developer/ vendor (if development of in-house software is not possible)
- Develop own website/Internet access

4 Resource Sharing:

- Network with local libraries,

- Network with similar institutions
- Creation of union catalog accessible electronically
- Develop policies/agreements for mutual resource sharing

5 Interlibrary Loan and Document Delivery:

- Classic mantra of library philosophy with electronic access
- Photocopy of the document when only text required.
- Electronic delivery of digitized resources
- Policy for timeliness delivery of documents electronically or manually

6 Reference Service:

- Develop competency in staff to respond to customer's query
- Staff's willingness to help users and deliver prompt service
- Staff's Timely response to users' queries

With this model we are trying to integrate the traditional and high-tech resources for the efficient and effective service delivery. The excellent resources and facilities will not achieve success unless the staffs are knowledgeable and responsive and empathetic to attend customer needs.

CONCLUSION

The methods and process of accessing information is changing fast. Information overload, information quality, information management and speed of accessibility are key issues of IT driven world. Remote/open/global access is today's buzzword as the users are finding lesser and lesser time to come to library for free or leisurely reading. It is clear that access to the information infrastructure, the ability to produce and consume are the determinants of individual's economic success and social mobility. Libraries need to understand the dynamics of service delivery to users and make sincere attempts to provide speedy access to both electronic and print resources. These two resources sometimes supplement or sometimes compliment each other. As print resources still dominate the scholarly publishing, libraries need to balance between the two resources. The requirements for print access and storage should be efficiently handled and providing electronic access via the desktop needs to be enhanced.

Good quality library services form an essential component of the universal access and libraries have a responsibility to facilitate access to expressions of knowledge and intellectual activity. Thrive on ongoing improvement in process, operations and service delivery to the customers. To accomplish this we should manage the library to performing up to their potential looking for opportunities and make them better and translating these opportunities into realities. Traditional library professionals should stop worrying on declining trend for use of print materials and become proactive to grab the opportunities available to them. This calls for genuine commitment and initiation from library professionals to develop a system, which allows users to access the information not only within four walls of physical library but also from remote corner through a mouse click. The also necessitates the professionalism in librarians and management's interest and commitment to provide adequate financial support and encouragement.

REFERENCES

1. Arms, William Y (2000): Economic Models for Open Access Publishing. *iMP Magazine*, March 22: 1-7
2. Baeza-Yates, Ricardo and Ribeiro- Neto, Berthier (1999): Modern Information Retrieval. Boston: Addison-Wesley-Longman Publishing Co. Chap 3.
3. Brown, John Seely and Duguid, Paul (2000): The Social Life of Information. Boston: Harvard Business School Publishing: 171-200
4. Cairncross, Frances (1997): The death of Distance: how the communications revolution will change our lives. Boston: Harvard Business School Publishing: i-xiv.
5. Campbell, Paul et al (1994): Information Access- a corner stone for web publishing. In Electronic Proceedings of the Second World Wide Web Conference '94: Mosaic and the Web organized by the Information Technologies Division (ITech) at the National Centre for Supercomputing Applications (NCSA), University of Illinois at Urbana-Champaign

6. Coogan, Elizabeth et al (1998): Service to Users Task Force Report submitted to Brown University Library in October.

7. Hukill, Mark; Ono,Ryota and Vallath, Chandrasekhar (2000): Electronic Communication Convergence. New Delhi: Sage publications India Pvt. Ltd.: Chap 2.

8. Humphrey, David (1998): Avatars and Navigation Strategies. *Information Services and Use* 18(3): 159-161.

9. Lederer, Albert L; Mirchandani, Dinesh A and Sims, Kenneth (2001): The search for strategic advantage from World Wide Web. *International Journal of Electronic Commerce*. 5(4), Summer: 117-133.

10. McGuinnes, Claire (2000): Can Students Navigate the Information Universe? *Information World Review* (120), Oct.: 10-11.

11. O'Day, Vicki L and Jeffries, Robin (1993): Orienteering in an information landscape: how information seekers get from here to there. In *Proc. of the INTERCHI '93*, Amsterdam, Netherlands, April 1993. IOS Press.

12. Satyanarayana, P.V (1986): Business Information: Great Lacuna. *Business World* 4(13), Sep 16-29: 56-57.

13. Seibert, Scott E; Kraimer, Maria L and Liden, Robert C (2001): A Social Capital theory of Career Success. *Academy of Management Journal* 44(2) April: 219- 237.

14. Wresch, Williams (1998): Information Access in Africa: Problems with Every Channel. *Information Society*, 14(4), Oct-Dec: 295-301.

5

Library And Information Science Research In The Changing Scenario Of Digital Information And Communication Technologies

Dr. M. Nagarajan

Reader,
Department of Library and Information Science,
Annamalai University,
Annamalai Nagar.

Dr. S. Surianarayanan

Librarian (Selection Grade),
Sri Paramakalyani College,
Alwarkurichi.

ABSTRACT

This paper deals with the Research activities in the field of Library and Information Science in the changing scenario of digital Information and Communication Technologies. The changing global environment due to the adoption of Internet and its supporting ICTs e-mail, EDI and Online Data Access in the research in LIS reduce the laborious and hectic works in unnecessary routines. This paper clearly describes the digital resources available on net for the research activities in LIS. Details of various databases, e- joumals and statistics and statistical tools available on www in the field of LIS have been discussed.

This paper also describes the usage of ICT in various routines in the field of LIS research ranging from choosing the problem, literature collection, data collection, and data analysis to submission of thesis. Some valuable suggestions and recommendations for the better usage of ICT in LIS research have been given. The URL of various web sites where the databases, e-journals, statistical tools for doing research are available have been given along with the titles. IT environment in the LIS will create a good and fruitful atmosphere for developing research activities and carrying research projects through the ICT.

INTRODUCTION

In any field, the research is the scholarly one developed on the basis of certain earlier findings and derived concepts by framing the objectives and formulating suitable hypotheses with systematic methodology of research design, review of literature, data collection, data analysis and reveal the findings with suitable suggestions and recommendations. A good research should also give the guidance for the future research avenue in the same field. The research activities can be speeded up and finished within the shortest time and stipulated period if the ICTs used for carrying out the research projects are powerful.

LIBRARY AND INFORMATION SCIENCE RESEARCH IN EARLY DAYS

Research in the field of Library and Information Science falls under the category of Social Sciences and hence a suitable research design and ways and means have been derived for doing research in this field. Since the Social science research is mainly dealt with the human problems, knowledge, thought and experience in the society, powerful qualitative evolution methods have to be introduced and suitable statistical tools also have to be used in testing the hypotheses. The researchers will also have to spend lot of money, manpower, material, and minute for literature collection, data collection and analysis etc.

LIS RESEARCH IN THE CHANGING SCENARIO OF DIGITAL ICTS

The revolution in the field of Science and Technology has created tremendous changes in the field of Information and Communication by introducing computers and networking facilities. The emergence of Digital technology has cleared the way for the entry of the digital ICTs like Internet, e-mail, EDI, Online Data Access that have become the powerful channels for spearheading the data transmission.

The hectic work of doing research in the field of Library and Information Science in those days has been made easy with the help of digital ICTs. These ICTs help the researchers from the very beginning of choosing the research problem to till the submission of thesis in easy ways without much difficulty.

DIGITAL RESOURCES FOR LIS RESEARCH

Internet is the backbone of all the other digital ICTs and a large number of digital resources are available on Internet for doing research in the field of Library and Information Science. Various web sites providing information on General Resources, National and State libraries, Library homepages and gophers, Library online catalogues, Research and Reference services, Technical services, Special collections, Digital library activities, Professional organizations, Professional journals and Library Vendors. Some of the details of the digital resources and their URLs are given below:

a. Databases

A large number of citations and full text databases are found on the Internet, which are useful to know the latest research trends in LIS, identify the research problem, collect the previously published literatures available on the specific topics. The following are some of the databases available on www, which are useful for researchers in doing research in LIS.

1. ACM Digital Library
   http://www.acm.org/dl/
2. Adobe PDF Document Search Interface
   http://searchpdf.adobe.com/
   - Ø It allows searching of over a million PDF documents located on the web.
3. Australian Digital Theses Program
   http://www.acer.edu.au/library/theses_frameset.html
4. Collection of Computer Science Bibliographies
   http://liinwww.ira.uka.de/bibliography/
   - Ø The collection currently contains more than one million references (mostly to journal articles, conference papers and technical reports) and consists of 660 MBytes of BibTeX entries.
5. COPAC
   http://www.copac.ac.uk/
   - Ø COPAC provides FREE access to the merged online catalogues of 21 of the largest university research libraries in the UK and Ireland.
6. Information Science Abstracts (ISA) http://www.library.pitt.edu/resources/database_info/isa.html
7. Library and Information Science Abstracts (LISA) http://www.library.pitt.edu/resources/database_info/lisa.html
8. Networked Digital Library of Theses and Dissertations (NDLTD) *http://www.ndltd.org/*
   - Ø The goals of the NDLTD are as follows: "To improve graduate education by allowing students to produce electronic documents, use digital libraries, and understand issues in publishing.
9. ResearchIndex
   http://citeseer.nj.nec.com/cs

- Ø It is a digital library that aims to improve the dissemination, retrieval, and accessibility of scientific literature.

10. UNESDOC: UNESCO Full Text Documents

    http://unesdoc.unesco.org/ulis/

    - Ø It Provides access to full-text documents published by UNESCO, many on issues related to library and information science, such as copyright, access to information, and so on.

b. Journals

There are large numbers of journals available on Internet. Some of them are giving only abstract of the articles and some are giving full text articles. Some of the journals are print versions published also in digital forms while some are online journals published only in digital forms. The following are some of the LIS journals available on Internet.

1. Ariadne

   http://www.ariadne.ac.uk/

2. BUBL Journals: Library and Information Science

   http://bubl.ac.uk/journals/

3. Bulletin of the American Society for Information Science

   http://www.asis.org/Bulletin/

4. College & Research Libraries

   http://www.ala.org/acrl/c%26rl.html

5. Computers in Libraries

   http://www.infotoday.com/cilmag/ciltop.htm

6. Cybermetrics: International Journal of Scientometrics, Informetrics and Bibliometrics

   http://www.cindoc.csic.es/cybermetrics/

7. Digital Information in the Information Research Field

   http://informationr.net/fr/freejnls.html

8. D-lib Magazine
   http://www.dlib.org/
9. EContent
   http://www.ecmag.net/
10. e-OnTheInternet
    http://www.isoc.org/oti/
11. IFLA Digital Libraries: Electronic Journal and Text Archives
    http://www.ifla.org/II/etext.htm
12. Information Research
    http://informationr.net/ir/
13. Information Today
    http://www.infotoday.com/it/itnew.htm
14. Informing Science
    http://inform.nu/
15. Intranet Professional
    http://www.infotoday.com/IP/default.htm
16. Journal of Digital Information
    http://jodi.ecs.soton.ac.uk/
17. Journal of Southern Academic and Special Librarianship
    http://southernlibrarianship.icaap.org/
18. KMWorld Magazine
    http://www.kmworld.com/publications/magazine/
19. Learned Publishing
    http://www.alpsp.org.uk/journal.htm
20. Library Philosophy and Practice
    http://www.uidaho.edu/~mbolin/lp&p.htm
21. LIBRES: Library and Information Science Research Electronic Journal
    http://aztec.lib.utk.edu/libres/

22. MLS: Marketing Library Services
    http://www.infotoday.com/mls/mls.htm
23. NewJour
    http://gort.ucsd.edu/newjour/
24. ONLINE
    http://www.onlineinc.com/onlinemag/index.html
25. Research Resources on American Periodicals
    http://home.earthlink.net/~ellengarvey/rsapresource1.html
26. Searcher: The Magazine for Database Professionals
    http://www.infotoday.com/searcher/default.htm
27. Sociosite/ICAAP Journals Database and Distribution Centre
    http://www.icaap.org/database/journals.html
28. Studies in Bibliography
    http://etext.lib.virginia.edu/bsuva/sb/
29. Transforming Traditional Libraries
    http://www.lib.usf.edu/~mdibble/ttl/
30. Journal server
    http://www.journalserver.org
    - Ø It is web site created by Oxford university for putting international reputed scholarly journals in various fields for the benefit of research scholars.

c. Statistics and Statistical Tools

Statistics is one of the powerful weapons in the field of research, which helps to attain the required result and test the reliability and validity of the arrived results. The manual way of doing the statistical calculations have been replaced by the ready-made software packages those make the process quickness and save the time. On Internet, large numbers of web sites are available for giving various statistical data and reports relating to library collections, expenditures, personnel, enrollment, etc. Apart from that some websites are found giving the guidance, instruction and illustration to calculate various statistical methods. The following are some of the examples of web sites relating to statistics and statistical tools available on net.

- Ø Statistics Every Writer Should Know
  http://www.robertniles.com/stats/
- Ø Rice Virtual Lab in Statistics
  http://www.ruf.rice.edu/%7Elane/rvls.html
- Ø Quantitative Data Analysis: An Introduction
  http://www.gao.gov/special.pubs/pe10111.pdf
- Ø Multivariate Statistics: A Practical Guide
  http://www.pfc.cfs.nrcan.gc.ca/profiles/wulder/mvstats/index.html
- Ø Internet Crossroads in the Social Sciences — Data and Program Library Service
  http://dpls.dacc.wisc.edu/internet.html

LIS RESEARCH ROUTINES IN THE DIGITAL ICT ENVIRONMENT

The Research routine of Library and Information Science has accommodated the latest digital ICTs environment and in each and every parts of routine the ICTs are more used to achieve the goal quickly.

Choosing the Problem

In choosing the research problem in the field of LIS, the digital databases available on Internet are being used. Most of the abstracts and Current contents are available in online and back issues are in CDs.

Literature Collection

Review of literature is one of the important aspects in the research routine. For that the back issues of the scholarly journals, Project reviews, Conference proceedings, and dissertation abstracts will have to be consulted. To obtain these resources the scholars need not go to far away big libraries and research centres. They can access them through Internet as large number of e-journals, Project reviews, Conference proceedings, abstracts and working papers are available on net.

Scholars can contact the Big libraries and Research centres through e-mail and collect the resources. More over information from abstracts available in the digital forms in most of the foreign universities can be got through EDI.

Data Collection

The data collection work in the field of Library and Information Science can be done with the help of digital ICTs more effectively and quickly. The e-mail, which is considered as the cheapest, and quickest communication technology can be, used for communicating to the samples to speedup the data collection. The Interview schedule may be put up on the net by creating a web site. The data collection may be organised by Online Data Access by applying the real time technology on the web.

Data Analysis

The Data analysis may be organised by creating digital databases in suitable software such as Visual Fox Pro, MS-Access, d-Base III etc. The software packages available for statistical testing such as SPSS, EXCEL, and LOTUS may be used to find the statistical out puts quickly.

Online data analysis can also be organissed with the help of the Computer and Information Personals. The statistical resources and tools available on the Internet such as. Simple Interactive Statistical Analysis (SISA), Data Desk, MODSTAT, S-PLUS, Statistica, XLISP-STAT, UCLA Stat page etc can also be utilized for data analysis and statistical testing.

Submission of Thesis

Apart from the printed version most of the Universities are instructed the candidates to submit the thesis in the form of CDs.

In some Universities the candidates are asked to produce the thesis in CDs for quick evaluation. The e-mail and EDI are used to send the thesis for valuation in many Universities.

SUGGESTIONS FOR BETTER USAGE OF ICTS IN LIS RESEARCH

The Research in LIS has been increased because of the usage of digital ICTs in research works. Even though the ICTs save the time and reduce the cost, the utilization of ICTs has not become full-fledged. It is due to the services of these ICTs that are not available fully to all the researchers in all parts of the country. The following are some of the suggestions and recommendations for the better usage of ICTs in LIS Research.

The Researchers should have familiar with the operation of all digital ICTs

The data transmission speed is very low in most of the places and it can be raised by increasing the bandwidth of the server.

The Internet should be made accessible by Local Calls in all places.

Grant may be provided to the Researchers for getting IT environment for doing research.

Workshops may be organised for accessing digital resources both in online and offline.

Telephone charges may be reduced or even cancelled for accessing Internet for research purpose.

OFC lines may be strengthened in all places for the better data transmission.

CONCLUSION

The digital ICTs have played a major role in changing the Research in Library and Information Science. The revolution occurred in the global environment facilitates that most of the resources are made available in www which can be accessed by any one from any where in the world. The digitisation of library resources and emergence of digital libraries and virtual libraries really become the backbone to Research activities. E- Journals also play a prominent role in satisfying the Researchers' literary needs. The digital ICTs Internet, e-mail, Electronic Data Interchange and Online Data Access have reduced most of the burdens of the Researchers, help them to pay more attention and concentration in their research problems and make them to bring the successful outcomes quickly.

REFERENCES

1. My facts page: Library and Information Services. Refdesk, 2002. [Online], available: *http://www.refdesk.com/*
2. Online Writing Lab: Internet Research starting points. Purdue University, 1995. [Online], available: *http://owl.english.purdue.edu/internet/tools/research.html*
3. Researching Librarian: Web resources helpful for librarians doing research. 2000. [Online], available: *http://www2.msstate.edu/kerjsmit/trl/*
4. Software for Statistical Analysis. 2002. [Online], available: http://www.kdnuggets.com/software/statistics.html
5. University Library System: Library science subject guide. University of Pittsburgh, 2002. [Online], available:
6. UTA Libraries Online: Research resources. Arlington: University of Texas, 2002. [Online], available: *http://www.uta.edu/library/research/*
7. http://www.library.pitt.edu/subjects/social/library/#stand.

   Core Print Resources

6

Electronic Information Sources : With Special Emphasis on e-journals

C.P. Ramasesh
Deputy Librarian,
Mysore University Library.

Y. Venkatesh
Lecturer,
Department of Studies in Library and Information Science,
University of Mysore.

ABSTRACT

Getting access to precise, relevant and authoritative information has become a tedious task. Segregation of redundant and irrelevant information from the mass of precise and accurate information is the need of the hour. Paper highlights popular databases of full text journals with explanation in brief. Also explained are the various content page and abstracting services available for academic and research libraries in India. The special features of each of these databases are pointed out and their merits are highlighted. The digital database of theses of UMS Proquest and its salient features with statistical details are indicated in the paper. The paper concludes with the suggestions that as a measure to face the inflation, libraries in India can resort to content page services which is comparatively economical.

Access to information is a necessity. Of late, there are barriers or constraints in getting access to information which is precise, relevant and authoritative. This is mainly because of four major factors.

- Overabundance of information
- Scatter of information
- Seepage of information
- Pollution of information

Scientist Mayoka is of the opinion that if you are able to segregate irrelevant mass of information from the relevant, precise information the very act may be called research process. Quite a number of research data, as well as the reference sources are now being made available in electronic format and on-line access is being provided for the digital libraries. The present trend is in creating digital libraries in the specified disciplines and providing on-line access to them.

A great majority of the popular libraries, which are conventional, is crumbling to dust because of the extensive use of electronic media and on-line databases. The Library of Congress, Washington D.C, with a collection of 118 million documents, 6000 staff, ¾ of them are professional. The library is being under utilized and 8.5 lakh documents are thrown away from the library every year as ephemerals retaining only 1.5 lakh documents in the collection. The same trend exists as regards state archives and traditional libraries.

The cost of 32 volume set of Britannica Encyclopedia is Rs. 36,000/-. The same 32 set volume of information on CD-ROM costs just Rs.1900/- However, access on the web is free of charge. Therefore, now-a-days academicians and scientists tend to rely on Internet rather than investing on hard copies of books and journals.

Today, most of the current facts and day-to-day information is much available on the web than printed sources. It is rather quick and easy to get information or write up on "Angle of Justice", "National Fruit", "National Tree" on internet. It is hard and time consuming to search for the write-up in printed reference sources.

FULL-TEXT E-JOURNALS

There are quite a number of digital libraries or digital databases for full text electronic journals. The popular ones are indicated here.

* **IEEE (Institute of Electrical and Electronic Engineers)** – regularly brings out 80 periodical publications. The journals are available on-line with back files right from the inception of each of the titles.
* **Proquest / ABI** – There are several packages of journals discipline wise and user category wise. The Academic Research Library package covers 2600 titles, including all major disciplines of knowledge. The back files date back to the year 1971 and the same is also made available on CD-ROM disc.
* There are other packages for several disciplines. Business Library, Medical Library, Computer Library, and the like. The database of 'Medical Library' and 'Business Library' are huge ones covering thousands of full text journals.
* **EBSCO** – Another popular database of journals which provides access to 6000 titles of all disciplines, specialized service called "Pay Per Exposure" is also introduced here by which one can seek access to relevant articles from some selected journals of current origin. The service will be delivered to the e-mail address of the individual. This is an economical means of getting access to full-text.
* **Emerald Library** –covers 55,000 recently published articles from journals in the areas of management science and library and information science. The Emerald Library database is popular one and widely accessed by researchers and professionals in the area of management science and public administration.
* **Science Direct** – Provides on-line access to 1200 core journals in basic sciences. It is said to be the widely used database of

journals especially by the academicians and research in science disciplines.

* **Ingenta** – A popular site for variety of information / data / statistical details covering all most all major subjects. It is said to have covered summaries of 25,000 publications and also establishes links to about 6000 full text journals of recent origin.
* **GaleNet** – A popular database for quite number of subjects. However, it is widely accessed for reference works, multi-volume sets and composite works in the area of English literature (commonwealth literature, Canadian literature, poetry, drama, prose including what do children read next? Shakespeare literature, contemporary authors and biographical information.
* **Medline** – A common site for on-line access to publications in medicine and allied disciplines. The database is also available on CD-ROM. The coverage is of 9 million of records/ documents from 4000 journals. The database is managed and regularly up-dated. In fact, "Medline" happens to be the first on-line information retrieval system in the world started in 1962. During those days information used to be stored on micro-fische as the optical laser technology was not there for CD-ROM diskettes.
* **IDEAL** – Provides access to 300 full text journals in Economics and allied disciplines. The database is said to have covered very important and often sought journals in economics. In addition to this, the journal database of London School of Economics with a collection of 250 core journals will satisfy the user groups and create customer delight.

CONTENT PAGE SERVICE:

Printed sources are gradually

* Increase in conversion rates
* Increase in package and postage charges

* Corresponding increase in agency commission / handling charges

To cope with the inflation trend and to overcome the inadequate budgetary provisions, libraries in India are resorting to "content page services". Some of the popular services are;

* **Inside on Web** – covers 20,000 journals being procured currently to the British Library, London. The coverage is 13,000 science journals and 7,000 journals in Social Science and Humanities. In addition, it also gives the details of the holdings of the British Library as to 70,000 conference proceedings and 2,50,000 back-log of journals.

The content page details can be accessed on Internet and the text of the desired articles can be had on fax or by international courier (photocopy). The individual or the institution must be prepared to pay 9 pound to per articles through fax or 14 pound per articles through courier post.

* **COPSAT** – Contents of periodicals in science and technology from UGC-INFLIBNET center, Ahmedabad. The coverage is about 4,500 titles in Science and Technology. Every month the subscriber will receive from NCSI, Bangalore the contents with abstracts on floppy. It is also available in paper format. The subscription is Rs.3,500/- for every 40 titles selected from the list.
* **CAPS** – Contents together with abstracts in the disciplines of science and technology is offered from INSDOC, New Delhi. The service covers 7,500 titles in Science and Technology. The subscriber in case wishes to get full text, the photocopy of the article will be supplied at nominal charges. Subscription to CAPS is found useful and economical. For 25 titles the annual charges is Rs. 25,00.00.
* **Current Contents from SNDT Women's University** – The Women's University in Bombay is offering contents and abstract service covering few disciplines in social sciences including library and information science. Now they have

started extending abstracting services (LISA, Sociological Abstracts etc) on web on consortia subscription, reducing the price by almost 50%.

* **Article Alert** – USIS is offering the content page and photocopy services to the researchers and academicians. As and when the latest issues of the journals are released, the photocopy of the content pages will be sent to the user group. Each user indicates by mailing a post card the desired articles. In the next stage, the Xerox copy of the full articles will be sent by mail. The service is well received and appreciated in the academic environment. The user have to select articles from a list of about 400 journals covering all disciplines. However, a greater part belongs to American Society, politics and public administration, literature, including many all branches of social sciences.
* **RGUHS : Journal Database** – Created recently for providing on-line access to the contents of 250 medical journals. This happens to be a controlled database since the user institutions (medical) have to contact the university and get the user ID and Password for on-line contents, access to the core foreign journals with back files for a period of 5 years.
* **J-Gate** – Content and Abstracting service from Informatics India, Bangalore covering 10,000 journals, Indian and Foreign. For 1600 titles, the database establishes links to the full text on the web which are free of charge. The service is found most useful for academic and research libraries. Moreover, the service is also made available on CD-ROM at almost 1/3 of the subscription value of the web access.

DIGITAL DISSERTATIONS

Proquest (UMI), Ann Arbor, Michigan, USA started its dissertation abstracts service way back in 1929. The coverage is right from the first US thesis submitted in the year 1869 upto the last term submissions. Now the institution encourages researchers to submit their thesis in digital format.

As of today, the digital database has more than 1.6 million theses of Canadian and American Universities. The full text can be downloaded from the web. If desired, the UMI is ready to supply full text of the theses in variety of formats.

* Xeroxgraphy
* Microfilm 16 M and 35 MM
* CD-ROM disc

CONCLUSION

- Online access to full-text e-journals eliminates the usual constraints of the traditional libraries. Delay in postal transit, misplacement of issues, non-receipt of issues, storage space and the like.
- Libraries and institutions can save to a great extent by having web subscription when compared to the print subscription.
- To cope with the inflation trend, especially with reference to the foreign journals libraries can relay on the content page and photocopy services to a great extent.
- The number of journals covered or specified by the aggregators is though more, a huge number comprises of periodicals like newsletters and house magazines which are not scholarly. Therefore, the users have to use the database on free trail offer for some time, carefully evaluate, and then select the titles for which subscriptions are to be paid.
- The aggregator / agency in case of on-line access to digital libraries establishes links to the full text titles that allow free on-line access. Therefore, the users easily get access to the titles at one stretch, without wasting the time.

WEBLIOGRAPHY AND BIBLIOGRAPHY

1. Ramasesh, C.P. et al. Librarianship in the new IT environment. LIS Education in the Internet Era. XVII National IATLIS seminar, 7-9 Feb 2001, Tiruvananthapuram, pA4.1-9.
2. Biswas, S.C. Will our university libraries transform ? Deccan

Herald, April 16, 2000, p.6.

3. MCLC News, Vol. 2 (4), 1999, pp. 3-4.
4. Ramasesh, C.P. and Y. Venkatesh : On line access to doctoral dissertations. Trends in achieving bibliographic control and creation of electronic databases. International conference on problems and prospects of IT professionals in the new millennium. Jan. 14, 2002, University of Mysore, (CIST).
5. Jayakumar, C et al., Accessing on-line electronic journals. Seminar on recent trends in library and information science – Technology Tiruchanapalli, Bishop Heber College, 2002, pp. 152-56.
6. http://www.informindia.com
7. http://www.ieee/d.org
8. http://www.inflibnet.ac.in
9. http://www.global.umi.com/dissertations
10. http://www.galenet.com
11. http://www.ebsco.com
12. http://www.afs.edu.gr/ELINON/journals.htm
13. http://www.bl.uk/inside
14. http://www.proquest.umi.com
15. http://www.ncsi.iisc.ernet.in
16. http://www.keesings.com
17. http://www.annularer.com
18. http://www.ncbi.nlm.nih.gov/pubmed
19. http://www.standards.ieee.org
20. http://www.americanlibrary.in.library.net
21. http://www.acm.org
22. http://www.epnet.com

7

Information Access or Chaos or Both? Choice is Yours!

Prof. S. Seetharama
17, Varadarajulu Street,
Chennai.

ABSTRACT

Access to information is one of the prime objectives of librarianship and libraries were providing access to traditional documentary sources for last many decades. Developments in the area of Information Communication Technology comprising of the concept of Information Super Highway, WWW, Internet, Electronic Library, Virtual Library etc. has made great implications on all walks of life especially on the traditional librarianship. This paper discusses the concepts of Information Access and Dilemmas of Information Professionals in the newly emerged IT based Library and Information environment. Some of the captions highlighting the issues and dilemmas confronting the modem information professionals are also reproduced.

INTRODUCTION

In the last few years, several developments have taken place in the area of Information and Communication Technologies (ICT) like the concepts of Information Superhighway, World Wide Web, Internet, Electronic Library, Virtual Library, etc which seem to have had a great impact in all walks of life. As a matter of fact, Tony Blair, the U.K. Prime Minister has recently stressed the importance of information revolution to that of agricultural and industrial revolutions. However, in every revolution, development has largely been due to the distribution mechanism. Thus. it may be said that the key feature of the information society is not the computer, but the development of networks, which allow global distribution of information. All these developments have had profound implications, shaking the very foundations of traditional librarianship. " This has largely been due to the paradigmatic shift of library as a place ... towards the information to which it can provide access ", a natural consequence of the digital icon replacing the icon of books in modern times (Brown 1997, Ashraf 2000). This situation seems to have worsened with the arrival of Internet on the library scene.

Perhaps, it is almost impossible to read a book or pickup a magazine or periodical without a mention of Internet or World Wide Web - - possibly because one of the strengths of the Web is that it is a multimedia environment.

In other words, it is time that the versatility and power of ICT - - in providing universal and speedy access to information, in improving existing services, ability for the generation of new services, facilitating cooperation, and in providing for an integrated approach to information without regard to format, location, or medium through which it is served, which can be lightheartedly be called " One-step information shopping " can stand in good stead for quality and productivity in information services and products. Nevertheless, the information professionals seem to face some dilemmas / questions, which are largely due to conflicts and contradictions, encountered which has resulted in chaos.

This paper intends to address the concepts of information access and dilemmas of information professionals in the IT-based library and information environment.

INFORMATION ACCESS

Access to information and information resources has been one of the objectives / functions of the libraries and librarians and this is fairly exemplified by Ranganathan's famous Five Laws of Library Science. While libraries have been doing a good job of providing access to traditional documentary sources for a number of years, the application of ICT to the generation, processing, storage, retrieval, and dissemination / transmission of information has radically changed the situation, and has altered, for example, the objectives and strategies, the nature of sources and services, operational / organisational structures, and the ways in which service(s) is delivered.

In recent times, increasingly, some of the libraries have been providing access to electronic resources which " have expanded from a few dozen computerized bibliographic databases to include the overwhelming information available on the Internet," (Fecko, 1997). In addition, thanks to electronic publishing, authors including academics are producing scholarly papers and teaching materials which are being placed in the institutional (if not public) domains without resorting to the traditional publishing process. Further, the accelerated growth of institutional Internets, or Intranets have facilitated access to information. Thus, one can see efforts underway to facilitate all types of access - - bibliographical access, physical access, intellectual access, and networked access to resources and services - - thereby enhancing use of information,

ACCESS PERSPECTIVES

Access to information resources - - traditional and / or electronic - - needs to be considered from different perspectives - - users, subject, information providers and the available technical infrastructure. Further, users will demand access from different locations, such as, the office, library, laboratory or home using different hardware and software platforms. In this context, Foster's comment that " the interface to the resources of the electronic library be developed to a lowest common denominator, or will it be acceptable to expect every user to download and / or install an additional software products necessary to view the resources? Alternatively, should different front ends be provided to different user groups or for different resource types? ". In an effort to tackle the problems of resource access, many projects have been undertaken - - European Decomate II project, for example, is developing an end-user service that provides access to heterogeneous information resources over different libraries in Europe using an uniform interface leading to a working demonstrator of the European Digital Library for economics.

In the not too distant a future, one can envisage various levels of access to electronic resources - - those in great demand are made permanently accessible through a campus network and others can be accessed remotely via campus network when needed, for example, through the Internet (Lancaster & Sandore, 1997).

The above mentioned developments have led to a change in the current library landscape projecting a need for the formulation of a Strategic Plan where the emphasis should be on information access and development of new, innovative and value-added services.

CONFLICTING ISSUES / DILEMMAS

While the impact of ICT is leading towards a paperless society, bookless libraries, digital information centres, virtual libraries, etc, it is not true to say that "information utopia" is round the corner as there are numerous technical, economical, legal and ethical issues to be dealt with. As rightly commented by Henry Ford II ",,, the economic and technological triumphs of the past few years, have not solved as many problems as one thought they would and in fact, have brought new problems one did not foresee."

Some of the dilemmas faced by information professionals causing confusion in their minds is largely due to conflicts and contradictions encountered which has resulted in chaos are mentioned below.

CAPTIONS / HEADLINES IN MEDIA

Some of the captions highlighting the issues and dilemmas confronting the modern information professionals are reproduced below:

- Computer Blues: Do computers spoil creativity?
- "Confidentiality / Privacy of client"; "Privacy, a casualty"
- Cyber Terrorism
- Chaos, thy name is Internet
- Do libraries and librarians have a future?
- Does copyright have any future on the Internet?
- De-institutionalization and De-professionalisation in a networked environment
- Employer surveillance of computer files
- Hacking - - a crime?
- Information Technology, a boon or bane?
- "Introduction of new technology can reduce quality of life"
- Is preservation or archiving of digital information possible?
- Making a resource technologically accessible does not necessarily make it intellectually accessible!
- Who is responsible for the authenticity of information on the net?
- Who is the user in an IT-based environment - - employer, inside users or outside users or all?
- Web of Deceit
- The old form is dead, Long live the Virtual Library

Clearly, the conflicting issues / dilemmas relate to PRIVACY / CONFIDENTIALITY, HACKING, COPYRIGHT, MANPOWER, ORGANISATIONAL STRUCTURES, OWNERSHIP Vs ACCESS, CYBER CRIMES / SECURITY, PRESERVATION,

RESPONSIBILITY FOR CONTENT OF INFORMATION. Etc. Some of these have been discussed in detail elsewhere. (Seetharama, 2002).

CONCLUSION

While introduction of ICT in libraries and information centres have facilitated the quest for quality and productivity of library and information sources and services and thereby to information access - - bibliographical access, physical access, intellectual access and networked access to resources and services - - a reality, it has brought in a host of conflicting issues to the forefront. Some of the questions, which seem to disturb the information professionals, are:

1. How does one maintain privacy and confidentiality in relation to the client / user / worker in an organisation?
2. How does one ensure strength and stability to flat structures created by IT introduction, which has contributed to the breakdown of traditional structures?
3. How to prevent de-professionalisation, a consequence of reduction in quality of life brought about by IT?
4. What should be learnt and what should be unlearnt?
5. When is one violating copyright in the context of electronic forms?
6. Who owns the information in a network-based environment?
7. How does one tackle cyber terrorism?
8. How to overcome security concerns?
9. How and what to preserve irt electronic information / forms?
10. Is it possible to teach the user / clientele complete knowledge about how to use the many databases?
11. How to tackle computer failures?
12. How to distribute information when one is not sure of its accuracy and reliability? How to validate?

13. How to resolve the conflict between censorship and freedom of speech?

14. When end-users have direct access to sources and services through user-friendly software, is it necessary to develop collections and / or generate information services?

In short, the various developments that have been taking place in the current library landscape have led to instability and unpredictability - - a chaotic state, so to say - - and has left many a librarian / information professional in a state of confusion.

While it is the fashion today to submit to a "destiny' imposed by machines, it would be appropriate to quote Brown "…As we wire ourselves into a hivish network, many things will emerge that we, as mere neurons in the network, don't expect, don't understand, can't control, or don't even perceive … but, this would bring a cultural distance from reality … The great paradox is that these electronic bridges designed to span geographical and temporal space, can also interpose a terrible buffer between those who wish to communicate. The Internet, in its current shape, is probably still a force more for good than evil. But, it is only a small part of a wider and far more powerful information space - - one whose sprawling topology actually undermines that quality of trust that lies at the core of all relationships, families, and communities … Already it begins to seem as if the more we "interact" by digital means, the more we are disconnected from each other."

In spite of the above, we must create a powerful paradigm - - a way of looking at IT - - that is based on a simple but enduring tenet. The profession should while working in tandem create the synergy that is essential.

Perhaps, one should know when to "lock kiya jaaye" (with apologies to KBC) in relation to information Technology in the context of libraries and information centres!

To conclude, Information Access and Chaos (to be overcome later) seems to be the only choice now available to us !!!

BIBLIOGRAPHICAL REFERENCES

1. ASHRAFF (T). The new digital paradigm: A challenge to librarianship. (In Second National Convention of MANLIBNWT on "Challenges 2000". Ahmedabad. 3 – 5 Feb, p 26 – 32.)
2. BROWN (D). Cyber Trends. 1997. Penguin books.
3. FECKO (MB). Electronic Resources: Access and Issues. 1997. London, Bowker Saur.
4. FOSTER (W). Towards the electronic library.
5. LANCASTER (F W) and SANDORE (B). Technology and management in library and information services. 1997. Library Association Publishing. London.
6. SEETHARAMA (S). Information Science and Information Technology: Chaos, Conflicts and Contradictions. (In Press).

8

Internet Use Among Women: A Study

S. Ally Sornam

Head,
PG Department of Library and Information Science,
Bishop Heber College,
Tiruchy.

K. Nithiakalyani

Student,
PG Department of Library and Information Science,
Bishop Heber College,
Tiruchy.

ABSTRACT

The present study aims to analyse the Internet use pattern of women in Trichy city. Main objectives of the study are: To identify the women internet users based on age, status and academic background; to rank Internet Service Providers based on usage; to rank the reasons for using Internet; to find out the frequency of usage of Internet; to identify the number of hours spend for Internet browsing and the choice of timings; to find out the amount of money spend on internet; to find out the search engines highly used and to assess the knowledge about special web sites for women. Major findings are also listed.

Indian society is undergoing a basic metamorphosis. Changes in educational system, political ideology, legal system and socio cultural values have influenced the traditional value system. New technology and scientific innovations accelerated the changes. The social changes have not left the women untouched. The traditional position she enjoyed in society, the roles she was expected to perform and the status she carried in her family have all been affected by the factors. Indian women are slowly emerging out of the centuries old darkness, shaking off their shakles of tradition and man determined and man imposed rules and are increasingly raising their voice to demand their rightful place in society.

India is one of the very few countries where perfect equality between the sexes form one of the fundamental principles and rights generated by the constitution. In spite of this Indian women are still at a considerable disadvantage demographically, socially and economically. The main purpose of women studies is to discover, acquire and accumulate knowledge about women which in turn helps to improve the status and position of women. The present study aims to analyse the internet use pattern of women in Trichy city.

Net is the fastest growing medium globally. While radio took 35 years, net crossed that milestone in just five years. Internet economy has become the worlds third economy. Net removes time, space and socio economic barriers to learning. Upto date information on every considerable source from any part of the world is possible today. With each new medium, has come a new opportunity for social learning, a new way to achieve common understandings. Internet is used to reach a large heterogeneous audience of widely dispersed people. This article studies the mode of internet use among women. The following objectives were formed for the study.

OBJECTIVES OF THE STUDY

1. To identify the women internet users based on age, status and academic background.
2. To rank Internet Service Providers based on usage

3. To rank the reasons for using internet.
4. To find out the frequency of usage of internet.
5. To identify the number of hours spend for internet browsing and the choice of timings.
6. To find out the amount of money spend on internet.
7. To find out the search engines highly used.
8. To assess the knowledge about special websites for women.

RESEARCH TOOL AND SAMPLE

The present study employs questionnaire as the tool for data collection. The questionnaire contains two parts. Part I contains personal data and Part II contains information on Internet use. A total of 15 questions were formed. The universe consist of 100 women respondents belonging to various states of life such as professionals, students, housewives etc. 75 filled in questionnaires were received, thus the rate of response was 75%.

MAJOR FINDINGS

1. Majority of the respondents fall under the age group 21 – 25 (57.33%). This is followed by the age group 36 and above. (20%)
2. Majority of the women internet users are students (53.3%) followed by working women (21.7%)
3. Majority of the women internet users have post graduate degree and that too in science discipline (81.7%)
4. VSNL is ranked first among the Internet Service Providers. Satyam, Dishnet and HCL follows.
5. Majority use internet for emailing (53%). This is followed by chat (13%), educational purposes (11%) and to view latest news (6%).
6. Regarding the frequency of usage, majority use once a week, (42.6%) followed by daily usage (18.4%).
7. Majority of the women spend a minimum of one hour for

internet (45%). 25.3% of women spend 2 hours per week. They prefer to use internet during evening hours.

8. 44% of women respondents spend Rs.100 per month for internet use. 39% spend upto Rs.200 per month.
9. Yahoo is the highly used search engine (40%) followed by Google (19%) and Altavista (13%).
10. Majority of the women internet users are not able to mention a single website for women (73.4%). 26.6% cited a single website for women.

CONCLUSION

Internet is a conglomeration of networks spanning a vast, global communication system and an information super high way consisting of people, information and computers. Indian women are passing through a paradigm shift. Internet has been a blessing to many women. The study reveals the awareness among women towards internet use for the settlement of their social, academic and personal lives. Comparing to the speed at which the influence of internet grows every day – the women respondents (mostly educated!) of the present study have found to be using it in a small way. E-mailing is the popular service which has attracted women in general. But there are many other potential areas in internet which could be powerfully utilized by women society. One could expect concrete potential outcome from women who use internet regular. A well planned awareness programme on the utility of internet could be conducted in higher educational institution.

BIBLIOGRAPHY

1. ELSHTAIN (Jean Bethka), Private Women in Social, Political thought, 1981, Martin Robinson Inc, Oxford.
2. SHASHI JAIN, Status and Role Perception of Middle Class Women, 1988, Allied Publication, New Delhi.
3. SUBRAMANIYAN (B) Information Technology : Issues and Trends, 1998, Cosmo Publications, New Delhi.
4. "Women find the going tough", Hindu Dec.7, 1996.

9

Cliches of Wireless Technology

R. Dhanapal,

Head, Department of Computer Science,
Bishop Heber College,
Tiruchirappalli.

ABSTRACT

In recent years, wireless telecommunications have become very popular. The new trend in technology is to provide users with the ability to have all they could possibly need in a pocket sized device. Smaller and smaller PDAs (Personal Data Assistants), Laptop Computers and Mobile phones are hitting the market, incorporating brand new features designed to let the users work and access documents. In the late eighties and nineties, mobility was associated with the ever-reachable mobile phones. This concept expanded with the advent of the Global System for Mobile communications (GSM). Blue Tooth is a new technology that is designed to provide common way to connect mobile devices such as PDAs, Laptop and Mobile phones in a wireless mode.

Today Internet access has primarily been a desktop activity done with a physical telephone line and modem. Mobile Internet access using a Laptop or hand helps computer using a wireless modem is the primary technology. That is offered by WAP (Wireless Application Protocol). The cell phone manufacturers and the computer device manufacturers are starting to build hand held devices, smart phones, full blown programmable computers embedded in the hardware with the wireless communication capabilities. The main objectives are small, lightweight, inexpensive mobile computing device that are equally suitable for high quality voice communication, modest bandwidth (5 to 10 kbps.) data communication, seamless internet connectivity and access to all it services and general purpose, programmable computing devices that can run custom applications. The Internet protocols (TCP/IP and HTTP) are far from being suitable for use with the mobile communications.

INTRODUCTION

The recent years, have witnessed a radical shift in the way we work, play and communicate. Today, the wireless technology allows people to exchange messages at the speed of light and access information from any source around the globe. The new trend in technology is to provide users with the ability to have all they could possibly need in a pocket sized device. Smaller and smaller PDAs (Personal Digital Assistants), Laptop Computers, Mobile phones and Internet are hitting the market, incorporating brand new features designed to let the users work and access documents whatever situation they are in. The internet and the World Wide Web services are always on, always available and easy to use. They are also relatively affordable, requiring only a simple browser, desktop personal computer and modem. The power of these services and their global reach is enriching people's personal lives and reducing costs for businesses.

Mobility is the ability to access the information and services anytime, anyhow, anywhere. People around the world have jumped to wireless communications at a frenzied pace. Today, cellular telephones are critical companions for active consumers and mobile professionals. In fact, many people have abandoned their wire line telephones altogether, drawn in by the lower costs and greater convenience afforded by wireless handsets. In many parts of the world that don not have sufficient terrestrial telephone service, cellular infrastructure represents an inexpensive, easy-to-deploy alternative to the traditional telephony infrastructure. According to industry analysis, there will be "over 1 billion wireless subscribers" by 2003, and with the introduction of micro-browsers on wireless devices many believe there will be more people accessing the wireless internet using WAP-(Wireless Application Protocol) enabled devices that PCs around that same time as well. In just three short years the WAP has become the defacto worldwide standard that can provide wireless Internet services on digital mobile phones, pagers, personal digital assistants and other wireless devices. Wireless devices represent the ultimate constrained computing devices with limited CPU, memory and battery life and a need for a simple user interface.

THE MOBILE INTERNET

The expansion of the Internet's reach and the burgeoning of mobile communications are now converging into the mobile Internet. The mobile Internet extends the traditional Internet to wireless devices such as cellular phones, Personal Digital Assistants (PDAs) and even automobiles. It brings information and services to user's fingertips when and where they need it, anytime, anywhere.

Today almost 60 percent of U.S. households have Internet access from their homes. Each household spends an average of 12.2 hours per week online. In Europe, 50 million users will have web access by the end of 2002. Even more people are expected to go online in the future, with the user population reaching a total of 171 million people in 2004. Furthermore, nearly 8.3 million businesses are projected to be Internet-enabled by 2004. The growth of the Internet has resulted, in part from its simplicity. To get onto the Information Superhighway, the user requires only a simple browser on a desktop terminal with a modem connection. This ease of accessibility, along with the wealth of Internet Services available for both consumers and businesses, has made the Internet into one of the most valuable technology tools.

Now, instead of using a desktop PC, we are running an Internet browser on a device that is portable, mobile and most importantly wireless. With the click of a button we can not only connect to the World Wide Web, but also reach from our desktop. Moreover, this device would be nothing more than the handy cellular mobile phone or Personal Digital Assistant (PDA). It is always turned on, meaning that the browser does not require a lengthy "boot up" procedure every time we want to reach the Internet or access information such as our list of contacts.

CONVERGENCE BETWEEN THE WIRELESS AND WIRED

Just as the online industry has boomed over the last few years and continues to grow at a rapid pace, the wireless telecommunication has experienced a tremendous growth spurt in the past decade. The convergence between the wireless and wired leads to the notion of mobile internet services, which would empower the user to access the same suite to rich value-added applications at work, at home, and on the road. Such a blended market offers more opportunities than the sum of the two individual worlds: access to services at any moment in time, from any device, at any place, instantly, and over any network. By 2004, the device of choice for accessing information will be the handheld mobile phone, as shown in Figure(1).

The browsers and applications running on mobile devices need to be easier to use than those on the desktop. After all, mobile users typically operate in a highly dynamic environment and may not be as tightly focused on the task at hand. Achieving an enhanced user experience on this mobile Internet therefore necessitates that highly personalized value-added services be made accessible with just a few key clicks. In contrast to the classic Web, the Mobile Internet delivers value by providing services dynamically based on the user's preferences or contest, including the current location, and by integrating voice telephony with asynchronous notification features.

SHORT MESSAGE SERVICE

Historically, the market for Wireless data has been driven primarily by the evolution of technology. In contrast, the World Wide Web, while a "disruptive innovation", is being driven primarily

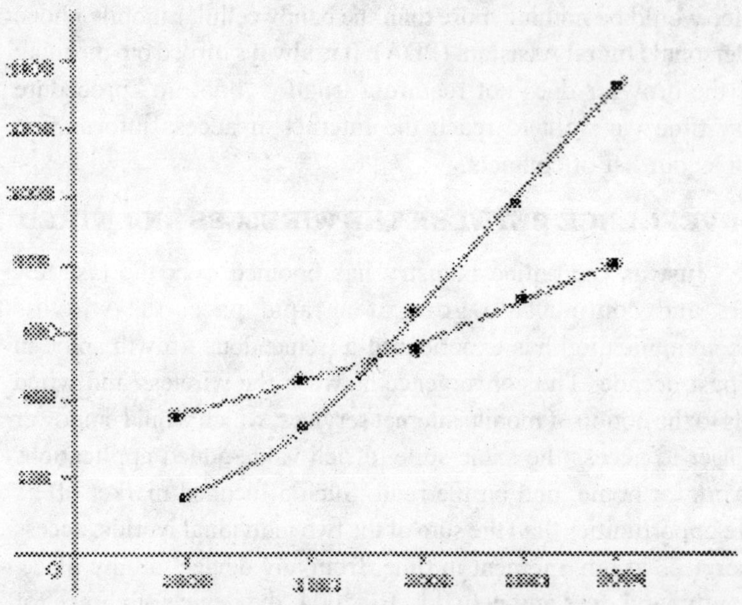

Fig. 1. Connectivity to the Internet

by a demand for electronic business. Mobile Internet will continue to improve business's bottom line and enhance people's lifestyles. In the early days of wireless data, the first people to accept new gadgets were high-end business users known as Early Adopters. These users were willing to pay more to explore untested technology to realize significant improvements in their productivity or achieve a sizable competitive advantage. Now, however, the Mobile Internet capability is poised to "cross the chasm". The emergence of Short Message Service (SMS) capability combined with the advent of location technology and browser enabled mobile devices offer prospects for accelerated growth within the main stream consumer market. Figure(2) shows, SMS services will generate almost $82 billion in revenue over the next two years.

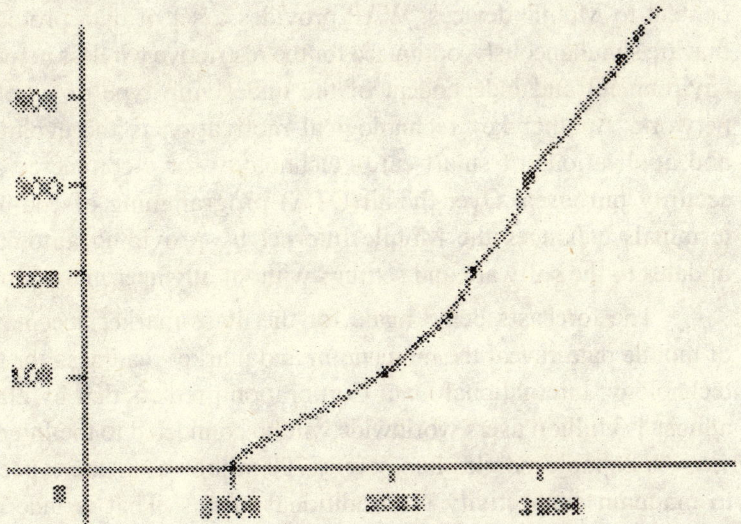

Fig. 2. Forecast for location-dependent services

Table 1. Summarizes some of the key drivers that will allow this market to thrive.

Table 1 Summary of the Drivers Enabling Convergence

Technology drivers	* Emergence of standards.
	* Network ubiquity and interconnection.
Usage drivers	* Mobility needs among business professionals, such as access to intranet information while at a customer site.
	* Need for people to be in touch with friends and family all the time.
Business drivers	* Explosive growth of the Internet
	* Opportunity for new revenue models.
	* Need to expand reach to new customers.

One key technology driver focuses on the emergence and standardization of the wireless data network infrastructure, application development and rendering technologies. At the forefront of this movement lies the Wireless Application Protocol (WAP). This suite of specifications enables the delivery and rendering of web-based content to Mobile devices. WAP provides a set of data protocols that are simultaneously, optimized for the restrictive wireless network environment and independent of the underlying type of wireless network. Another key technological motivation is the evolution and applications of smart-card technology for e-commerce and security purposes. Over-the-air(OTA) programming of end-user terminals enhances the Mobile Internet by providing automatic updates to the software and settings without any user intervention.

The forecasts being made for the mass-market acceptance of mobile data reveal the momentum and market readiness for this technology. International Data Corporation predicts that by 2004, almost 1.3 billion users worldwide will be connected to the Internet via web-capable mobile phones; only 700 million users are expected to maintain connectivity via traditional means. That is indeed a large number of eyeballs from mobile devices, which naturally attracts businesses striving to capture a share of the market.

Innovation often brings with it new markets and revenue opportunities, new channels of distribution, new partners and management teams and most importantly new business models. The life cycle for high technology markets is typically characterized by three phases. The first phase is the "tools" phase, where products-primary tools and utilities are targeted toward the Early Adopters. It is followed by the "platforms" phase, during which infrastructure providers bring products to market and seek increasing returns by focusing on the Early Majority users who are looking for pragmatic solutions to business problems. These two phases together account for 50 percent of the market. However, the most profitable phase is the "applications" phase, where the focus is on value-added applications.

APPLICATIONS FOR THE MOBILE INTERNET

The Mobile Internet-enabled by the Wireless Application Protocol-allows users to access services over high-latency, low-bandwidth cellular networks from thin-client terminals such as mobile phones and Personal Digital Assistants(PDAs). The applications may deliver data that is currently available on enterprise intranets, the World Wide Web, and any other repository on an Internet Protocol (IP) network. Applications may also deliver data that is specifically valuable in the mobile context, this data may be time-sensitive, location-sensitive, or secure in nature. Whatever the circumstances, the user experience depends on the usability of the applications themselves, as well as the devices ability to render that information. Table 2 summarizes these applications. We expect several more types of value-added services to emerge as WAP becomes more ubiquitous.

Although wireless networks and mobile communication can be used for many applications, particular application environment seem to be predestined for their use. Some of them are,

- Vehicles
- Emergencies
- Business
- Replacement of wired networks
- Infotainment and more
- Location dependent services
- Mobile and wireless devices

CONCLUSION

WAP is in its infantry stage, predicting the future direction of any technology and its impact is always risk factors. All the usual clichés regarding technological change apply to WAP and a range of other wireless technologies, rapid change and development, huge speculative investments by an enormous range of companies from tiny startup to some of the largest companies in the world such as NOKIA, Panasonic, Microsoft, enormous uncertainties, huge potential market opportunities to fight for etc., In many ways they mirror the emergence and growth of the internet with its associated changes and opportunities however, we are currently at a stage where we can identify a number of key elements that will

Table 2. The Applications for the Mobile Internet.

Category	Application	Explanation
Productivity applications	E-mail/text messaging.	**Native access to electronic mail, with features such as reading a message, replying to it and so on.**
	Personal Information Management(PIM)	**Access to calendar for schedule and appointments, reminders and notifications, address book and contacts and to-do lists.**
	Unified messaging and universal inbox	**Integration of voice mail, e-mail and fax into the same inbox that can be accessed by the user by various means.**
	Instant messaging	**Awareness of online users and instant messaging with them**
Information and transactional services	**Kiosk to content**	**News, stock quotes, weather, traffic updates, sports scores, directions to restaurants and ATMs, bus and train schedules, and other information. Also includes searching for directory information such as that found in the white or yellow pages.**
	E-Commerce	**Online transactions such as banking, purchase of goods and services, day trading, bill payment and so on.**

Life-enhancing applications	**Telematics**	**In-vehicle information systems that enable navigation, infotainment services, and roadside assistance**
	Entertainment services	**Games, puzzles, ring tones, image downloads, betting services and recipes.**
	Multimedia services	**Video mail, graphical directions, traffic reports and speech synthesis.**
	Enhances telephony applications.	**Visual voice mail, multi-way conference setup and incoming call treatment.**
Telephony, account and subscription	**E-care**	**Electronic customer care for billing information, service-related information, service plan options, minutes of use and other applications.**
Vertical services	**Fleet management and dispatch**	**Ability for the fleet to receive and view information about schedules, location of pickups and drop-offs and so on.**

have an impact on the development of the wireless data market in the months and years ahead. The precise balance of these forces, in terms of their relative impact and importance is in a state of flux. However, each of them form a part of the overall wireless date jigsaw, which in turn will Influence the future role of WAP. The internet and wireless communications are converging to meet the needs of anywhere, anytime access to information and services. Wireless data services promise to unleash a broad consumers and businesses. The wireless Application protocol will provide a common foundation that will enable the rapid development of these mobile data applications. Hence time is the primary factor that should decide on all developments.

REFERENCES

1. Wideband Wireless Digital Communications by Andreas F. Molisch.
2. Professional WAP by Charles Arehant, Nirmal Chidambaram, Shashikiran Guruprasad, Richowell.
3. Programming Applications with WAP by Stevemann.
4. The Wireless Application Protocol. by Sandeep singhul, Thomas Bridgman, Lalitha Suryanarayana, Daniel Mauney, Jim chan. Websites

   http://wap.colorline.no/wap-faq

   http://www.wap.com/share/osas/cache/antid 150220.html

   http://www.wapforum.org/

   http://www.wirelessdevnet.com/training/wap www.ericsson.se

10

WLAN and Its Application in University Library Services

Noushad Ali P.M.,
Lecturer,
Department of Library and Information Science,
Aligarh Muslim University,
Aligarh—202002.

Musthafa. K.M.,
Department of Library and Information Science,
Aligarh Muslim University,
Aligarh—202002.

ABSTRACT

The advantages of Wireless Local Area Network is discussed. Wireless LAN offers productivity, convenience and cost advantages over traditional wired networks in Libraries highlights the components of WLAN. Wireless LANs augment rather than replace wired LAN networks, often providing the final few meters of connectivity between a wired network and the mobile user.

In the IT age rather mobile age, notebook computers with PC cars and mobile phones put the information you need, at your finger tips, wherever you are, whenever you need it. Wireless Local Area Network (WLAN) is a new product of modern technology, which can be used for the data transmission without wired environment, using radio frequency (RF) technology, microwave or infrared technology. WLAN technology gives live networked environment without cable connections from virtually anywhere in the building or campus and which will make possible to be get connected with the data source wherever you go[1].

The notable significance of wireless LAN in libraries is, the users can access shared information without looking for a place to plug in, and libraries network managers can set up or build up networks without installing or moving wires. Using the laptop and notebook computers, the real time information transmission as well as data processing is possible to the centralized host computer. Another advantages of WLAN is it is possible to make inside or outside the library building and still remain connected to the internet or to other computing devices on the network.

COMPONENTS OF WLAN

Wireless LANs use electro magnetic airwaves (radio or infrared) to communication information from one point to another without relying on any physical connection. Radio waves are often referred to as radio carriers because they simply perform the function of delivering energy to a remote receiver. The data being transmitted is super imposed on the radio carrier so that it can be accurately extracted at the receiving end. Once data is super imposed (modulated) onto the radio carriers, the radio signal occupies more than a single frequency, since the frequency or bit rate of the modulating information adds to the carrier[2].

To set up a WLAN technology in a university library needs the following components.

1. Access Point:

A device, which used as transmits/receiver is called access point or transceiver. This connects to the wired network from a fixed location using standard cabling. The access point working as a mediator between the wireless LAN and the wired network infrastructure. Usually single access point can serve a small group of users and within a small area.

2. Adapter:

Adapters provide an interface between the client network operating system and the airwaves via an antenna. The forms of adapters are variant according to the type of computers as PC cards, as cards desktop computers and in hand held computers as integrated.

3. Network Operating Software (NOS):

A pre-designed well programmed network operating software is essential for any network, either wired LAN or Wireless LAN. It should be capable to organize the system and devices attached to the WLAN. The efficiency and effectiveness of a WLAN is mainly depending upon the quality and performance of the operating system.

4. Input/Output Devices:

The input/output devices with computers in their variant frames are another required component of WLAN. In Wireless Local Area Network the portable computers and wireless devices are more popular.

5. Network Connection:

The individual system have to be connected with the server: A WLAN uses a high-speed, redio-frequency (RF) network access technology to transmit and receive data over waves, a radio receiver tunes in one radio frequency while rejecting all other frequencies.

WHY WLAN IN LIBRARIES

Wireless LANs offer the following productivity, convenience and cost advantages over traditional wired networks.

- **Mobility:** WLAN systems can provide library users with access to real-time information anywhere in their organization. This mobility supports productivity and service opportunities not possible wit wired network.
- **Installation speed and simplicity:** Installing a wireless LAN system can be fast and easy and can eliminate the need to pull cable though walls and ceilings.
- **Installation flexibility:** Wireless technology allows the network to go where wire can not go.
- **Reduced cost-of-ownership:** While the initial investment required for wireless LAN hardware can be higher than the cost of wired LSN hardware, overall installation expenses and life-cycle costs can be significantly lower. Long term cost benefits are greatest in dynamic environments requiring frequent moves and changes.

The WLAN is more suitable in libraries where we can not install cable and offer mobility because of physical terrain obstacles, architecture that is unfriendly to wiring, and the users are in different places or not constant at anywhere. The users of library and information centres are mainly students, research scholars, teaching staff policy makers, technologists and other supporting staff.

WLAN allows more mobility in the system. The librarian can control all the sections of the library sitting in his/her chamber without any constraints of cables and connections. For users, can search their information in OPAC from anywhere, within the library s well as outside the library within the control of WLAN. If it is more powerful, it is useful to provide access to OPAC as well as other services even from different departments of a university.

Students in the campus can access catalogue of the central library as well as other department libraries through WLAN. They can conveniently search the online catalogue as well as CD-ROM databases anywhere in the campus even in the classroom. Students holding class on a campus can also access the internet to consult the catalogue of the Library of Congress. Research scholars in the Universities are more productive because hand held or not book computers with wireless LAN capability deliver latest information instantly. Online and CD-ROM databases, OPAC and Internet can also be accessible through WLAN server, which facilitate the internet connection. Scientists can have interaction with library staff whenever they need or the specific and recent information.

Teachers can use OPAC, databases and other library services through WLAN while sitting in their chambers. They can give references and bibliography on a particular subject while class is in progress. Other users of the university library can also have their own information without moving anywhere. The users can save the time of moving to the library and OPAC terminals, this time can utilize for more effective activities.

Using WLAN, librarians can make assisting the library users more efficiently, instead of taking library users to the terminals he can take the terminals to the right user. They can use for collection of serial usage of data and book selection.

In meetings library authorities can make quicker decisions because they have real time information at their finger tips.

Apart from the above mentioned advantages the WLAN can be used in various sections of the library such as reference, circulation, serial control, documentation and information services to provide better service and fast transaction of information.

CONCLUSION

WLAN provide services beyond the physical restraints of wall and buildings. Mobility and flexibility are the two boons, WLAN promise. As a new technology WLAN has its own limitations like it works within a few meters of connectivity between a wired network and the mobile user. There are some companies which provide complete range of IEEE 802.11b compliance product for

WLAN such as CISCO (*www.cisco.com)*, D-link (*www.dlink_inida.com)*, 3COM (*www.3com.com)*, TATA TELECOM etc. application of WLAN in the information dissemination will facilitate easy and effective service in university libraries, which is the need of the hour.

Wireless LANs have gained wide popularity in a number of fields, including, the health-care, business, manufacturing, ware housing and academia. Wireless LANs frequently augment rather than replace wired LAN networks often providing the final few meters of connectivity between a wired network and the mobile user.

REFERENCES

1. Wireless LAN – it's a part of your future. *Information Technology*, March 2001, p,20-24.
2. White paper on what is Wireless LAN. *www.proxim.com/learn/library/ whitepapers.*
3. SHARMA(SK), WLAN: Access to digital libraries without wires.*CALIBER 2002,* 14-16 Feb., 2002, p. 139-46.
4. The wireless LAN Alliance (WLANA). *www.wlana.com.*
5. Wireless Networking in our homes. *Information Technology,*March 2001, p. 26-27.

11

Freedom of Information, Copyright and Data Protection, and Intellectual Property Rights in Informatics Policies: UNESCO-FID Survey

Prof. A. Neelameghan

Hon. Visiting Professor,
DRTC, ISI, 8th Mile,
Mysore Road,
Bangalore.

ABSTRACT

A summary overview of the common elements of Informatics Policies, especially relating to freedom of information, copyright, data protection, and intellectual property right, of several countries, developing and developed countries, included in the survey carried out by the International Federation for Information and Documentation under a UNESCO contract. Presents the contextual background to the specific issues.

SCOPE OF THE PAPER

Education, science, culture, informatics and communication are the core functional areas and global involvement of UNESCO. Hence, as part of this involvement the Organization has been supporting programmes and study projects in such areas as patenting and patent documentation, cross-border data flow, copyright, freedom of information and access to information. More often these are accomplished in collaboration with such other international organizations as the World Intellectual Property Organization (WIPO), International Federation for Documentation and Information (FID), International Council on Archives, etc.

Ten years ago, UNESCO, based on its extensive experience, especially in developing countries, of advising and assisting in the formulation of national information policies and the available documentation, prepared and published a handbook entitled National Information Policies, by Victor Montviloff [1]. The preface to the book noted:

"The advance of new technologies and the rise of service economies as opposed to manufacturing economies are two important events that have marked the socio-economic development of the world during the second half of the century. These remarkable changes have generated a significant evolution in the attitudes of governments towards information activities, pressing them to revise their national priorities and to establish new policies. The government policy makers are facing at present the formidable challenge of adapting the new ways and means of providing and exploiting information resources in their national development strategies. They increasingly recognize that in order to make information resources and services more responsive to the economic, social and political needs the former must be carefully planned and managed; hence their increasing interest for the formulation of national information policies which would guide the development of information activities within their respective countries."

Resolution VII.15 adopted by the UNESCO General

Conference at its 28th session (1995) relates to the new information and communication technologies (ICTs) as a factor of socio-economic and cultural development of Member states. One of the resolutions invites the Director-General:

> "to promote a deontological approach which is in keeping with UNESCO's ethical mission and which is aimed at achieving harmonious development of these technologies while ensuring respect for linguistic and cultural pluralism and for the right to privacy."

Unesco's World Information Report 1997/98 [3], an intended brief biennial global survey (similar to UN World Development Report) on matters relating to libraries, archives, information centres and services, the emerging ICTs technologies, superhighways, etc. The seven chapters (20-26) in Part 3: Issues and Trends considers matters relating to copyright, right to information, privacy and other legal aspects. The contribution by Charles Oppenheim (chapter 26) deals specifically with the complexities of implementing laws and regulations relating to copyright, intellectual property rights, security, privacy, etc. in the emerging digital environment, where different countries have different governance structure and regulatory mechanisms, and operating in different political social, economic and cultural milieu. There are complex issues relating to copying and transmitting multimedia, for example, on the Internet. UNESCO's new programme 'Information for All', replacing its General Information Programme and the Intergovernmental Informatics Programme, seeks to define the role of the Organization in the information society. The programme's objective is

> "...to ensure that everyone has access to the information needed to participate equitably in a global information society and to enjoy the free exchange of ideas and knowledge. New method of processing and accessing information affect its quality, reliability and diversity and can result in imbalances depriving certain sectors of society from equitable access to information.

"Information and knowledge are instrumental in bridging the gap between the information rich and information poor. They constitute a global public good and are essential in advancing education, science and culture as well as in fostering democracy. By developing an appropriate infrastructure for the preservation and global sharing of information and knowledge by citizens of all countries, UNESCO will enable all citizens to contribute to and fully enjoy their culture. At the same time, the Organization must ensure that mechanisms are set up for the fair-use and protection of intellectual property rights, and the privacy and security of personal data." [6].

Over the past decade rapid developments in ICTs and their widespread applications have had a significant impact on the economic, industrial, commercial, social, and cultural life of nations. In view of this, a number of countries have been either reviewing and/or formulating new national information policies. Other international agencies, such as, the International Development Research Centre (IDRC), Canada, have been actively advising and assisting developing countries (e.g. in Africa) in this regard. The European Commission has also taken steps in formulating information policies [4,5].

More recently, the International Federation for Information and Documentation (FID), under a UNESCO contract, carried out a survey and analysis of informatics policies in selected countries, and the results compiled by Stephen Parker was published in 1999 [2]. It covers twenty-five countries some developed and some developing countries. Many more countries have formulated and/ or revised their national informatics policies during the past decade. However, the analytical study has noted a remarkable commonality in the elements covered and of policy formulations of these countries. Of course, there is variance among countries in the details and emphasis and also in the implementation of the policies and benefits derived there from. In the past, it has been noted that some countries with relatively poor or no information policy have developed good information infrastructure; on the other hand, other countries with good information policy formulations and implementation have developed good information infrastructures too. However, the value of formulating comprehensive national informatics policy appears to be recognized in an increasing measure in most countries. The document uses the term 'Informatics' to denote 'information technology.'

In the earlier policy document [1] the general information policy issues discussed and proposed covered the following:

- Role of information in national development
- Development of national information resources
- Development of national information services and systems
- Organization of information
- Access to information
- Development of information manpower
- Use of information
- Participation in international programmes and services

These issues and related strategies continue to be valid and important to all Countries; this presentation, however, highlights the commonality of concerns of most nations with particular reference to such issues as 'Freedom of access to information,' 'Freedom of (use) of information', 'Copyright and data protection', and 'Intellectual property rights' vis a vis the merging information society and digital environment, as evidenced in the FID document

The discussion on the above specific issues is prefaced by a brief overview of the context in which the policy formulations have to be considered.

THE CONTEXT

Context of Convergent Technologies

Informatics policies cannot be independent of the characteristics of the national societal and development milieu. The FID document observes:

"Informatics policies need to reflect and be in harmony with overall national policies and goals, which themselves must reflect the culture and traditions of the country concerned. They not only need to take account of the social, cultural and political realities, but also be realistic in terms of available resources and capacities, particularly so far as their main technical component – the development of the information infrastructure – is concerned."

It implies that the information infrastructure should be attainable and sustainable within the particular national context.

Implications to national development policy formulation is that:

"Policy makers therefore need to be aware of and understand the potential impact of converging information technologies on the development of the information society, and their implication for the further transition to a knowledge society.

Whatever the limitations that may be imposed by a country's economic, social or political situation,... a country which ignores or neglects the opportunities and challenges offered by the information society – still more, the 'knowledge society' – will face a grim future."

"The widespread introduction of informatics into a society, touching as it does on almost all aspects of daily life, requires that informatics policies make proper provision with regard to the legal aspects of the use of informatics, including such aspects as computer crime and the use of computers in evidence as well as the legal implications of the use of informatics in relation to copyright law."

Responsibility for Policy Formulation

In free market economies, the private sector is given more responsibility in national informatics policy formulation, its promotion and implementation, the government playing an enabling and regulating role. Even in centrally planned economies it is felt desirable to involve the private sector and all other kinds of institutions and private individuals in policy formulation and implementation.

It is posited that this approach would give them a sense of 'ownership' with respect to policy, and that would help to ensure its successful implementation.

Preserving and Promoting Democracy

The nature of modern informatics systems and networks makes it difficult for governments to restrict or prevent the exercise of democratic rights by their citizens. Thus ICTs can help create and sustain greater and wider awareness about the idea of democracy among people at different levels of society.

SPECIFIC ISSUES

Freedom of Access to Information

Promotion of democracy and ensuring equality of opportunity cannot be sustained unless steps are taken to avoid the creation of an 'information poor' subclass who, for whatever reasons, do not have access to the emerging ICTs. The occurrence and widening of the gap between the 'information rich' and the 'information poor' is not merely an issue between the developed and developing nations but it is so even within a nation whether developed or developing, especially where the use of ICTs is widespread. The document observes: "This is one area where market forces alone can rarely be the determining factor; the provision of access to the poor, to old people, to those living in remote areas or those with physical disabilities, is always a matter for the public authorities and – at least to some extent – the public purse."

Freedom of Information

While *freedom of access* to information is essential it is of limited value if there are too many restrictions on the use of the information accessed. *Freedom of information* is deemed a fundamental right in some countries. In any case public policies and laws should ensure "the maximum possible freedom to create, publish, disseminate, transmit, store and retrieve information, subject only to the limitations imposed by laws or cultural traditions concerned with such aspects as public decency, the protection of minors, national security and the protection of personal (and corporate) privacy." P.K. Dey in a recent essay on the Freedom of Information Bill (India) discusses the exceptions to transparency, accountability and the right to information in relation to defence and intelligence agencies (*The Hindu*, 31 Oct. 2000, Open page, OB-1).

Data Protection

In the context of the growing volume of digitized data in databases and transacted over networks, which can be more easily manipulated and misused, special provisions are necessary to ensure that sensitive data are protected from unlawful intrusion or "that personal and commercial data supplied to the authorities for legitimate purposes are not subsequently divulged or misused."

Intellectual Property Rights

In many countries there already exist laws, regulations, and/or policies to protect copyright and other intellectual property rights. However, it the context of ICT developments, it is necessary to revisit these to ensure that they are adequate to prevent the abuse of the facility that ICTs provide to copy documents and other copyrighted information resources. Where such laws do not already exist they should be formulated and incorporated as an integral part of the national informatics policy.

REFERENCES

1. Montviloff, Victor. National information policies – a handbook on the formulation, approval, implementation and operation of a national policy on information. Paris, FR: Unesco, 1990. 160 p.
2. Parker, Stephen, Comp. National informatics policies and strategies: report on a study carried out on behalf of UNESCO by the International Federation for Information and Documentation (FID), The Hague, The Netherlands: FID, 1999, 91 p.
3. World information report *1997/98*. Paris, FR: Unesco, 1997. 190 p.

4. Hoere, T. An assessment of long –term solutions in the context of copyright and electronic delivery services and multimedia products. Luxembourg: European Commission, 1995. 56 p.

5. Vercken, G. *Practical guide to copyright for multimedia products.* Luxembourg: European Commission, 1996. 226 p.

6. Information for all: a UNESCO new programme. Information, Informatics, Telematics, UNISIST Newsletter, 28 (1); 2000; 4-5.

12

Information Technology-Misuse and Abuse

Noufal. P.P.,
Research Associate,
Indian Institute of Management,
Kozhikode.

ABSTRACT

Information Technology is changing our society, along with all the exciting positive things that IT can do. The interesting thing is that they can also have negative effects. Information Technology has raised a multitude of negative issues ranging from illegal copying of software programs to planned surveillance of employer's electronic mail files. Over the years, new and more advanced forms of misuse and abuse have emerged. Misuse and abuse of Information Technology is the threat to humanity. It thus presents major challenges to ethical use of IT. Cyber crime poses serious threats to the integrity, safety and quality of any system. Conventional security measures are inadequate to cope with criminals using modern technologies. High Tech security systems are therefore vital for survival in the modern day scenario where crime, burglary and theft have increased substantially. This Paper examines damaging effects of the malicious IT misuse and abuse and also presents some broad recommendations towards addressing the problems.

Today IT is playing a significant role in the society. Global Information networks are now an integral part of the way in which modern business and organizations operate. Internet is the best example of the trend. It reduced the distances and lead to a Global village. As a consequence, there is now widespread dependence on computer and networks technology, with the ability to communicate and receive information via these Channels being recognized as an ingredient for competitiveness in the global market. Unfortunately the dark side of the IT is revolutions of cyber crimes and other problems. In the wake of frequent cyber crimes, business and organizations are trying to cope with the intricacy and mystique that surrounds the computer system.

Information Technology can have a beneficial effect as well as negative effect in each area. It emphasis that the use of IT has major impacts on society, and these raised serious ethical considerations in areas such as individuality, employment, working conditions, privacy and crimes etc.

IT and Individuality

A frequent criticism of IT is that it affects the individuality of the people. In the modernized computer friendly organizations the human relationships are very less. Although it is more efficient for an information system to deal with an individual as a number than as a name, many people feel a loss of identity when they seem to be as" just another number". The negative impact of IT on individuality is reinforced by horror stories that describe how inflexible computer-based systems are when it comes to rectifying their own mistakes.

IT and Working Conditions

One of the most explosive ethical issues concerning the quality of work is Computer Monitoring. That is, computer is used to monitor the productivity of employees. It seriously violates the workers' privacy and personal freedom. Computer monitoring stress on employees who must work under constant electronic surveillance.

Privacy Issues

The power of IT to store and retrieve information can have a negative effect on the right to privacy of every individual. For examples confidential e –mail messages of employees are monitored by many organizations. Personal information is being collected about individuals every time they visit a site on the WWW. Information on individuals contained in centralized computer databases by credit bureaus. Government agencies and organizations have been misused, resulting in the invasion of privacy, fraud and other injustice. Some people are widely misusing The Virtual Network Computing software to reveal privacy of others. Internet is notorious for giving its users a feeling of anonymity. Information about Internet users is captured automatically each time you visit a Website or News group recorded as "cookie files" on your hard disk. Then Website owners or online auditing service like 'Web Track' and 'Double Click' may sell the information from cookies files.

Cybercrimes

The rapid developments in computer and telecommunications and other technologies has lead to growth of new forms of crimes. The potential extent of cyber crime is as broad as the extent of the international communication systems. Cyber crimes have virtually no boundaries and do or may affect every country in the world. There are a large number of definitions for cyber crime. The simple definition is "unlawful acts wherein the computer is either a tool or a target or both".

Let us examine the various cyber crimes

Money theft: Many cyber crimes involve the theft of money. This is a threat to every organization. The scope of such financial losses is much larger than the incidents reported. Most companies don't reveal that they have been either victims of cyber crime. They fear the customers and shareholders

Service theft

The unauthorized use of computer and internet is called service theft.Net work monitoring software called 'Sniffers' is frequently used to monitor network traffic to evaluate the network capacity as well as reveal proof of misuse also.

Software Theft

Computer programs are valuable property. Unauthorized copying of software i.e. software piracy is also a major issue of software theft. Unauthorized copying is illegal because software is intellectual property that is protected by copyright law and user licensing agreement. We need to consider three copyright related matters; Software network piracy. Plagiarism and ownership of images; sounds and other media. Network piracy is using electronic networks to distribute unauthorized copyrighted materials in digitized form. Piracy tends to increase prices. If you use the pirated copies, you will face the following problems:getting up-to- date versions; ability to get help;Risk of getting a virus;and risk of getting caught. Plagiarism is expropriation of another writers text, findings etc. Manipulations of sounds images and video are also included in this category.

Hacking

Hacking is a generic expression. A hack is a quick fix or clever solutions to restrictions. Hackers are people who gain unauthorized access to computer or telecommunication system for the challenge or even the principle of it. A hacker's greatest asset is that he can easily transcend all physical barriers. According to NASSCOM chief Dewang Metha " The concept of countries has no meaning for a cyber criminal". Hackers who broke into BARC were traced to have roots in England. Hackers are also helped by the fact that most countries are yet to come up with laws to counter cyber crimes. Hackers are used the 'Sniffer' programs which sat silently within the computers for four weeks monitoring its activities. This could allow the hackers to give unauthorized access to every computer on the networks

Cracking

Crackers also gain unauthorized access to IT , but do for malicious purposes. Crackers attempt to break into computers and deliberately obtain information for financial gain, shut down hardware, pirate software or destroy data.

Email spoofing

A spoofed e-mail is one that appears to originate from one source but actually has been sent from another source. Spoofing the mails could spoil the people relationships. These kinds of e-mail can cause monetary damage also.

Cyber stalking

Stalking means "pursuing stealthily". Cyber stalking involves following a person's movements across the internet by posting messages on the bulletin boards frequented by the victim, entering the chat rooms frequented by the victim, constantly bombarding the victim with e mails.

Data Diddling

This kind of an attack involves altering the raw data just before it is processed by a computer and then changing it back after the processing is completed. Electricity Board in India have been victims to data diddling programs inserted when their systems were being computerized by private parties.

Pornography

The pornography is the output of abuse of computers. A lot of people use

IT to communicate about sex. 'Yahoo', the internet Directory Company says that the word "sex" is the most popular search word on the net. A special problem is that children may participate in sexual conversations, download hard- core pictures encounter odious adults tempting them into a meeting. Many companies are concerned about the loss of productivity and the risk of sexual harassment as workers spend time online looking at sexually explicit materials.

SOME POSSIBILITIES TO PREVENT THESE INCIDENTS

Blocking the software

Some software developers have discussed a golden opportunity in making programs like 'SurfWatch', 'Net Nanny' and 'CyberPatrol'.These filters screen out objectionable matters. And in the case of children some programs also prevent kids from giving out personal informations such as address and credit card numbers.

Browsers with rating

Another method provision in browser software that contains builtin ratings for and www Files. Parents could choose a browser that has been endorsed by the Online Service Provider. Special browsers include 'ChiBrow', 'Kid Desk' and 'Surf Monkey'.

Spams and Virus threat

One such threat is unsolicited electronic mail, Already burdened by dozens of legitimate email messages daily, and workers can find themselves with junk mails known as Spam's.

Another threat by misuse of technology is virus. A virus is a piece of computer code or program that is hidden within an existing program. Virus attacks are in different forms. Some viruses just produce fanciful message such as "happy birth day joshi" on your screen. Some virus has the power to format your system within seconds. Viruses are passed in two ways by discs and networks. Virus may take several forms, the three main ones are: Boot sector viruses, file viruses; and multipartite viruses. A more recent one is the macro virus, which attacks the documents rather than programs. E.g.: Laroux

Boot Sector Viruses

The boot sector is that the part of the system software

containing most of the instructions for booting or powering up the system. The boot sector virus replaces these boot instructions with some of its own. Once the system is in turned on, the virus is logged into memory before start of the operating system.

Example of boot sector virus is 'Ant Cmos', 'Anti EXE' and 'NYB'.

File Virus

File virus attach themselves to executable files those that actually begin a program while it is run .The virus starts working get into main memory and infect other files.

Multipartite viruses

Multipartite virus is a hybrid of the file and boot sector types. The multipartite virus infects both files and boot sector, which works better at spreading and more difficult to detect. E.g.: 'Junkie', 'Parity Boot'.

Micro Virus

Micro virus take advantage of a procedure in miniature program known as macros, are embedded inside common data files such as those created by e-mail or spread sheets. Micro viruses are sent over computer network, until recently, such document has typically been ignored by anti-virus software.

E.g.: '*Concep't* with Word document.

'Laroux' with the Excel document.

Logic Bomb

Logic Bomb differ from other virus in that they are set to go off at a certain date and time.

Eg: Chernobyl Virus

Antivirus

The tool for protecting your system from computer viruses

is to install and use anti-virus software. Variety of virus fighting programs is available in the market. Across the web we will find many companies selling anti-virus software.Two of the best known and most commonly used ant-virus programs are 'Norton AntiVirus'and 'McAfee VirsScan'.You can use virus –protection software in one of two ways.First, whenanother user gives you a disk or file, you can run your virus-protection software and direct to scan the file for viruses.If the software detects a virus,it will ask you how you want it to proceed.Most virus-protection software can delete the file or possibly remove the virus from the program.You can also direct most virus-protection programs to run continuosly.so that the software scans each file you plan to open,run,save, and so on.

Security Solution

Safeguarding computers and telecommunications.

Security is a system of safeguards for protecting IT against disasters, system failure, non-authorized access that can result in damage of loss.

Components of Security:

1) Identification and access
2) Encryption
3) Protection of software and data

Identification and Access

There are three ways a computer system can verify that you have legitimate right of access. Some security systems use a mix of these technologies. The system tries to authenticate your identity by determining.

1. What you have
2. What you know
3. Who you are

Encryption

PGP is a computer program often used for encrypting a computer message-pulling them into secret code. Encryption or enciphering is the altering of data so that it is not usable unless the change are undone. PGP(Pretty Good Privacy) is good that it is practically unbreakable. I t can be download from *http://www.nai.com* Other encryption softwares are available such as *SynCript.* When you encrypt something, you scramble it, to decrypt it you unscramble it. Both activities require a key, like password. Encryption is clearly useful for some organizations especially those concerned with trade secrets, military matters and other organizations.

PROTECTIONS OF SOFTWARE AND DATA

Organizations are very careful to protect their data. This includes educating employees and makes back-up discs, protecting against and so on.

Other security procedures:

a) Control of access

b) Firewalls

For security organization with their own intranet networks often install guarded gateways known as firewalls. A firewall is a software or hardware that prevent hackers and others from infiltrating a computer or network from out side network. A firewall admits only those outside communication you decide to select. If you want to close off your network except some you can do that.

c) Audit controls

Many networks have audit controls to track which programs and servers were used, which files opened and so on. This creates an audit trial, a record of how transactions were handled from input through output.

CONCLUSION

It goes without saying that the prevention of cyber crime is more effective than treatment. Implementing control as identified in a security policy would indeed detect computer misuse. However, IT abuse is different in the sense that it represents a deliberate attempt by one party to inflict damage on others. We must modify our attitudes and give the issue a similar level of consideration to that which we already give to other types of crime. In the end we must realize that IT misuse is a cultural and human resources issue that cannot be solved by technology or policy alone. Instilling a positive culture and making the awareness is the only sure way to eradicate the technology misuse.

REFERENCES

1. *http://www.internetmisuse.com*
2. Johnson,Deborah G, Computer ethics.
3. Karis Jamsa, Personal computers.
4. Toffler,A. The third wave
5. *http://www.privacyinternational.org*
6. *http://www.cybercrime.org*
7. Jonathan Rosenoer, Cybeer Law
8. David Bell, The cyber cuIuturs reader
9. Gregory Giagnocavo, Child safety on internet
10. *http://www.difgitalcentury.com*

13

Assessing the Quality of Information Sources and Services in Academic Libraries A New Management Technique for Librarians in the Technological Age

Abdul Majeed. K.C.,
Lecturer,
Dept. of Library & Inf. Science,
Farook College, Calicut.

Dr. M. Bavakutty,
Professor in Library Science and University Librarian,
University of Calicut.

ABSTRACT

Library is a service organization dealing with tangible assets and intangible services. The tangible assets of a library includes the library building, furniture, equipments, information resources and staff, and the intangible services includes all services rendered by library staff to its users. Both tangible assets and intangible services are evaluated in the light of changing face of libraries and users. The Internet, Private Lending Libraries, Commercial and non-commercial information products and services, Escalating price of information sources, Budget cut, Competition from other libraries and information centers, etc are some of threats to our libraries. Hence the librarians, have to change their mind and be ready to evaluate the tangible assets and intangible services in the library to attract more and more users. Providing excellent service to users is the best solution to keep our library exists in the changing world. This paper discusses how the quality of services provided in libraries can be measured and used for improving library services and attract more users. The results of the study conducted in a postgraduate college library to see how far the service quality determinants are applicable in libraries are also discussed.

INTRODUCTION

Libraries and information centers are service organizations charged with the responsibility of providing different information services based on a collection of suitable resources. It contains tangible assets of a library namely library building, furniture, equipment, information resources and staff, and intangible services, all services rendered by library staff to its users. Today all these tangible assets and intangible services are evaluated in the light of changing face of libraries and users. The Internet, private lending libraries, commercial and non-commercial information products and services, escalating price of information sources, budget cut, competition from other libraries and information centers, etc. are some of the threats to our libraries. As a result librarians are forced to adopt suitable strategies and techniques of the business and management and started to restructure their library in most economical and attractive way. Now we have started to use and talk about management terms such as *Intellectual Property, Accountability, Information Resources, Library Management, Library Manager, Marketing of Information Products and Services, Library Customers, Quality of Library Services*, etc. in Library and Information Science.

Librarians are ready to evaluate the collections and services, the tangible and intangible assets and services, in the library to attract more and more users. Providing excellent service to users is the only solution to keep our library exists in the changing world. This paper discusses how the quality of services provided in libraries can be measured and used for improving library services and attracts more users.

QUALITY CONCEPT IN LIBRARIES

Quality of services offered decides the level of utilization of libraries by the users. It can have a strong reputation among its users only when the services offered are in good quality. Special Libraries and libraries attached to Research and Development Organizations are offering quality library services compared to academic libraries and public libraries. In academic libraries, university and post-graduate college libraries are offering better services compared to school and junior college libraries. Public libraries are mainly concentrating in traditional services. Concept of quality is not measured properly in libraries, not because it is lacking in libraries, but because quality is very difficult to describe or measure in libraries.

The concept of quality, developed by Edward Deming, is recently adopted in library context. There are two different ways of applying quality concept to library services. First one is measuring the performance of libraries with quantifiable data collected from library records and users. This method can be used to evaluate in-house use, availability of information sources, use of library tools, services offered, etc. The other one is the application of Total Quality Management to library works and services. Quality concept is not applied in libraries mainly due to the reluctance of librarians to accept the fact that the users of library services are solely responsible to determine the quality of the service provided.

Users or customers are the sole judges of service quality. But many marketing experts have observed that services generally are intangible. It is said that quality can be measured with a pre-determined set of specifications and such pre-determined specifications are not available for library services. It is also true that the quality of a product can be tested, verified and improved further before its sale. But there is no chance of ascertaining the quality of library and information services before the delivery because it is the users of these services who have to determine the quality of services, non the service provider, the librarian. It is because of the fact that locating user's needed information (production) and using of that information (consumption), the two parts of information services, are inseparable. So user's perception about the library and information services provided is to be collected and analyzed to ascertain the quality of services provided in libraries.

METHODS FOR MEASURING USER'S PERCEPTIONS OF SERVICES

There are a number of methods available to collect data from users about the quality of library services offered, most widely used among them are:

Interview with Individual Users

In this method, the users are interviewed in person or by telephone and collect their perceptions about the library services offered.

Focus Groups

In this method, a group of 8 to 12 persons are formed and discuss the matter under the direction of a moderator. This method can be used to discover why people do not use certain library services offered.

Un-Obstructive Observation

It is a method in which factual questions are asked to users and required data/ answers are collected. This method will acknowledge the existence of service problems and so measures to improve the services can be easily derived.

User Surveys

A user survey is to have quantifiable data about the services offered in libraries. It can cover a large number of users and will enable the researcher to make valid judgments on the services offered. It is easy to conduct, easy to understand, and also inexpensive. It is considered as the oldest and most enduring method of research on libraries. It comprises techniques like Questionnaire, Interview,

Observation etc.

LIBRARY SERVICE QUALITY

Measuring the quality of libraries is a basic problem. It has got two sides. One is the difficulty to describe the library goals for quality in precise terms and the other one is lack of true and tried tools and methods to measure quality. The quality of services provided in a library can be assessed well through questionnaires containing questions on library service quality determinants developed by library experts like Thomas Sea, Danuta A. Nitecki etc. based on the work of Parasuraman, Zeithaml and Berry. [Parasuraman and others (1988) have developed an instrument called SERVQUAL in the form of a questionnaire, which contains 97 statements addressing expectations about service that should be offered followed by 97 statements addressing perceptions about actual service received. The formula is Q = P – E Where Q represents Quality, P represents Perceptions and E represents Expectations.]

The service quality determinants suitable for libraries are as follows:

1. Reliability.

It involves delivery of the promised library service dependably and accurately. It means that the library services performed by staff members are for the first time and the library collections contain information appropriate to the needs of the users. It involves

a). Giving correct information asked

b). Making relevant information available

c). Keeping records consistent with actual holdings

d). Keeping databases up and running

e). Making sure that overdue notices and fine notices are accurate

2. Responsiveness

It indicates the readiness of library staff to provide services timely. It involves:

a). Making new information available

b). Checking in new journals and newspapers promptly

c). Contacting a user immediately once the requested document or information is received in the library

d). Re-shelving books quickly

e). Minimizing the time needed for inter library loan.

3. Assurance

It refers to the knowledge and courtesy of the library staff and their ability to convey confidence. It involves politeness, friendliness, skill to provide information about collection and services. It involves:

a). Valuing all requests for information equally and convey worthiness of the inquiry to the users;

b). Clean and neat appearance of staff;

c). Thorough understanding of the collection;

d). Familiarity with working of equipment and technology;

e). Learning the user's requirements;

f). Providing individual attention to users; and

g). Recognizing the regular users.

4. Access

It means that there are sufficient numbers of staff and equipment as well as hours of operation. It involves:

a). Waiting time in circulation check out line is minimal;

b). Computer terminals;

c). Library hours; and

d). Location of the library is central and convenient.

5. Communications

It means keeping the customers informed in language they can understand and listening to them. It demands the use of language understandable to different category of users. It involves:

a). Avoiding unnecessary library jargons;

b). Understanding the user's needs precisely;

c). Using precise and clear instructions;

d). Teaching library skills to users; and

e). Assuring users that their problems will be handled properly.

6. Security

It means freedom from danger, risk or doubt. It involves:

a). Physical safety within the library; and

b). Library dealings are confidential.

7. Tangibles

It includes maintenance of physical facilities and serviceability of equipment. It involves:

a). Physical conditions of library buildings like heat, light, ventilation, etc.;

b). Conditions of equipment like microfilm reader, copiers, computers etc.; and

c). Impact of other users in the library.

In addition to these determinants, there are determinants like competence, credibility, understanding the customers etc suitable for service organizations.

In this method, the comments of users are classified and categorized each into one of the service quality categories or determinants. Then each of these comments is assessed for its positive or negative attribute. The comments of each user will be given in 5 score scales. That is, the questionnaire will contain quantifiable 5 score scaled questions. So the survey result becomes a good basis for defining quality library services.

Libraries are slow to recognize that a reputation for quality is built on the perception that library users have about the library staff as well as the service itself. When a library breaks a service promise, the users lose confidence in the library's ability to deliver services accurately and dependably. Dependability and accuracy are the two important characteristics influencing the user's thinking about quality of services.

The search for quality begins with a focus on library users. So far librarians have measured services in terms of quantity of services performed during particular period or per user. Today librarians searching for quality take the help of users to judge service quality and try to meet user's quality expectations.

ASSESSING THE QUALITY OF A COLLEGE LIBRARY; A CASE STUDY

In order to assess the feasibility of service quality determinants in libraries, a study was conducted in a reputed college library under the University of Calicut. A questionnaire comprising of 38 questions grouped under 5 service quality determinants were prepared. These determinants were: Tangibles: appearance of physical facilities, equipment, personnel, and communication materials; **Reliability**: ability to perform the promised service dependably and accurately; **Responsiveness**: willingness to help customers and provide prompt service; **Assurance**: knowledge and courtesy of employees and their ability to convey trust and confidence; and **Empathy**: the caring, individualized attention the firm provides its customers.

The questionnaire has got two parts. Part I contained 19 questions on service quality expectations and Part II contained 19 questions on service quality perceptions. A sample of 65 users (32 postgraduate students and 33 faculty members) was covered by the study. Maximum attention is paid to give due representation to different disciplines (Arts 26, Science 32 and Commerce 7) and sex (Male 40 and Female 25). The data were analyzed with simple statistical techniques like mean, mode and standard deviation and ANOVA and MANOVA tests were conducted to see the relationship between the variables. The results of the study are as follows:

Qualities of a Good Library; User Expectations

Users expectations are the essentials about the availability of library services and they are very important in measuring service quality. The data on users expectations were obtained through the questionnaire and the details are as follows:

The users were requested to indicate the extend to which the features mentioned through the 19 SERVQUAL statements were essential for a good college library.

The analysis of individual features on mean scores indicates the priorities in users expectations. The features related to 'adequate number of required books and periodicals', 'the willingness of staff to help the users', 'easy access and convenient working hours', 'excellent facilities and services' and 'prompt service to users' are the most important features identified by the user community. A user expects these services more than to other services from a good library. At the same time 'feeling of users to depend on staff' and 'personalized attention to users' were viewed as the least essential features for a good library. The details are given in Table 1.

Table 1. Qualities of a Good Library; User's Expectations

Q.No.	Statements	Mean	SD	Rank
1	Modern building and furniture are required for a good library	3.85	1.11	16
2	Excellent facilities and services will be provided in a good library	4.57	0.75	4
3	Adequate number of required books and periodicals will be available in a good library	4.82	0.50	1
4	The books, periodicals and other documents will be attractively displayed in a good library	4.14	1.04	12
5	Whenever a good library promise to do something by a certain time, it will do	4.02	0.91	15
6	Whenever user has a problem in locating a document, the staff in a good library will show keen interest in locating the same.	4.52	0.81	6

7	A good library will provide right book the very first time	4.18	0.92	11
8	Presence of an error free record is essential for a good library	4.28	0.98	9
9	The staff in a good library will always be willing to help the users	4.68	0.66	2
10	The staff in a good library will give prompt service to users	4.57	0.66	5
11	The staff in a good library tells precisely when the document requested would be available	4.25	0.66	10
12	The staff in a good library will inform the user as soon as the requested document is available	4.38	0.63	7
13	The staff in a good library will never be too busy to respond to users	3.78	1.26	17
14	The behaviour of staff in a good library will develop confidence in users	4.34	0.85	8
15	The staff of a good library will have the knowledge to answer user's questions	4.12	1.01	13
16	Users of a good library will feel they can depend on the staff	3.52	1.24	18
17	The staff in a good library will give personalized attention to the users	3.20	1.45	19
18	A good library will have easy access and convenient working hours	4.62	0.60	3
19	The staff in a good library will understand the specific needs of the users	4.11	0.90	14

The overall mean, standard deviation and median score on the individual features are 4.21, 1.00 and 4.00 respectively. The mean is above to the neutral level, i.e. neither agrees nor disagrees and the standard deviation also shows that the differences of opinion among the users are negligible. . It indicates that all users expect good quality services from their library and the differences on expectation among users are negligible.

The analysis of the SERVQUAL statements of expectations according to the SERVQUAL determinants namely Tangibles, Reliability, Responsiveness, Assurance and Empathy shows that Tangibles are very important compared to other determinants of service quality. Among the five dimensions Tangibles scored the highest and Empathy the least. The details are given in Table 2.

Table 2. User Expectations; Determinants Wise Analysis

Rank No	Determinants	Mean	SD
1	Tangibles	4.34	0.57
2	Responsiveness	4.33	0.48
3	Reliability	4.25	0.58
4	Assurance	3.99	0.70
5	Empathy	3.97	0.70

The over all mean, SD, and median scores of the SERVQUAL determinants are 4.18, 0.63 and 4.33 respectively. The mean score indicates very high expectations of users and the standard deviation score indicates the negligible difference between the user's responses. It indicates that differences among the users are very negligible. The mean scores of individual statements under each determinants shows that, the mean scores of the statement contributing to the ranking of Tangibles and Responsiveness are above to the median score.

QUALITIES OF A GOOD LIBRARY; EXPECTATIONS OF STUDENTS AND TEACHERS

The user wise analysis of the statements and SERVQUAL determinants were conducted to see whether there is any difference in the expectation of teachers and students. The statement wise analysis showed that the student community expect features, 'willingness to help the users' and 'adequate number of required books and periodicals' very high from a good library. At the same time the students do not expect much personalized attention from the staff and they do not think that they can depend much on the library staff for any help. The teacher wise analysis indicates that they expect 'adequate number of books and periodicals' and 'excellent facilities and services' from a good library. But they do not expect 'personalized attention' and 'depend the staff' from a good library. More details are available from Table No.3.

Table 3. Qualities of a Good Library; Expectations of Students and Teachers

Q. No	Students Mean	SD	Rank	Teachers Mean	SD	Rank
1	3.63650	0.612499	17	3.46262	1.622597	15
2	4.59682	0.328362	4	4.04747	1.820223	2
3	4.73452	0.447353	2	4.11414	1.841645	1
4	4.11269	0.518601	13	3.87575	1.759476	9
5	4.22936	0.487456	9	3.56414	1.649248	12
6	4.59246	0.256866	5	3.94949	1.789901	5
7	4.27103	0.372737	7	3.54747	1.608792	13
8	3.90277	0.570866	16	3.89646	1.750632	8
9	4.77063	0.155822	1	3.95454	1.783187	4
10	4.30198	0.546242	6	3.97525	1.788833	3
11	4.13333	0.188561	12	3.85656	1.753022	10
12	4.26626	0.137931	8	3.91313	1.769225	7
13	4.15714	0.733976	11	3.40252	1.625181	16
14	4.16230	0.581797	10	3.93939	1.776973	6
15	3.99603	0.479296	15	3.48181	1.608409	14
16	3.18055	0.879109	18	3.23888	1.525680	18
17	2.89603	0.534220	19	3.02121	1.395832	19
18	4.72222	0.284043	3	3.70606	1.695746	11
19	4.07976	0.348568	14	3.34848	1.497780	17
OVER ALL	4.1443400	0.4798156		3.6997607	0.3011321	

The overall mean (4.14) of student community is very high and the variations (0.47) in expectations among them are very negligible. At the same time the over all expectations of teachers are high (mean 3.7) but less than to the expectations of students.

The determinant wise analysis showed that Responsiveness

followed by Tangibles is the major expectations of students and teachers and they expect Assurance and Empathy very least. There is no difference in the expectations of teachers compared to student's expectations. More details are available in Table 4.

Table 4. Expectations of Students and Teachers; Determinants Wise Analysis

Determinants	Students Mean	SD	Rank	Teachers Mean	SD	Rank
Tangibles	4.27013	0.43262	2	3.87500	0.25347	2
Reliability	4.24890	0.24428	3	3.73939	0.18463	3
Responsiveness	4.36805	0.24077	1	3.92487	0.04533	1
Assurance	3.77962	0.42901	5	3.55336	0.29042	4
Empathy	3.89933	0.75637	4	3.35858	0.27967	5

QUALITIES OF A GOOD LIBRARY; SEX WISE ANALYSIS OF EXPECTATIONS

The analysis of statements according to the user's sex indicates that there is some difference in the expectations of male and female users. The male users expect 'adequate number of books and periodicals' and 'easy access and working hours' very high from a good library. At the same time they do not expect 'personalized attention' and 'modern building and furniture much from a good library. The female users expect 'willing to help users' and 'adequate number of books and periodicals' very much from a good library. At the same time they do not expect much on' depend on staff' and 'personalized attention' from a good library. More details are available in Table 5.

Table 5. Qualities of a Good Library; Sex wise Analysis

Q. No	Male			Female		
	Mean	**SD**	**Rank**	**Mean**	**SD**	**Rank**
1	3.66262	0.765986	18	3.43650	1.675785	17
2	4.74747	0.309941	3	3.89682	1.895324	3
3	4.91414	0.093295	1	3.93452	1.919149	2
4	4.40909	0.393680	8	3.57936	1.829955	12
5	4.04747	0.536805	13	3.74603	1.834539	6
6	4.68282	0.245796	6	3.85912	1.903098	4
7	4.28080	0.403663	12	3.53769	1.711588	14
8	4.31313	0.301237	11	3.48611	1.788854	15
9	4.72121	0.111175	4	4.00396	1.944617	1
10	4.69191	0.371892	5	3.58531	1.834934	11
11	4.32323	0.217384	10	3.66666	1.854723	7
12	4.37979	0.225973	9	3.79960	1.877886	5
13	3.95252	0.731070	15	3.60714	1.753378	10
14	4.47272	0.561554	7	3.62896	1.863742	9
15	3.81515	0.402363	17	3.66269	1.797536	8
16	3.82222	0.784234	16	2.59722	1.462873	19
17	3.25454	0.543602	19	2.66269	1.466947	18
18	4.87272	0.144	2	3.55555	1.714642	13
19	3.98181	0.324246	14	3.44642	1.675883	16
OVER ALL	4.28133397	0.4397297		3.5627610	0.3574996	

The overall mean of male and female users are 4.28 and 3.56 respectively which indicates that the male users expect more than to the female users and the variation in the expectation of individual users are very negligible as the standard deviation is less than one.

The SERVQUAL determinant wise analysis showed that both male and female users expect Responsiveness and Tangibles more compared to other determinants. They least prefer assurance and Empathy. The variation in the expectation among the male users is very negligible but there is some significant variation among the female users. More details are given in Table 6.

Table 6. Expectations of Male and Female Users; Determinant Wise Analysis

Determinants	Male			Female		
	Mean	SD	Rank	Mean	SD	Rank
Tangibles	4.433	0.390726	2	3.712	1.830053	2
Reliability	4.330	0.371875	3	3.657	1.809520	3
Responsiveness	4.528	0.231606	1	3.764	1.878040	1
Assurance	3.836	0.582717	5	2.866	1.708050	5
Empathy	4.036	0.337283	4	3.221	1.619157	4

QUALITIES OF A GOOD LIBRARY; EXPECTATIONS ACCORDING TO DISCIPLINE

The statement wise analysis showed that there are differences in the expectations of users in Arts, Science and Commerce disciplines. The users in Arts discipline expect prompt service and willingness of staff to help users very high, but the expectation of users in Science discipline is different. They expect adequate number of books and periodicals in a good library. In the case of users in Commerce discipline, they expect adequate number of books and periodicals and excellent facilities and services from a good library. All the users in Arts, Science and Commerce disciplines agree that they do not expect personalized attention from a good library. More details are given in Table 7.

The overall mean score is 4.23, 4.27 and 3.25 for Arts, Science and Commerce discipline respectively. It indicates that the users in Arts, Science and Commerce disciplines expect much from a good library. Compared to Arts and Commerce, the users in Science discipline expect more from a good library. The variations in the expectations of individual user in all disciplines are very negligible.

The determinant wise analysis showed that users in Arts and Science discipline consider Responsiveness and Tangibles most important compared to other determinants in a good library. At the same time the users in Commerce discipline think that Tangibles and Reliability are more important than to other determinants. All

Table 7. *Qualities of a Good Library; Expectations according to Discipline*

Que.No	Arts			Science			Commerce		
	Mean	SD	Rank	Mean	SD	Rank	Mean	SD	Rank
1	4.01666	**0.385116**	14	3.54870	**0.669246**	17	3.08333	0.288675	9
2	4.54166	**0.748125**	5	4.75811	**0.239855**	3	3.66666	0.288675	2
3	4.65416	**0.594132**	3	4.86883	**0.205367**	1	3.75	**0**	1
4	4.10833	**0.706402**	12	4.37435	**0.522292**	11	3.5	**0.552771**	4
5	4.03333	**0.260762**	13	4.24025	**0.416539**	12	3.41666	**0.552771**	5
6	4.54583	**0.497152**	4	4.68376	**0.427464**	4	3.58333	**0.288675**	3
7	4.22916	**0.235505**	11	4.16525	**0.194961**	14	3.33333	**0.486938**	6
8	3.97916	**0.421197**	15	4.38636	**0.583565**	10	3.33333	**0.333333**	6
9	4.65833	**0.430584**	2	4.84610	**0.270384**	2	3.58333	**0.333333**	3
10	4.69583	**0.333995**	1	4.63668	**0.11099**	5	3.08333	**0.57735**	9
11	4.39999	**0.357333**	9	4.41818	**0.349448**	9	3.16666	**0.288675**	8
12	4.47916	**0.276214**	7	4.53993	**0.355051**	7	3.25	**0.333333**	7
13	3.73333	**0.29449**	17	4.10616	**0.664448**	15	3.5	**0.5**	4
14	4.32916	**0.557179**	10	4.57337	**0.401547**	6	3.25000	**0.552771**	7
15	4.40833	**0.524257**	8	4.05844	**0.53049**	16	2.75000	**0.720889**	11
16	3.72916	**0.300585**	18	3.14999	**0.119539**	18	2.75	**0.720889**	11
17	3.5	**0.055305**	19	3.04253	**0.079357**	19	2.33333	**0.866025**	12
18	4.52499	**0.494561**	6	4.53409	**0.382515**	8	3.58333	**0.288675**	3
19	3.91250	**0.651938**	16	4.22987	**0.43963**	13	3	**0.57735**	10
Over All	4.2357456	**0.3471250**		4.2716336	**0.5068899**		3.2587719	**0.3544771**	

users in Arts, Science and Commerce disciplines agree in the fact that Assurance and Empathy are not much important for a good library. More details are available in Table 8.

QUALITIES OF A GOOD LIBRARY; USER PERCEPTIONS

User perceptions is viewed as user's experience or feelings about the services provided by the library. Understanding the user's perception is necessary for measuring service quality. Users perceptions towards the library services were measured by tabulating the responses of 19 SERVQUAL statements given in the questionnaire.

The analysis of these questions showed that the staffs were always willing to help the users, but the staffs did not understand the specific needs of the users. The mean scores of the perceptions of users indicates that 'willingness of staff to help the users and 'easy access and working hours' were ranked first. On the other hand, the users are not satisfied with the 'building and furniture available' and 'understanding the specific needs of users by library staff'. More details of analysis are given in Table 9.

Table 8. Expectations according to Discipline; Determinant wise Analysis

Determinants	**Arts**			**Science**			**Commerce**		
	Mean	**SD**	**Rank**	**Mean**	**SD**	**Rank**	**Mean**	**SD**	**Rank**
Tangibles	4.33020	0.27258	2	4.38750	0.51787	2	3.5	0.25685	1
Reliability	4.19687	0.22189	3	4.36891	0.19840	3	3.41666	0.10206	2
Responsiveness	4.55833	0.12272	1	4.61022	0.15665	1	3.27083	0.18980	3
Assurance	4.15555	0.30322	4	3.92727	0.58844	5	2.91666	0.23570	5
Empathy	3.97916	0.42110	5	3.93549	0.64352	4	2.97222	0.51068	4

Table 9. Qualities of a Good Library; Perceptions of Users

Q.No.	Statement	Mean	SD	Rank
1	My Library has Modern building and furniture	3.12	1.05	18
2	My library has Adequate number of required books and periodicals	3.40	1.21	10
3	My library provides me Excellent facilities and services	3.26	1.22	14
4	The books, periodicals and other documents are attractively displayed in my library	3.54	1.05	8
5	Whenever my library promise to do something by a certain time, it will do so	3.31	1.09	13
6	Whenever I have a problem in locating the document, my library shows keen interest in locating the same.	3.68	1.03	5
7	My library provides me the right book at the very first time	3.26	1.14	15
8	My library has error free catalogue	3.60	1.03	7
9	The staff in my library are always willing to help me	3.92	0.96	1
10	The staff in my library give me prompt service	3.77	1.01	4
11	The staff in my library tells me precisely when the document requested will be available	3.32	1.08	12
12	The staff in my library informs me as soon as the document requested is available	3.43	1.06	9
13	The staff in my library never too busy to respond to my requests	3.38	1.18	11
14	The behaviour of staff in my library gives me confidence in library matters	3.63	0.96	6
15	The staff in my library has the sufficient knowledge to answer my questions	3.22	1.27	16
16	I fell free and comfortable to depend my library staff for some help	3.78	1.02	3
17	The staff in my library gives me personalized attention	3.18	1.04	17
18	My library has easy access and the working hours are convenient to me	3.80	1.06	2
19	**The staff in my library understands my specific needs**	**3.03**	**1.09**	**19**

The overall mean, standard deviation and median score on the individual features are 3.46, 1.11 and 3.00 respectively. The mean score is very below to the maximum level score 5. It indicates that the perceptions of all users are good. The SD score above to one that indicates that there are variations among the individual users' perception slightly.

The analysis of the SERVQUAL statements of perceptions according to the SERVQUAL determinants namely Tangibles, Reliability, Responsiveness, Assurance and Empathy shows that Responsiveness are very important compared to other determinants of service quality. Among the five determinants, Responsiveness scored the highest and Tangibles scored the least. It indicates that the library staff is always ready to respond to the questions of users. It also indicates that users are not very much satisfied with the Tangibles such as building and furniture, collection, services and facilities. The details are given in Table 10.

Table 10. Qualities of a Good Library; Determinant Wise Analysis of Perceptions

Rank No	Determinants	Mean	SD
1	Responsiveness	3.57	0.82
2	Assurance	3.54	0.88
3	Reliability	3.46	0.81
4	Empathy	3.34	0.92
5	Tangibles	3.33	0.86

The over all mean, SD, and median scores of the SERVQUAL determinants are 3.45, 0.86 and 3.60 respectively. The mean score is just above to the neutral level score 3, which indicates that the perceptions of all users about service quality determinants are very low to the maximum level score fixed. The SD score indicates that variations among the individual users are negligible.

QUALITIES OF A GOOD LIBRARY; PERCEPTIONS OF STUDENTS AND TEACHERS

Analysis of the data establishes that the perceptions of students and teachers about the quality of a good library vary. The students are very much satisfied with the 'willingness of library staff to help' them followed by the 'display of documents available in the library'. But they are not at all satisfied with the 'personalized attention given by library staff' and the 'present library building and furniture'. At the same time the teachers are very much satisfied with the 'willingness of library staff to help' them and they are very much sure that they can 'depend the library staff for any help' needed. But they are not satisfied with the 'knowledge of library staff to answer their questions' and the library does not provide the 'right book at the very first time' from the library. More details are given in Table 11.

Table 11. Qualities of a Good Library; Perceptions of Students and Teachers

Question No	Student			Teacher		
	Mean	SD	Rank	Mean	SD	Rank
1	2.84	0.699	16	3.105	1.483	8
2	3.58	0.626	6	2.975	1.354	11
3	3.556	0.728	7	3.095	1.456	9
4	3.91	0.335	2	2.951	1.403	15
5	3.405	0.309	10	2.973	1.408	12
6	3.621	0.438	5	3.21	1.506	5
7	3.118	0.658	14	2.821	1.341	18
8	3.523	0.469	9	2.966	1.451	13
9	3.963	0.448	1	3.445	1.555	1
10	3.863	0.498	3	3.241	1.482	4
11	3.141	0.599	13	2.915	1.360	16
12	3.405	0.447	10	2.96	1.349	14
13	3.171	0.721	12	3.045	1.452	10
14	3.536	0.520	8	3.331	1.511	3
15	3.341	0.623	11	2.691	1.291	19

16	3.58	0.542	6	3.385	1.549	2
17	2.811	0.458	17	3.111	1.442	7
18	3.816	0.292	4	3.201	1.441	6
19	2.888	0.449	15	2.871	1.324	17
OVER ALL	3.425	0.130		3.068	1.429	

The overall mean score is 3.4, which indicates that the students and teachers are almost satisfied with the collection, services and facilities offered to them. The SD score (0.13) indicates that the variations between the perceptions of individual users are negligible. It also indicates that students are more satisfied than the teachers.

The determinant wise analysis shows that the students and teachers are satisfied with the Responsiveness and Assurance. But the students are not satisfied with the factors related with Empathy and Reliability. At the same time teachers are not satisfied with Reliability and Tangibles. More details are given in Table 12.

Table 12. Qualities of a Good Library; Determinant Wise Analysis of Perceptions

Determinants	Student			Teacher		
	Mean	SD	Rank	Mean	SD	Rank
Tangibles	3.471	0.390	3	3.031	0.068	4
Reliability	3.417	0.188	4	2.992	0.139	5
Responsiveness	3.593	0.335	1	3.140	0.215	1
Assurance	3.486	0.103	2	3.136	0.315	2
Empathy	3.172	0.456	5	3.061	0.139	3

QUALITIES OF A GOOD LIBRARY; SEX WISE ANALYSIS OF PERCEPTIONS

The sex wise analysis shows that there are differences in perspectives of male and female users of the library. The male users are very much satisfied with the 'easy of access and working hours' and 'willingness of library staff to help' them. But they are not satisfied with 'personalized attention given to them' and the way in which they are informed the availability of requested document precisely. At the same time the female users are very much satisfied with the 'willingness of library staff to help them' and the 'prompt service' they get from the library. But they are not satisfied with the 'provision of right book' they requested and the 'understanding of their specific needs' by library staff. More details are given in Table 13.

Table 13. Qualities of a Good Library; Sex Wise Analysis of Perceptions

Question No	**Male**			**Female**		
	Mean	**SD**	**Rank**	**Mean**	**SD**	**Rank**
1	3.188	0.739	14	2.756	1.443	17
2	3.791	0.448	5	2.763	1.296	16
3	3.578	0.498	9	3.073	1.543	7
4	3.818	0.458	3	3.043	1.425	10
5	3.573	0.435	10	2.805	1.299	15
6	3.76	0.449	6	3.071	1.452	8
7	3.505	0.367	12	2.435	1.252	19
8	3.566	0.287	11	2.923	1.480	12
9	3.928	0.358	2	3.48	1.589	1
10	3.808	0.314	4	3.296	1.552	2
11	3.081	0.603	18	2.975	1.365	11
12	3.21	0.263	13	3.155	1.431	5
13	3.128	0.712	17	3.088	1.459	6
14	3.581	0.426	8	3.286	1.533	3
15	3.175	0.500	15	2.858	1.402	13
16	3.685	0.581	7	3.28	1.515	4
17	3.078	0.585	19	2.845	1.401	14
18	3.951	0.137	1	3.066	1.393	9
19	3.171	0.400	16	2.588	1.274	18
OVER ALL	**3.504**	**0.451**		**2.989**	**1.427**	

The over all mean score for male is 3.5 and for female is 3, which indicates that male users are more satisfied with the library collection, services and facilities than to the female users and their level of satisfaction is very level to the maximum level fixed. The SD score (0.45 for male and 1.4 for female) indicates that the variations in the perception of individual male users are very negligible, but there are considerable variations in the perception of individual female users.

The determinant wise analysis shows that male users get more satisfaction on Reliability factors followed by Tangibles. Empathy and Assurance are the least scored in the level of satisfaction they attained. Female users are very much satisfied with Responsiveness and Assurance. Reliability and Assurance are the least scored determinants to them. More details of the analysis are given in Table 14.

Table 14. Qualities of a Good Library; Determinant Wise Analysis of Perceptions

Determinants	Male			Female		
	Mean	SD	Rank	Mean	SD	Rank
Tangibles	3.594	0.536	2	2.909	1.427	3
Reliability	3.601	0.384	1	2.808	1.371	5
Responsiveness	3.507	0.385	3	3.226	1.484	1
Assurance	3.480	0.502	4	3.141	1.483	2
Empathy	3.400	0.374	5	2.833	1.356	4

QUALITIES OF A GOOD LIBRARY; PERCEPTIONS ACCORDING TO DISCIPLINE

The perceptions of Arts, Science And Commerce students show certain differences. The statement wise analysis and determinant wise analysis clearly showed that users in Arts and Commerce discipline agree in the most satisfied statement and determinant. And Arts and Commerce students are much satisfied with the 'willingness of library staff' to help them. At the same time the users in Science discipline are more satisfied with 'error free catalogue' available in the library. But users in Arts discipline are not at all satisfied with the 'error free library catalogue' available in the library. According to the users in Science discipline, the library staff is not able to 'understand the specific needs of the users'. The users in Commerce discipline are not satisfied with the 'right book provided by the library at the very first time' and the 'personal attention' given to them. More details are given in Table 15.

Table 15. Qualities of a Good Library; Discipline Wise Analysis of Perceptions

Q. No	Arts			Science			Commerce		
	Mean	SD	Rank	Mean	SD	Rank	Mean	SD	Rank
1	3.395	0.773	13	3.272	0.713	17	2.25	1.479	14
2	3.495	0.690	9	3.587	0.374	8	2.75	1.605	7
3	3.945	0.491	2	3.282	0.776	16	2.75	1.605	7
4	3.675	0.341	7	3.452	0.457	11	3.165	1.832	2
5	3.257	0.182	18	3.395	0.376	15	2.915	1.721	5
6	3.542	0.361	8	3.705	0.647	6	3	1.732	4
7	3.337	0.603	14	3.405	0.404	13	2.167	1.385	15
8	3.112	0.515	19	3.955	0.315	1	2.667	1.581	8
9	4.032	0.100	1	3.83	0.465	2	3.25	1.891	1
10	3.83	0.251	6	3.742	0.510	4	3.085	1.817	3
11	3.27	0.286	16	3.397	0.424	14	2.417	1.588	11
12	3.425	0.376	11	3.54	0.371	9	2.582	1.533	9
13	3.432	0.396	10	3.475	0.749	10	2.417	1.588	10
14	3.855	0.147	5	3.615	0.597	7	2.832	1.707	6
15	3.405	0.737	12	3.23	0.582	18	2.415	1.400	12
16	3.887	0.274	3	3.727	0.661	5	2.832	1.707	6
17	3.267	0.285	17	3.45	0.734	12	2.167	1.385	15
18	3.875	0.258	4	3.82	0.160	3	2.832	1.658	6
19	3.275	0.192	15	3.03	0.688	19	2.335	1.395	13
OVER ALL	3.542	0.382		3.521	0.527		2.675	1.611	

The over all mean score for Arts, Science and Commerce disciplines are 3.54, 3.52 and 2.67 which are very below to the maximum score level. This indicates that the users in Arts, Science and Commerce disciplines are not well satisfied with the collection, services and facilities available in the library. The SD score indicates that the variation among the individual users in Arts and Science discipline are quite negligible (less than 1), but there are some variations among the individual users in Commerce discipline.

The analysis of the perceptions of users in Arts, Science and Commerce discipline according to service quality determinants indicates that there is no much difference among the disciplines. For the users in Arts discipline, Assurance is the most satisfied determinant. At the same time it is Responsiveness for Science and Commerce disciplines. But for Arts, Reliability is the least scored determinant. For Science, it is Tangibles and for Commerce it is Empathy. More details are available in Table 16.

DIFFERENCE BETWEEN USER PERCEPTIONS AND EXPECTATIONS

The service quality of a library can be clearly assessed by analyzing the difference between the user's perceptions and expectations of facilities and services. The difference between them indicate how well the facilities and services provided in the library match the users expectations. The results of the analysis are as follows:

The statement wise analysis shows that users perceptions about the library collection, services and facilities are below to their expectations. However there is no wide gap between them. The users perceptions about the library staff and the help they provide is more than to their expectation. The user can feel free to depend the library staff for somc help. The personal attention they get in the library is also up to their expectation. But the users perception about the services and facilities followed by the books and periodicals available in the library are much below to their expectations. More details of the gap between the two are given in the Table 17.

Table 16. Qualities of a Good Library: Determinant Wise Analysis of Perceptions

Determinants	Arts			Science			Commerce		
	Mean	SD	Rank	Mean	SD	Rank	Mean	SD	Rank
Tangibles	3.627	0.574	3	3.398	0.580	5	2.728	1.630	2
Reliability	3.312	0.415	5	3.615	0.435	2	2.687	1.605	4
Responsiveness	3.639	0.253	2	3.627	0.443	1	2.833	1.707	1
Assurance	3.715	0.386	1	3.524	0.613	3	2.693	1.604	3
Empathy	3.472	0.245	4	3.433	0.527	4	2.445	1.479	5

Table 17. Qualities of a good library; Difference between user perceptions and expectations

Q.No.	Mean (Perception)	Mean (Expectation)	Mean Difference	Rank
1	3.12	3.85	-0.73	7
2	3.4	4.57	-1.17	16
3	3.26	4.82	-1.56	17
4	3.54	4.14	-0.6	4
5	3.31	4.02	-0.71	6
6	3.68	4.52	-0.84	10
7	3.26	4.18	-0.92	12
8	3.6	4.28	-0.68	5
9	3.92	4.68	-0.76	7
10	3.77	4.57	-0.8	8
11	3.32	4.25	-0.93	13
12	3.43	4.38	-0.95	14
13	3.38	3.78	-0.4	3
14	3.63	4.34	-0.71	5
15	3.22	4.12	-0.9	11
16	3.78	3.52	0.26	1
17	3.18	3.2	-0.02	2
18	3.8	4.62	-0.82	9
19	3.03	4.11	-1.08	15

The Determinant wise analysis shows that the perception about Assurance is equal to their expectations. But their perceptions about the Tangibles are very low compared to their expectations. The difference mean score indicates that except Tangibles all service quality determinants are more or less equal to the users perceptions and expectations. The details are given Table 18.

Table 18. Qualities of a good library; Determinant Wise Analysis of User perceptions and expectations

Determinants	Mean (Perception)	Mean (Expectation)	Mean Difference	Rank
Tangibles	3.33	4.345	-1.01	5
Reliability	3.462	4.25	-0.78	3
Responsiveness	3.61	4.47	-0.86	4
Assurance	3.543	3.543	0	1
Empathy	**3.336**	**3.976**	**-0.64**	**2**

QUALITIES OF A GOOD LIBRARY; DIFFERENCE BETWEEN EXPECTATIONS AND PERCEPTIONS OF STUDENTS AND TEACHERS

The user wise analysis of the difference between the user's perceptions and expectations indicates that both the students and teachers perceptions about the 'help provided by library staff' and the 'personal attention given' to them are more than to their expectation. But the students perception about the 'understanding of their specific needs' and the 'facilities and services provided' are very low compared to their expectations. The teacher's perception about the library collection, facilities and services are not reached up to their expectations. More details about the gap between the students and teachers are given in Table 19.

The determinant wise analysis of the user's perceptions and expectations reveals that there is difference between the students and teachers. All the determinants are found below to the users expectations. In the case of students Assurance has got the least gap between perceptions and expectations. But in the case of teachers, perceptions on Empathy is nearer to their expectations. In the case of students Reliability shows maximum gap from its expectations. On the other hand it is Tangibles for teachers. More details are given in Table 20.

Table 19. Difference between perceptions and expectations of Students and Teachers

Q. No	Student				Teacher			
	Mean(Perception)	**Mean (Expect)**	**MeanDiff.**	**Rank**	**Mean(Perception**	**Mean(Expect)**	**MeanDiff.**	**Rank**
1	2.84	3.637	-0.79	8	3.105	3.463	-0.35	3
2	3.58	4.597	-1.01	16	2.975	4.05	-1.07	16
3	3.556	4.734	-1.17	18	3.095	4.11	-1.01	15
4	3.91	4.113	-0:20	3	2.951	3.88	-0.92	12
5	3.405	4.229	-0.82	10	2.973	3.56	-0.58	7
6	3.621	4.592	-0.97	13	3.21	3.95	-0.74	11
7	3.118	4.271	-1.15	17	2.821	3.55	-0.72	9
8	3.523	3.903	-0.37	4	2.966	3.896	-0.92	12
9	3.963	4.77	-0.80	9	3.445	3.955	-0.51	6
10	3.863	4.302	-0.43	5	3.241	3.975	-0.73	10
11	3.141	4.133	-0.99	15	2.915	3.857	-0.94	13
12	3.405	4.266	-0.86	11	2.96	3.913	-0.95	14
13	3.171	4.157	-0.98	14	3.045	3.402	-0.35	3
14	3.536	4.162	-0.62	6	3.331	3.939	-0.60	8
15	3.341	3.996	-0.65	7	2.691	3.481	-0.78	11
16	3.58	3.181	0.399	1	3.385	3.239	0.146	1
17	2.811	2.896	-0.08	2	3.111	3.021	0.090	2
18	3.816	4.722	-0.90	12	3.201	3.706	-0.50	5
19	**2.888**	**4.079**	**-1.19**	**19**	**2.871**	**3.348**	**-0.47**	**4**

Table 20. Qualities of a good library; Determinant Wise Analysis of Perceptions and expectations of students and teachers

Determinants	Student Mean (Percept)	Student Mean (Expect)	Student Mean Diff.	Student Rank	Teacher Mean (Perception)	Teacher Mean (Expect)	Teacher Mean Diff.	Teacher Rank
Tangibles	3.471	4.27	-0.79	4	3.031	3.875	-0.84	5
Reliability	3.417	4.249	-0.83	5	2.992	3.739	-0.74	3
Responsiveness	3.593	4.368	-0.77	3	3.140	3.925	-0.78	4
Assurance	3.486	3.779	-0.29	1	3.136	3.553	-0.41	2
Empathy	3.172	3.899	-0.72	2	3.061	3.356	-0.29	1

QUALITIES OF A GOOD LIBRARY; SEX WISE ANALYSIS OF USER EXPECTATIONS AND PERCEPTIONS

Sex wise analysis of the users' expectations and perceptions shows that there are differences between their perceptions and expectations on all library matters. But the mean score difference indicates that most of the matters are up to their expectations. Both the groups admit that the library staff is always ready to help them at any time and so it is more than to their expectations. They also admit that they get 'personalized attention' more than to their expectations. The perception about the facilities and services of the male users are far below to their expectations. In the case of female users, their perceptions about the 'collection of books and periodicals' and the 'availability of right book at the very first time' are far below to their expectations. More details of the gap between the two variables are given in Table 21.

The service quality determinant wise analysis of male and female users shows that except Responsiveness, other determinants are up to their expectations. Assurance has got prime position in the order of nearness to expectations. The male users noted that the Responsiveness is very low to their expectations. At the same time the female users' perceptions about Assurance are above to their expectations, but Reliability is very low to their expectation. More details are given in Table 22.

Table 21. Difference between perceptions and expectations of Male and Female Users

Q. No	Male				Female			
	Mean (Perception)	**Mean (Expectation)**	**Mean Diff.**	**Rank**	**Mean (Perception)**	**Mean (Expectation)**	**Mean Diff.**	**Rank**
1	3.188	3.663	-0.47	3	2.756	3.437	-0.68	11
2	3.791	4.747	-0.95	14	2.763	3.897	-1.13	19
3	3.578	4.914	-1.33	17	3.073	3.935	-0.86	16
4	3.818	4.409	-0.59	4	3.043	3.579	-0.53	8
5	3.573	4.047	-0.47	3	2.805	3.746	-0.94	17
6	3.76	4.682	-0.92	13	3.071	3.859	-0.78	13
7	3.505	4.28	-0.77	7	2.435	3.537	-1.10	18
8	3.566	4.313	-0.74	6	2.923	3.486	-0.56	9
9	3.928	4.721	-0.79	8	3.48	4.004	-0.52	7
10	3.808	4.692	-0.88	11	3.296	3.585	-0.28	3
11	3.081	4.323	-1.24	16	2.975	3.667	-0.69	12
12	3.21	4.379	-1.16	15	3.155	3.8	-0.64	10
13	3.128	3.953	-0.82	10	3.088	3.607	-0.51	6
14	3.581	4.473	-0.89	12	3.286	3.629	-0.34	4
15	3.175	3.815	-0.64	5	2.858	3.663	-0.80	14
16	3.685	3.22	0.465	1	3.28	2.597	0.683	1
17	3.078	3.255	-0.17	2	2.845	2.663	0.182	2
18	3.951	4.873	-0.92	13	3.066	3.556	-0.48	5
19	**3.171**	**3.982**	**-0.81**	**9**	**2.588**	**3.446**	**-0.85**	**15**

Table 22. Determinant Wise Analysis of perceptions and expectations of Male and Female Users

Determinants	Mean (Perception)	Male Mean (Expect)	Mean Diff.	Rank	Mean (Perception)	Female Mean (Expect)	Mean. Diff	Rank
Tangibles	3.594	4.433	-0.83	4	2.909	3.712	-0.80	4
Reliability	3.601	4.330	-0.72	3	2.808	3.657	-0.84	5
Responsiveness	3.507	4.528	-1.02	5	3.226	3.764	-0.53	3
Assurance	3.480	3.836	-0.35	1	3.141	2.866	0.275	1
Empathy	3.400	4.036	-0.63	2	2.833	3.221	-0.38	2

QUALITIES OF A GOOD LIBRARY; DIFFERENCE BETWEEN USER EXPECTATIONS AND PERCEPTIONS ACCORDING TO DISCIPLINE

The discipline wise analysis of users' expectations and perceptions shows some differences among the different groups. The users in Arts and Science discipline admit that they get 'personalized attention' from the library staff. But for the users in Commerce discipline, it is the 'dependability of library staff' for some help. At the same time the perception of users in Arts and Science discipline about the 'understanding of their specific needs by library staff' is very low compared to their expectations. For the users in Commerce discipline, 'rightness of the book they received' on request is very low. More details of the analysis are given Table 23.

The determinant wise analysis of the users in different disciplines indicates that there is no difference in their opinion about the determinant, which is nearer to their expectations. Assurance is up to their expectations. The perception of users in Arts discipline about Responsiveness is far below to their expectation. For Science discipline it is Tangibles and Responsiveness and for Commerce it is Empathy. More details of the analysis are given in Table 24.

SUMMARY OF FINDINGS

1. Most of the users expect *adequate number of books and periodicals* and *help of staff* from a good library. This argument is fully supported by majority of the postgraduate students, female users and users in Science discipline. However, majority of the teachers, male users and the users in Arts discipline do not expect much help from library staff. Instead excellent facilities and services, easy access and convenient working hours, and prompt service are expected from a good library.
2. Majority of users except male users admit that *personalized attention* should not be expected from a good library. They also convinced that it is not necessary to depend the library

Table 23. Difference between user perceptions and expectations according to discipline

Q. No	Arts				Science				Commerce			
	Mean (Perc.)	Mean (Expt.)	Mean Diff.	Rank	Mean (Perc.)	Mean (Expt.)	Mean Diff.	Rank	Mean (Perc.)	Mean (Expt.)	Mean Diff.	Rank
1	3.395	4.017	-0.62	5	3.272	3.549	-0.27	2	2.25	3.083	-0.83	11
2	3.495	4.542	-1.04	14	3.587	4.758	-1.17	17	2.75	3.667	-0.91	12
3	3.945	4.654	-0.70	6	3.282	4.869	-1.58	19	2.75	3.75	-1	13
4	3.675	4.108	-0.43	4	3.452	4.374	-0.92	11	3.165	3.5	-0.33	4
5	3.257	4.033	-0.77	8	3.395	4.24	-0.84	9	2.915	3.417	-0.50	6
6	3.542	4.546	-1.00	13	3.705	4.683	-0.97	13	3	3.583	-0.58	7
7	3.337	4.229	-0.89	11	3.405	4.165	-0.76	7	2.167	3.333	-1.16	15
8	3.112	3.979	-0.86	10	3.955	4.386	-0.43	4	2.667	3.333	-0.66	8
9	4.032	4.658	-0.62	5	3.83	4.846	-1.01	15	3.25	3.583	-0.33	4
10	3.83	4.696	-0.86	10	3.742	4.637	-0.89	10	3.085	3.083	0.002	2
11	3.27	4.4	-1.13	16	3.397	4.418	-1.02	16	2.417	3.167	-0.74	9
12	3.425	4.479	-1.05	15	3.54	4.54	-1	14	2.582	3.25	-0.66	8
13	3.432	3.733	-0.30	2	3.475	4.106	-0.63	5	2.417	3.75	-1.08	14
14	3.855	4.329	-0.95	12	3.615	4.573	-0.95	12	2.832	3.25	-0.41	5
15	3.405	4.408	-0.82	9	3.23	4.058	-0.82	8	2.415	2.75	-0.33	4
16	3.887	3.729	-0.42	3	3.727	4.15	-0.42	3	2.832	2.75	0.082	1
17	3.267	3.5	0.407	1	3.45	3.043	0.407	1	2.167	2.33	-0.16	3
18	3.875	4.525	-0.71	7	3.82	4.534	-0.71	6	2.832	3.583	-0.75	10
19	3.275	3.913	-1.2	17	3.03	4.23	-1.2	18	2.335	3	-0.66	8

Table 24. Determinant Wise Analysis of difference between the user perceptions and expectations according to discipline

Determinants	Arts				Science				Commerce			
	Mean (Perc.)	Mean (Expt.)	Mean Diff.	Rk	Mean (Perc.)	Mean (Expt.)	Mean Diff.	Rk	Mean (Perc.)	Mean (Expt.)	Mean Diff.	Rk
Tangibles	3.627	4.33	-0.70	3	3.398	4.387	-0.98	4	2.728	3.5	-0.77	4
Reliability	3.312	4.197	-0.88	4	3.615	4.369	-0.75	3	2.687	3.417	-0.72	3
Responsiveness	3.639	4.558	-0.91	5	3.627	4.61	-0.98	4	2.833	3.271	-0.43	2
Assurance	3.715	4.155	-0.43	1	3.524	3.927	-0.40	1	2.693	2.917	-0.22	1
Empathy	3.472	3.979	-0.50	2	3.433	3.935	-0.50	2	2.445	2.972	-0.52	5

staff for all. At the same time, male users do not consider *modern building and furniture* as a necessary item needed for good libraries.

3. In general, most of the users consider *Tangibles* as an important feature of good libraries. This argument is supported only by users in Commerce discipline. Other groups of users, such as Students, Teachers, Male and Female users and users in Arts and Science disciplines consider *Responsiveness* as the prime feature of good libraries.
4. *Empathy*, the service determinant, is not expected as an important feature of a good library by most of the users in general and users belonging to teacher group and Arts discipline in particular. At the same time, postgraduate students both male and female users, and users in Science and Commerce discipline think that *Assurance* is to be the least considered feature from a good library.
5. Most of the users in the college library strongly support the fact that they are *getting all sorts of help* from their library staff and it is true in the case of all categories of users under study.
6. Majority of users, in general, are not satisfied with the present *library building and furniture* and the level of understanding to library staff about their specific needs. Most of the postgraduate students, female users and users in Science discipline also have the same opinion about the library staff. Teachers, male users and users in Arts and Commerce discipline are of the view that the library staff does not have enough *knowledge to answer* their enquiries, and they are not providing *personalized attention* to them.
7. Most of the users strongly responded that they are getting immediate *response* to their enquiries from their library staff. This is true in the case of postgraduate students and teachers, female users and users in Arts and Commerce discipline. *Reliability and Assurance* is high rated features for male and users in Science discipline.

8. Most of the users in general noted *Tangibles* as the least considered feature in their library. Only the users in Science keep this view. For postgraduate students, male users, and users in Commerce discipline *Empathy* and for teachers, female users and users in Arts and Commerce discipline *Reliability* is least considered in their library.
9. User's perceptions about the *personal attention* given and *dependence made on library staff* are almost up to their expectation. *Library building and furniture, promptness of service provided and early response they received from library staff* is up to the expectations of users in Arts, Commerce and Science discipline respectively.
10. User's perceptions about the *library collection of books and periodicals* and the *services provided* are very low compared to their expectations. Postgraduate students, male and female users and users in Arts, Science and Commerce discipline strongly noted that *understanding of their specific needs* by library staff, *rightness of the books given* on request, and the speed in which the *staff responded* on their requests respectively are far below to their expectations.
11. The library offers *Assurance* to the maximum level to maximum users except the teachers who gets *Empathy* up to their expectations.
12. Most of the users are least satisfied with the *building and furniture* of their library. Teachers and users in Science discipline support this view. Most of the postgraduate students and female users feel that *Reliability* is very poor in their library. Male users and users in Arts discipline viewed *Responsiveness* very poor. At the same time *Empathy* is far below to the expectations of users in Commerce discipline.
13. Users expect *adequate books and periodicals, good services and maximum help from library staff*. At the same time they get only *maximum help* up to their expectations.

14. Expectation on *Tangibles* is very high to the users, but they do not get it from their library.
15. User's perceptions about the *help of library staff* are above to their expectations.
16. User's perceptions about *Assurance* are equal to their expectations.

CONCLUSION

The fact is that users expect certain types of services from a library. But the library are not able to provide these services, instead they provide something else. This will develop a gap between user's expectations and their perceptions. Once this gap is get widened, the very existence of the library may be questioned. So the library and information professionals have to see this gap very serious and do the needful urgently. Management techniques like Gap device, SERVQUAL, LIBQUAL+ etc are very suitable for assessing the gap between the user's perceptions and expectations about their library collections and services. Without giving proper consideration to the quality expectations of users, no libraries can succeed in coming years.

REFERENCES

1. Danuta A. Nitecki . SERVQUAL: Measuring Service Quality in Academic Libraries. *ARL Newsletter*, 191, May 1997. p1-2.
2. Banwet, DK and Datta, B. Effect of Service Quality on Post-Visit Intentions. *Annals of Library Science and Documentation*, 47(2), 2000. p41-48.

14

Online Research Tools and Resources in Life Sciences

Dr. R. Samyuktha

Deputy Librarian,
University of Madras,
Guindy Campus,
Chennai.

ABSTRACT

The fundamental purpose of any research library is to provide access to the organised record of knowledge and ideas. There has been a paradigm change of two kinds in research; those driven by needs and expectations of users of Library and Information Services and those driven by the changes in Technology. Researchers expect faster access to more complete sources delivered in a more timely way. There is clear evidence that they increasingly want to use digital material alongside traditional materials and want access from their desktop whenever they want and wherever they are. When such is the scenario, Libraries and Information Professionals have begun to take a much more proactive stance to their role. They are required to act as catalysts to guide the researchers who are perplexed not knowing all the information resources and research tools available and how to access them. This paper discusses some of the major Online Research Tools and Resources that are popularly used by researchers in Life Sciences. A listing of the major weblinks is also furnished which would be of prime importance to Life Science researchers.

INTRODUCTION

The fundamental purpose of any research library is to provide access to the organised record of knowledge and ideas. Great changes are happening in the ways that knowledge and ideas are communicated, recorded and accessed. Libraries have begun to take a much more proactive stance to their role. They are recognising the potential that exists for them to play a central part in addressing the opportunities the technological changes are bringing.

There is an environment of change; the changes being of two kinds: Those driven by needs and expectations of users of library and information services and those driven by changes in technology.

The needs and expectations of users for information and library services are growing more extensive and diverse. People expect faster access to more complete sources, delivered in a more timely way. In most of the developed world, computer literacy from school to workplace and into the home has become a reality. The Internet has experienced unprecedented growth. There is clear evidence that researchers in academia and industry, and educators and learners at all levels, increasingly want to use digital materials alongside traditional materials and want access from their desktop whenever they want and wherever they are.

When such is the scenario, We, the Information Professionals are guised with a new role of being guides to enhance the knowledge of the researchers in Information Access. It is quite a crucial role in the context of the time that we would save for the researchers, by periodically furnishing the current relevant information resources.

SCOPE

This paper focuses on the Online Research Tools and Resources accessed by Life Science researchers. Since the spectrum of scientific research is a broad horizon it is intended to concentrate on a segment of science, namely Life Sciences.

Life Sciences encompasses the *Biological Sciences, Botanical*

Sciences and *Zoological Sciences* and the major Online Research Tools and Resources of these disciplines which the researchers access in the various stages of research are discussed and their weblinks are further listed in this paper.

ONLINE RESEARCH TOOLS AND RESOURCES

Abstracts and Indexes

Journals

Research News

Industry News

Reviews

Patents

Research techniques

Computational Softwares

Conferences

Life Science Publishing

Grants

PDF News / Biocareers

ABSTRACTS & INDEXES

This basic research tool aids the researcher to get a comprehensive knowledge of the type of research already done in the field. Serves as a guide to select a research problem.

eg. *www.umi.com/hp/Products/Dissertations.html*

Proquest Online Dissertations

To browse what dissertation is available in a particular subject.

www.biosis.org/products-services/ba.html

Biological Abstracts

Produced by BIOSIS, the world's largest abstracting and indexing service for the Life Sciences. Coverage is of about 4000 serials every year.

More links Annexure

JOURNALS

Today's online readers demand for more than an electronic reprint of the paper -based journal – static web pages are no longer the norm. But as web sites grow in complexity, it is critical to ensure that the readers can leverage advanced features in ways that make research more efficient and productive. Just a few years ago, publishers placed journals online simply to establish a presence on the web. Today's researchers are experienced web users who look for online journals they can use rather than merely visit.

Some of the features of the online journals that generally interest the researcher are the etocs (electronic table of contents), abstracts of articles, full text of research papers, Instruction to Authors to aid in publishing papers and Impact factor of the *journal to know its ranking of usage.*

eg: *http://bioresearch.ac.uk/browse/mesh/detail/C0600646L1174978.html*

Electronic Journals (Publication Type) A-Z

www.indiana.edu/~liblife/ejournal.html

Life Sciences electronic journal list.

www.isinet.com/isi/products/cc/editions/cds

Current Contents / Life Sciences provides access to complete bibliographical information from articles, editorials etc in recently published editions of over 1370 of world's leading Life Science Journals and Books.

(For more details see the Annexure)

There are some Information Services / Consortias like Science Direct, Ovid, OCLC first search, Dialog, Highwire Press, Catchword, Ideal that provide the resources that researchers in academic institutions depend on. Libraries that go in for such consortias benefit the researchers who have a access to their wide range of products and services.

eg. *www.hw.ac.uk/libwww/irc/journals/scidir.html*

'Science Direct' service is a web database for scientific research that contains full text of more then 1000 Elsevier Science Journals in Life, Physical, Medical, technical and Social Sciences available through internet.

It contains abstracts from core journals in the major scientific disciplines and is the most comprehensive database of primary literature in the Sciences available today.

(For more details see the Annexure)

RESEARCH NEWS

What's news in Life Science research – Weekly current news is provided by quite a few websites maintained by professional scientists. Access to webcasts and online discussions are special features.

eg: *www.bio.com/Redirectors/LinkRedirect01_23.jhtml?link=10*

Bio.Com's live webcasts

*www.bio.com/newsfeatures/newsfeatures***research.jhtml**

All past In Focus webcast recordings and manuscripts

www.bioexchange.com/news/bioinformatics.cfm

Current Bioinformatics news and online Bioinformatics discussions.

INDUSTRY NEWS

www.progen.com.au/lifeSciences/index.cfm

Progen's Life Sciences business unit is a leading distributor of biological and chemical reagents and kits for use in molecular and cellular biology, diagnostic and biotechnology research. Access to free industry newsletters and conferences are also available.

www.bio.com/industryanalysis/industryanalysis_news.jhtml

REVIEWS

Research Reviews and Product Reviews express the experiences of biological researchers to add on to the knowledge and tools that they require.

eg: *http://reviews.bmn.com*

RESEARCH REVIEWS - BIOMEDNET REVIEWS

www.biowire.com

Product Reviews Patents

Intellectual property rights and comprehensive patent data available helps the researcher to avoid duplication in research and also get to know the procedures of patenting..

eg: *http://biotechpatent/com*

Patent news is published monthly and Patent Report six times a year.

(For more details see the Annexure)

RESEARCH TECHNIQUES

Research techniques such as PCR (Polymerize Chain Reaction) applications, Protocols, Microassays etc. are some of the prime research tools required by the researchers.

eg: *www.bioprotocol.com*

Protocols for Molecular biology, Neurobiology, Developmental biology, Cell biology, Microbiology, Plant biology, Biochemistry etc.

(For more details see the Annexure)

COMPUTATIONAL SOFTWARE

Some of the latest Life Science related softwares that are available have features to design primers for PCR, track and store Labdata, design Micoarrays, simplifies computational analysis of sequence information and so on.

eg: *www.bio.com/Redirectors/LinkRedirect03_27.jhtml?link=10*

Primer Premier V5 - Primer design software amplifies across species or defect pathogens, designs high amplification efficiency primer for PCR, sequencing and hybridization with a built-in automatic search mode that tailors stringency to the template and one can design primers for difficult templates at the click of a button.

(For more details see the Annexure)

CONFERENCES

There are quite a few professional websites providing conference news available by subject, date or location. They enable the research scholars to track call for papers from various universities and professional bodies. Online conferences also enhance information exchange between the researchers.

eg: *www.hum-molgen.de/meetings/meetings/subject/html*

Calendar for events in genetics, biotechnology, bioinformatics, biochemistry and immunology.

(For more details see the Annexure)

LIFE SCIENCE PUBLISHING

Writing and presenting research work necessitates knowledge of resources and guidance in writing, especially for scientific presentations. Online Writing Resource Links aids the researcher to access writing guides for technical / scientific writing, standard citation guides, range of advice on publication, writing style, refereeing etc.

eg: *www.medbioworld.com/advice/prsenting.html*

Provides links to online writing and presenting Research Work.

AWARDS / GRANTS / FELLOWSHIPS

Information regarding Project grants, Programme grants, Research Fellowships, Travel grants, Symposia grants, Equipment – only grants are provided by various organisations online.

eg: www.ocms.ox.ac.uk/ocms/funding.html

Oxford Centre for Molecular Sciences

(For more details see the Annexure)

PDF NEWS / BIOCAREERS

Researchers who want to pursue their post doctoral research or work as Research Associates Scientists in Life Sciences have a wide range of weblinks to keep track of what's new every week.

eg: *www.sciencecareers.org*

It is the premier job site for scientists. Every week one can find hundreds of new job postings, employer profiles, a resume/ CV database and career advice; all the tools needed to find a top job in the industry.

http://career.bio.com

CONCLUSION

There has been a paradigm shift in the methods of research in this electronic age. This scenario compels the scientists or researchers to keep pace with the technology to be in the race. The research tools especially online research tools are available in such a wide range that the researcher is perplexed not knowing all that is available and how to access or use them. Here comes our role of, 'We as Information Professionals' who can act as catalysts to guide them to the right source of information at the shortest time possible. To be such role players, keeping uptodate is warranted. In doing so, we would definitely be the inevitable guides to their successful research.

ANNEXURE

ONLINE RESEARCH TOOLS AND RESOURCES

http://biobenchhelper.hypermart.net

Collection of internet resources which one may consult when working in the biolab

http://bioresearch.ac.uk/browse

UK's gateway to high quality internet resources in Biological and biomedical research. Comprehensive data on Fungi regarding classification, collection, genetics and pathogenecity is available.

http://eelink.net/Endspp

Endangered species.

http://scarab.msu.montana.edu/extension/PEPLinks.html

Pesticide related weblinks.

http://world.std.com/~krahe

Herbs and Aromas – Medicinal plants and properties.

http://www.vims.edu/tcs/crust_links.htm

Crustacean – related resources on the web.

www.ala.org/acrl/resjun00.html

Extensive list of plant related web resources with descriptive annotations for each site.

www.aqualink.com/catalogs/wplants1.html

Aquatic plants.

www.ars-grin.gov/npgs/tax

Grin taxonomy.

www.bagelhole.org/article.php/Food/163

Edible and medicinal plants.

www.bio.com

Bio Online provides research news, industry news, market research, investment research. Areas covered are genomics, proteomics, bioinformatics, biotherapeutics, bioengineering, drug discovery and immunotechnology. Access to webcasts of discussions of current topics are also available.

www.biocompare.com

Resources of new technologies in Life Sciences.

www.biofind.com

Internet's one stop – shop for worldwide Biotech industry.

www.bioresearchonline.com

Digital market place for bioresearch. Is a premier information source for biological research industry.

www.biosis.org.uk/free_resources/resource_guide.html

A free guide to finding zoology related information on the net. Indudes infomation on organisms, an index to organism names, systematics and taxonomy and an excellent resource guide for mammals.

www.biospace.com

Specialized provider of web based products and information services to the Life Science.

www.biotechnet.co.uk/links.htm

Website for bioscience entrepreneurs.

www.derwent.com/lifesciences

Offers a choice of Life Science databases. Covering patents, journals and conferences used by research.

www.golgi.harvard.edu/Biolinks.html

Biology links.

www.herbalgram.org/browse.phys/medicinal-plant

Medicinal plant information.

www.keil.ukans.edu/~fungi

Mycological research.

www.marenet.de

Marenet is the worldwide Network of Marine Research Institutions and Documents.

www.nursery.umd.edu/plant.htm

Plant identification.

www.plantstress.com/admin/WRFiles/literaturewr.htm

Plant science literature, databases and online learning.

www.public.iastate.edu/~pedro/rt-journals.html

Pedro's biomolecular research tools.

www.rt66.com/hrbmoore/HOMEPAGE/HomePage.html

Medicinal plant images and databases.

www.scicentral.com

Scicentral – Biological Sciences – Metadirectory maintained by professional scientists.

www.wri.org/wri/biodiv/pharmacy.html

A short list of plant based medicinal drugs.

www.3.ibm.com/solutions/lifesciences

Discovery link gives access to 25 million assays and 400,000 compounds – answer in 15 seconds.

Aspects of GMO (Genetically Modified Organism) technology

http://biotech.info.net/index.html

www.colostate.edu/programs/lifesciences/Transgeniccrops

www.edmonds-institute.org

www.house.gov/science/smithreport04/300.pdf

www.percyschmerser.com

ABSTRACTS AND INDEXES

http://tls.il.proquest.com/hp/products/DisExpress.html

Dissertation Express

If the publication number, author or title of the dissertation that is required is known, Dissertations Express in the fastest and easy ordering service

http://wwwlib.umi.com/dissertations

Proquest Digital Dissertations

Free access to most current two years of citations and abstracts of the Dissertations.

www.biosis.org

BIOSIS Reviews,

Zoological Record – The world's premier source for animal science research. Coverage is 4500 serials every year.

www.biosis.org/products_services/ba.html

Biological Abstracts

Produced by BIOSIS, the world's largest abstracting and indexing science for Life Sciences; coverage is 4000 serials every year.

www.cabi-publishing.org/products/Database/Abstracts/Index.asp

CAB Abstracts is a bibliographic database compiled by CABI publishing. It covers significant research and development literature in the fields of forestry, human nutrition, animal health, management and conservation of natural resources. Coverage 4 million records.

www.csa.com/detailsv3/asfaset.html

Aquatic Science Fisheries Abstracts

www.derwent.com/biotechabstracts.index.html

Derwent's Biotechnology Abstracts provides details of advances in processes and applications of biotech research from journals, conferences and patents.

www.isinet.com/isi/products/derwent

Derwent's Innovations Index is a web accessible product that merges Derwent World Patent index and Patents Citation Index.

JOURNALS

http://apt.allenpress.com/aptonline

Biology journals online.

http://bioresearch.ac.uk/browse/mesh/detail/C0600646L1174978. html

Electronic Journals (Publication Type) A – Z

http://marenet.uni-oldenburg.de/MareNet/marejournals.html

Lists online available journals and newsletters related to Marine Science.

www.ejb.org

Electronic journal of biotechnology is a scientific pre-reviewed journal edited exclusively in electronic format. Research and Review articles available are free on the web.

www.elsevier.com/homepage/san/aqua/online/online.sht

AquaOnline – gateway to Aquatic biology and Ecology Research.

www.indiana.edu/~liblife/ejournal.html

Life Sciences electronic journal list.

www.isinet.com

Current Contents / Life Sciences provides access to 1370 of world's leading Life Science journals.

www.vsppub.com/journals/jn-Cru.html

Website for Journal Crustaceana which is the foremost journal in the world on Crustacean research.

INFORMATION SERVICES / CONSORTIA

www.catchword.com

'Catchword' provides internet access to full text of articles of almost 50 research journals published by a number of leading scholarly and academic publishers.

www.dialog.com

'Dialog' is the worldwide leader in providing online based information services. Their products are a combination of highly accurate online research tools offering access to unique and relevant database designed to meet the specific needs of a wide range of users.

www.highwire.stanford.edu

Delivers scientific and medical research online in high quality web environments.

www.hw.ac.uk/libwww/irc/journals/ap.html

'Ideal' service provides access to recent issues of about 170 journals published by Academic Press.

www.hw.ac.uk/libwww/irc/journals/scidir.html

'Science Direct' service is a web database for scientific research that contains full text of more then 1000 Elsevier Science Journals in Life, Physical, Medical, Technical and Social Sciences available through internet. It contains abstracts from core journals in the major scientific disciplines and is the most comprehensive database of primary literature in the Sciences available today.

www.oclc.org/firstsearch

'OCLC Firstsearch' connects a world of Libraries to a universe of information, gives library users instant online access to more than 70 databases with links to 5.9 million online full text articles, full image articles from over 3500 electronic journals.

www.ovid.com

'Ovid' provides the resources that researchers in universities and colleges depend on. Their coverage of databases in a broad range of subjects makes Ovid an ideal solution for Libraries and Consortia around the world.

RESEARCH NEWS

www.bio.com/Redirectors/LinkRedirect01_23.jhtml?link=10

Bio.Com's live webcasts

www.bio.com/newsfeatures/newsfeatures_research.jhtml

All past In Focus webcast recordings and manuscripts

www.bioexchange.com/news/bioinformatics.cfm

Current Bioinformatics news and online Bioinformatics discussions.

INDUSTRY NEWS

www.bio.com/industryanalysis/industryanalysis_news.jhtml

www.progen.com.au/lifeSciences/index.cfm

NEWSLETTERS

www.bio.com/newsletter

www.bioresearchonline.com

www.lifescipub.com/newsletter.htm

www.mnh.si.edu/botany/bcn/issue/175.html

Biological conservation newsletter.

www.uga.edu/~protozoa

Protozoology newsletter.

REVIEWS

http://reviews.bmn.com

Biomednet Reviews – World's largest resource for Life Science researchers.

www.biowire.com

Product reviews by scientists for scientists – definitive resource of knowledge and tools biological researchers need.

PATENTS

http://biotechpatent.com

Patent News - monthly publication, Patent Report - 6 times a year.

www.intellectual-property.gov.uk

www.patent.gov.uk

www.patentcafe.com

www.derwent.com/worldpatentsindex

Comprehensive database of patent documents published in the world.

PROTOCOLS

www.bioexplorer.net/methodsand_protocols

Collection of links to protocols used in biosciences

www.bioprotocol.com

Protocols for Molecular biology, Neurobiology,

Developmental biology, Cell biology, Microbiology, Plant biology, Biochemistry etc.

www.biovisa.net

Directory of protocols, journals and forums in the area of biology.

www.biowww.net

Comprehensive collection of lab troubleshooting resources, newsgroups and protocols in molecular biology.

www.cellbio.com

Links to useful and well organised sites for educational resources, methods and protocols and current research.

COMPUTATIONAL SOFTWARE

www.bio.com/Redirectors/LinkRedirect03_27.jhtml?link=10

Primer Premier V5 - Primer design software amplifies across species or defect pathogens, designs high amplification efficiency primer for PCR, sequencing and hybridization with a built-in automatic search mode that tailors stringency to the template and one can design primers for difficult templates at the click of a button.

www bio.com/Redirectors/LinkRedirect3_12.jhtml?link=11

DNA Microarray Software: Batch PCR primer design and hybridization probe design tool for Windows. Supports many specialized needs like ORF studies and SNP detection using primer extension. Can be used with DNA chip and gene chip arrays.

www.bio.com/redirectors/Linkredirect03_27.jhtml?link=12

LABTrack represents an exciting new development in Laboratory Information Management Systems (LIMS) – a new generation called Electronic Lab Notebooks. Typically, LIMS store only reduced and/or approved data. LABTrack can store all of the data that is produced in the lab – raw and reduced.

CONFERENCES

http://marenet.uni-oldenburg.de/MareNet

Conference links of the Network of Marine Research Institutions.

www.vims.edu/tcs

Crustacean related conference news.

www.hum-molgen.de/meetings/meetings/subject.html

Calendar for events in genetics, biotechnology, bioinformatics, biochemistry and immunology.

www.jeukmic.org/Soc.html

Conference links for protozoology

www.lib.ucdavis.edu/bioag/biotec.html

Conference links of biological and agricultural science.

www.papersinvited.com

World's largest listing of call for papers. Tracking the call for papers from various universities and professional bodies.

LIFE SCIENCE PUBLISHING

www.medbioworld.com/advice/presenting.html

Provides links to online writing and presenting Research Work.

AWARDS / GRANTS / FELLOWSHIP

www.erin.utoronto.ca/~w3msa

Mycological Society of America.

www.lifeSciences.umich.edu/values/lsvsp-links.html

University of Michigan Life Sciences, Values and Society Program.

www.nas.edu

National Academy of Sciences.

www.nsf.gov

National Science Foundation.

www.ocms.ox.ac.uk/ocms/funding.html

Oxford Center for Molecular Sciences.

www.reeusda.gov/crgram/biotechrisk/biotech.htm

USDA biotech risk assessment research grants.

www.uga.edu/~protozoa

Society of protozoologist.

PDF NEWS / BIOCAREERS

www.sciencecareers.org

Science Careers.org is the premier job site for scientists. Every week one can find hundreds of new job postings, employer profiles, a resume/CV database and career advice; all the tools needed to find a top job in the industry.

http://career.bio.com

WEBLIOGRAPHY

http://apt.allenpress.com/aptonline

http://biobenchhelper.hypermart.net

http://bioresearch.ac.uk/browse

http://bioresearch.ac.uk/browse/mesh/detail/C0600646L1174978.html

http://biotech.info.net/index.html

http://biotechpatent.com

http://career.bio.com

http://eelink.net/Endspp

http://marenet.uni-oldenburg.de/MareNet

http://marenet.uni-oldenburg.de/MareNet/marejournals.html

http://reviews.bmn.com

http://scarab.msu.montana.edu/extension/PEPLinks.html

http://tls.il.proquest.com/hp/products/DisExpress.html

http://world.std.com/~krahe

www.3.ibm.com/solutions/lifesciences

www.ala.org/acrl/resjun00.html

www.aqualink.com/catalogs/wplants1.html

www.ars-grin.gov/npgs/tax

www.bagelhole.org/article.php/Food/163

www.bio.com

www.bio.com/industryanalysis/industryanalysis_ews.jhtml

www.bio.com/newsfeatures/newsfeatures_research.jhtml

www.bio.com/newsletter

www.bio.com/Redirectors/LinkRedirect01_23.jhtml?link=10

www.bio.com/Redirectors/LinkRedirect03_27.jhtml?link=10

www.bio.com/Redirectors/LinkRedirect03_27.jhtml?link=12

www.bio.com/Redirectors/LinkRedirect3_12.jhtml?link=11

www.biocompare.com

www.bioexchange.com/news/bioinformatics.cfm

www.bioexplorer.net/methodsand_protocols

www.biofind.com

www.bioprotocol.com

www.bioresearchonline.com

www.biosis.org

www.biosis.org.uk/free_resources/resource_guide.html

www.biosis.org/products_services/ba.html

www.biospace.com

www.biotechnet.co.uk/links.htm

www.biovisa.net

www.biowire.com

www.biowww.net

www.cabi-publishing.org/products/Database/Abstracts/Index.asp

www.catchword.com

www.cellbio.com

www.colostate.edu/programs/lifesciences/Transgeniccrops

www.csa.com/detailsv3/asfaset.html

www.derwent.com/biotechabstracts.index.html

www.derwent.com/lifesciences

www.derwent.com/worldpatentsindex

www.dialog.com

www.edmonds-institute.org

www.ejb.org

www.elsevier.com/homepage/san/aqua/online/online.sht

www.erin.utoronto.ca/~w3msa

www.golgi.harvard.edu/Biolinks.html

www.herbalgram.org/browse.phys/medicinal-plant

www.highwire.stanford.edu

www.house.gov/science/smithreport04/300.pdf

www.hum-molgen.de/meetings/meetings/subject.html

www.hw.ac.uk/libwww/irc/journals/ap.html

www.hw.ac.uk/libwww/irc/journals/scidir.html

www.indiana.edu/~liblife/ejournal.html

www.intellectual-property.gov.uk

www.isinet.com

www.isinet.com/isi/products/derwent

www.jeukmic.org/Soc.html

www.keil.ukans.edu/~fungi

www.lib.ucdavis.edu/bioag/biotec.html

www.lifeSciences.umich.edu/values/lsvsp-links.html

www.lifescipub.com/newsletter.htm

www.marenet.de

www.medbioworld.com/advice/presenting.html

www.mnh.si.edu/botany/bcn/issue/175.html

www.nas.edu

www.nsf.gov

www.nursery.umd.edu/plant.htm

www.oclc.org/firstsearch

www.ocms.ox.ac.uk/ocms/funding.html

www.ovid.com

www.papersinvited.com

www.patent.gov.uk

www.patentcafe.com

www.percyschmerser.com

www.plantstress.com/admin/WRFiles/literaturewr.htm

www.progen.com.au/lifeSciences/index.cfm

www.public.iastate.edu/~pedro/rt-journals.html

www.reeusda.gov/crgram/biotechrisk/biotech.htm

www.rt66.com/hrbmoore/HOMEPAGE/HomePage.html

www.scicentral.com

www.sciencecareers.org

www.uga.edu/~protozoa

www.uga.edu/~protozoa

www.vims.edu/tcs

www.vims.edu/tcs/crust_links.htm

www.vsppub.com/journals/jn-Cru.html

www.wri.org/wri/biodiv/pharmacy.html

wwwlib/umi.com

15

Consortium of University Libraries in Kerala : A Proposal

Dr. M. Bavakutty,
Professor of Library Science and University Librarian,
University of Calicut.

Mohamed Haneefa. K.,
Junior Research Fellow,
Dept. of Library & Information Science,
University of Calicut.

ABSTRACT

The monopoly of libraries on information provision is over. Now, the focus of libraries is shifting from the acquisition of physical information resources to providing access to distributed information resources in a variety of formats. Libraries of developed countries formed consortia to achieve some common interests such as sharing the same system, sharing databases, to standardise policy in accessing commercial databases, etc. But libraries in India are lagging behind in realising the wonderful possibilities of library consortium. The main reason to form a library consortium is to improve information resources, to provide better services to the users and to gain financial benefits.

Libraries are now facing severe economic constraints. They are encountering budget-cut coupled with the escalating costs of resources and diverse needs of users. They are struggling to keep up their relevance in this fast changing information environment. University Libraries of Kerala are no exception to this phenomenon. Joining or forming a consortium can solve many of the problems faced by the University Libraries in Kerala.

The present paper makes a proposal for a consortium of university libraries in Kerala. The paper discusses the need for forming a library consortium, requirements of a library consortium and benefits of a library consortium.

INTRODUCTION

Information is a fundamental resource for social development and the progress of society. During the passage of years the mode of accessing information has changed. Technology in its broad sense is the main factor determining the development of information. Information is increasingly becoming a commodity and is viewed as something to be bought and sold. The explosive growth of information, proliferation of literature and specialization of subjects have compelled libraries to share their resources.

The local collections of libraries are not self-sufficient to meet the information requirements of their users. Therefore libraries no longer have a monopoly on information provision. Now, the focus of libraries is shifting from the acquisition of physical information resources to providing access to distributed information resources in a variety of formats. Technological change has made its impact on the ways through which information seekers find and receive information.

Libraries are now facing severe economic constraints. They are encountering budget-cut coupled with the escalating costs of resources and diverse needs of users. They are struggling to keep up their relevance in this fast changing information environment. Users can access a variety of information through electronic means from outside the library. Now, libraries are segregated by their type: public, academic and special and also with their collection. As far as information seekers are concerned these boundaries are artificial to their information requirements. The information needs and information seeking behaviour of users are changing. Now, new information requirements are arising by the inter-disciplinary nature of learning like Bioinformatics, Geoinformatics,

Biotechnology, etc. Under these circumstances libraries are not able to satisfy all the requirements of its users on their own. So some form of co-operation among similar type of libraries is very much essential.

Libraries can work together by forming consortia. Hundreds of local, regional and national library consortia are operational throughout the world. Libraries of developed countries formed consortia to achieve some common interests such as sharing the same system, sharing databases, sharing of e-journals or to standardise policy in accessing commercial databases. But libraries in India are lagging behind in realising the wonderful possibilities of library consortium.

LIBRARY CONSORTIUM

What is Library Consortium

Library consortia is a generic term to indicate any group of libraries that are working together towards a common goal, whether to expand cooperation on traditional library services (such as collection development) or electronic information services. The term is now used perhaps too broadly, and encompasses everything from formal legal entities (such as incorporated or governmental agencies) to informal groups that come together solely to achieve better pricing for purchasing electronic information (Arnold Hirshon, 1999) "A library consortium is a group of libraries that are established as a separate entity by incorporation under societies act, the companies' act or a memorandum of agreement among members. Library systems incorporated under the libraries act are not considered consortia. A consortium must have a budget and a staff member responsible for coordinating the activities of its members and act as the contact for its members" (Alberta Library, Canada).

Thus a library consortium is the association of libraries to achieve a common goal that is beyond what an individual library could achieve on its own. It has its own structure of governance and can act as a corporate body on behalf of all its members.

Why Library Consortium

The main reason for forming a library consortium is to improve information resources and services to the library users and to gain financial benefits. The standardised policy in collection development and bargaining power of a consortium can help to reduce costs of documents.

Libraries of a consortium can share a variety of resources. Following are some of the resources that can be shared:

- Sharing collections
- Sharing electronic resources
- Sharing databases
- Sharing e-journals
- Sharing storage resources
- Sharing archiving of resources
- Sharing expertise
- Sharing catalogue
- Collaborating on collection development
- Creation of digital collection
- Professional development
- New sources of funds

UNIVERSITY LIBRARIES IN KERALA

There are seven universities in Kerala: University of Kerala, Thiruvananthapuram; Mahatma Gandhi University, Kottyam; Cochin University of Science and Technology, Cochin; Sree Sankaracharya University of Sanskrit, Kalady; Kerala Agricultural University, Thrissur; University of Calicut, Thenhipalam; Kannur University, Kannur. All these universities except Kannur and Sree Sankaracharya University have well equipped university libraries. Since the Kerala Agricultural University (KAU) is a specialised one, its library resources may not be of much use to the users of other university libraries and vice versa. So KAU Library can be excluded from the proposed university library consortium.

The University of Kerala was established on 1st November 1957 as the University of Travancore. The main objective of the university was the reorganization of the education system of the state and to promote Kerala Arts and Culture. Presently university provides research facilities in Aquatic Biology, Biochemistry, Biotechnology, Botany, Chemistry, Environmental Science, Mathematics, Optoelectronics, Physics, Statistics, Zoology, etc. The library system of the Kerala University consists of a University Library at Palayam, a campus library at Karyavattam, libraries at departments and study centers. The campus library at Karyavattom was started in 1977. There are about 4 lakhs of books and other reading materials in the library. It subscribes about 400 periodicals in different subjects. It has certain special collections like Kerala Studies, Women Studies, World Bank Publications, Patents etc.

The University of Calicut is a premier institution for studies and research in the sciences, the humanities and the arts. It was established in 1968 with the objective of providing higher education and research facilities to the students of Malabar. The C.H. Mohammed Koya Library, the Central Library of the university was established to satisfy the information requirements of the academic community in the university campus, affiliated colleges, teacher education centres, study centres and outside graduates. The library system has a Central Library and libraries at all teaching and research departments, university study centres and the information centres at five district headquarters. The central library is computerised and fully automated. The library has a rich collection of documents including books, journals, theses, microfilms etc. The library provides a variety of services including Loan Service, Reference Service, Document Delivery Service, Internet facilities, Bibliographic Service, Reprographic Service, Current Awareness Service such as list of new additions, exhibition of new arrivals, exhibition of reading materials, etc.

The University of Cochin was established at Cochin in 1971. It has been reorganised and converted into a full-fledged Science and Technology University namely, Cochin University of Science and Technology (CUSAT) in 1986. CUSAT is a unitary type of university, national in character, international in pursuit of excellence in diverse fields such as Applied Science, Technology, Industry, Commerce, Management, Social and Marine Science. Specialisations exist in Mechanical, Electrical and Civil Engineering, Hindi, Foreign Languages, Traditional as well as Modern branches of Law, Human Rights, Marine Geology and Geophysics, Chemical and Physical Oceanography, Environmental Science, Environmental Engineering, Fishing Technology, Fish Processing and Packing Technology, Atmospheric Science, Applied Economics, Commerce, Business Management, Operations Research, Physics, Applied Chemistry, Computer Science, Information Technology, Instrumentation, Ship Building and Naval Architecture, Safety Engineering, Polymer Science, Rubber Technology, Engineering Statistics and Mathematics. The CUSAT Library was established in 1977. CUSAT library system consists of Central Library and department libraries functioning at different faculties. The Central Library is fully automated and the whole campus of 180 acres is networked. The main purpose of the library system is to support teaching, research and other academic and scientific activities carried out in the university. It has a good collection of books and periodicals, majority of which are foreign documents. The various services offered by the Central Library are: Loan Service, Inter-Library Loan Service, Literature Search, Compilation of Bibliographies, Reprographic Services, Reprint Request Service, Conference Alert Service, New Additions Alert Service, Patent Information, Reference Service, Consultancy Service, Internet, Browsing and e-mail Service and Information Desk.

Mahatma Gandhi University (M.G. University) came into existence on 2nd October 1983. The University has 26 teaching departments; three study centres and 92 affiliated colleges. The University Library system consists of a Central Library, Libraries at 26 Departments and Schools of thoughts. The main aim of the University Library is to support the information requirements of the students, research scholars and teachers in the university departments and the affiliated colleges. It has a good collection of books, periodicals and non-book materials. It provides a variety of services like User Awareness Service (CAS), Document Delivery Service (DDS), Content Page Service, Internet facilities, Selective Dissemination of Information (SDI) Service, etc.

Sree Sankaracharya University of Sanskit was established at Kalady in 1995 and the university library was started almost simultaneously to the establishment of the university. The organization of the university library is not satisfactory due to lack of professional expertise and functional organisation of the collection. The library provides services like Lending and Reference Service, Reprographic Service, Document Delivery Service and Literature Search Service.

Kannur University was established in 1995. Kannur University Library started functioning in the beginning of 1999. The library is not well organised and the functioning of the library is not satisfactory. There are several reasons for this such as lack of professional expertise, lack of a qualified and senior librarian and lack of proper interest of the university authorities. The library system comprises the Central Library and libraries at 3 teaching departments, 3 teacher education centres and legal studies.

CONSORTIA OF UNIVERSITY LIBRARIES: A PROPOSAL FOR KERALA

Joining or forming a consortium can solve many of the problems faced by the University Libraries in Kerala. The main goal of the consortium should be convenient access to information in whatever form and manner and wherever they are located at minimum cost and time.

The consortia activities may first start in the university libraries with higher level of library automation and electronic services. Only the computerised and automated university libraries can participate in the consortia because of the increasing relevance of digital information. A sound networking infrastructure with Internet connection is very essential to share the resources between the members of the consortia. Sharing of networked information resources through distributed access appears to be more economical. The University libraries and their users in Kerala are likely to benefit themselves by participating in the consortium. Common membership for all the users of the member libraries is the main attraction of the consortium. The consortium can issue a common library card to users and which will enable them to use any university library. The benefits that accrue from consortia are:

a) Reciprocal access to the collections by the users of the university libraries
b) Preferential treatment of inter library loan
c) More efficient collection development
d) Access to a wide range of electronic databases
e) Access to new electronic and print resources
f) Optimum utilisation of rare collections
g) Preparation of union catalogues
h) Provision of bibliographies
i) Saving of technical work and collections
j) Marketing of information services and resources in a better way.

Presently the Calicut University Library and CUSAT Library is computerised and fully automated. The computerization process of Kerala University Library and M.G. University Library is almost complete. Calicut University Library has a separate Internet Centre with V-SAT and ISDN connection and Kerala University Library is going to open such a centre in the central library. CUSAT Campus is networked and the central library has full time Internet connection. The libraries of Kannur University and Sree Sankaracharya University of Sanskit are in the infant stage and yet to be developed. It is better to form the consortium in two phases, because at present Kannur University and Sree Sankaracharya University Libraries are not able to participate in the consortium. In the first phase all the automated university libraries viz, Calicut University Library,

CUSAT Library, Kerala University Library, M.G. University library may be included in the consortium. The consortia activities may be monitored by a central agency with dedicated staffs. The Calicut University Library can act as the central agency, since they have enough infrastructure and professional expertise.

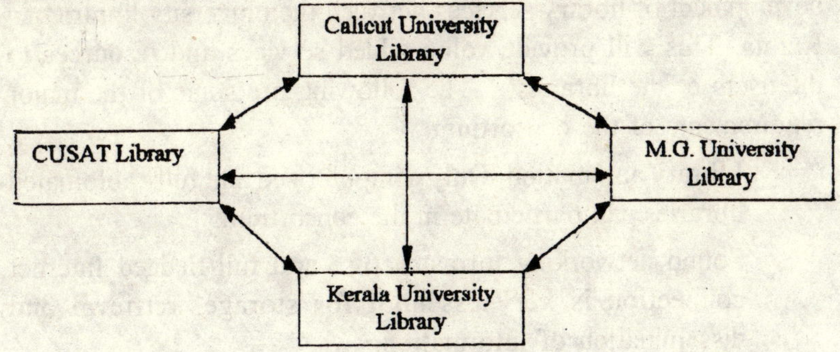

Structure of Consortium of University Libraries in Kerala – Phase I

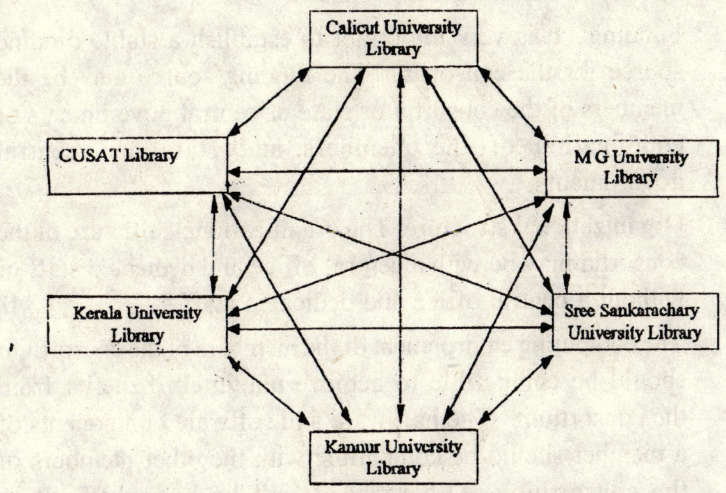

Structure of Consortium of University Libraries in Kerala – Phase II

In the second phase, Kannur and Sree Sankaracharya University Libraries can be included. By the time the first phase of the consortia gets activated they can equip themselves to become active participants of the consortia. In the first phase a careful monitoring of all the members and their users should be done. It will be helpful to assess how far the consortium is able to meet the information requirements of users and financial benefits achieved by members while being a member of the consortium.

The consortium will act as a platform for cooperation in the development of library services between the university libraries in Kerala. This will provide value added services and resources to the users of the libraries. The following are some of the major requirements of the consortium.

- Library automation: Only computerised and fully automated libraries can participate in the consortium.
- Sound networking infrastructure and full-fledged Internet connection is very essential for storage, retrieval and dissemination of information.
- Agreement: It is very essential to have some formal agreement between members of the consortium.
- Funding: It is very important to establish a stable funding source for the consortia. The funding source may be the members of the consortia or state or central governments or combination of the members and state and central governments.
- Organizational structure: The organizational structure of the consortia may be with a central office and dedicated staff or without a central office and dedicated staff.
- The computing environment of the members of the consortium should be compatible to achieve maximum benefits from the consortium. The hardware and software components of a member should be compatible with the other members of the consortium. Otherwise it will be very difficult to interconnect for a service.
- Security: It is very important to safeguard the computer and network of the consortium from unauthorised access. Only the members of the consortium should allow access to the resources.

Mutual understanding: The attitudes of the members of the consortium have a big impact on the success or failure of the consortium. Some members may have an attitude of protecting their individual collection. Such attitude exhibited by members is not favourable for the smooth sailing of the consortium.

- Skills of planning, organization and administration
- Human resources.

CONCLUSION

The monopoly of libraries on information provision is over; today no library is self-sufficient to meet all the information requirements of users. Library cooperation occurs when two or more libraries work together to provide more developed information resources and services to their users. Libraries and information centres in Kerala have wide variety of opportunities to cooperate and share their resources with other libraries. These opportunities offer exciting benefits to participating libraries. By setting up a consortium, the participating libraries can cooperate in collection development, sharing of physical resources, access to electronic information sources, etc. Such consortias should be able to change with the changes of the information environment. All members of the consortia should actively participate for the smooth sailing of the consortia. And all members should have a clear understanding of their users and their information needs and should assess how far the consortium is able to satisfy their information needs.

REFERENCES

1. Alberta Library, *http://www.thealbertalibrary.ab.ca/*
2. Anatolian University Library Consortium, *http://www.lib.metu.edu.tr/ankos*
3. Arnold Hirshon, Library Consortia Web Forum, *http://www.mcb.co.uk/services/conferen/webforum/mcb-lcm-forum6.html/*
4. Coalition of South African Library Consortia, *http://www.sabinet.co.za/library/ind_cosalc.html*
5. Cochin University of Science and Technology, *http://www.cusat.ac.in/*

6. Consortium of Academic Libraries in Manchester, *http://rylibweb.man.ac.uk/calim/calim2.html*
7. Consortium of Swiss Academic Libraries, *http://lib.consortium.ch*
8. Consortium of University Research Libraries-U K, *http://www.curl.ac.uk*
9. Council of Federal Libraries Consortium, *http://www.nlc-bnc.ca/cfl-cbgf/consort/*
10. Estonian Libraries Network Consortium, *http://www.utlib.ee/elnet*
11. J.K. Vijayakumar and M.G. Sreekumar, "Consortia approach among the higher education and research libraries in India: a dire need of the hour", *Library Co-operation in a Networked World: Papers presented in the National Seminar held at the University of Calicut,* ed. M. Bavakutty et. al (New Delhi: Ess Ess Publications, 2002) : 75-82.
12. M.D. Baby, "Library of future-today: CUSAT-a case study", *CALIBER-2000 Information Services in a Networked Environment in India : Papers presented at the seventh national convention for automation of libraries in education and research*, ed. R. Vengan, et. al. (Ahmedabad: INFLIBNET Centre, 2000) : 3.113-3.119.
13. Mahatma Gandhi University, *http://www.mguniversity.edu/*
14. Michigan Library Consortium, *http://mlc.lib.mi.us*
15. Ramesha and R.M. Vatnal, "Library co-operation among the university libraries in a networked environment", *Library Co-operation in a Networked World: Papers presented in the National Seminar held at the University of Calicut*, ed. M. Bavakutty et. al (New Delhi: Ess Ess Publications, 2002) : 11-23.
16. United Nations System Consortium, *http://www.unsystem.org/Index.html*
17. University of Calicut, *http://www.unical.ac.in/*
18. University of Kerala, *http://www.keralauniversity.edu/*
19. Yasar Tonta, "Cooperative collection development of electronic information resources in Turkish university libraries", *Paper presented at 66th IFLA Council and General Conference, Jarusalem, Israel* (IFLA, 2000).

16

Preservation of the Past for the Future

G.Dhanasegaran,
Deputy Librarian,
Dr.T.P.M Library,
M.K. University,
Madurai.

ABSTRACT

Explains the concept of conservation, preservation and restoration. Discusses the need for preservation – Brings out the causes of damage to library materials-Mentions the various hazards to information materials-Speaks about the various control measures for document preservation in libraries-Elucidates the methods of preservation of Non-Book materials-Highlights the responsibilities of librarians-Enumerates the suggestions for proper preservation of library materials.

INTRODUCTION

Libraries contain books, periodicals and information materials like maps, prints, photographs, microforms, slides, films, sound recordings and videotapes. "The book is the only immortality". Libraries are much concerned with preservation and restoration of all kinds of documents. Librarians should find out the causes that contribute to the deterioration of library materials.

The statutes of International Institute of Conservation, London, stated that conservation is a concept which includes two aspects viz., 1.Preservation 2. Restoration. Conservation process consists of control of the environment in which books are stored and the actual treatment of them.

Preservation is the maintenance of objects close to their original condition as far as possible. Preservation is the action taken to prevent, stop or retard deterioration. Restoration is the action taken to treat objects for the purpose of correcting any alteration they have undergone. It denotes those techniques and judgements used by the technical engaged in the making good of a library materials damaged by time, use and other factors.

NEED FOR PRESERVATION

In view of rarity and its importance the reading materials are preserved. One of the major functions of any library is to collect the documents of the past and of the present and to keep and maintain them so that they are available to the present and future users. Any material, which provides information should be taken care for preserving them. As the budgets shrink and the cost of books and other reading materials escalates, librarians are forced to see that their existing collections last as long as possible. Some collections became valuable over a time. Thus conservation and preservation of library materials have become major concerns of the librarians.

CAUSES OF DAMAGE TO LIBRARY MATERIALS

The following are the causes of damage to library materials:

Paper-aging	Damage in transport.
Environmental conditions	Damage by light.
Damage in storage.	Failure of air-conditioning system.
	Failure of fire fighting system.

HAZARDS TO INFORMATION MATERIALS

Tropical countries like India need much care and steps to preserve the library materials from various factors of deterioration. Library materials are considered to be susceptible to deterioration by the following factors.

Environment factors.

Biological factors.

Physical factors

Chemical factors

Human factors.

ENVIRONMENTAL FACTORS

The specific location and climate where a library is located and contributes the deterioration of library materials. The various environmental factors that cause the deterioration includes:

Pollutants
Gases
Normal Constituents

Pollutants

The atmosphere contains a host of pollutants such as dust, dirt, smoke and salt particles. These constitute a considerable hazard for library materials.

Gases

The various gases that cause deterioration are carbon monoxide, Nitric acid, Sulphur dioxide, Ozone, Paraffins, Hydrogen Sulfide, Amonia etc. These form the greatest hazard to library materials.

NORMAL CONSTITUENTS

Air

Air may be one of the worst enemies of the books. If it is too dry or too wet it is harmful.

Water

Water causes humidity of the atmosphere and does injury to the steel furniture due to rusting. During rainy season, rain water may enter the stack room either through the ventilators or windows or due to leakage of roofs.

Dampness

Excessive humidity is one of the concrete factors in the deterioration. Too much dampness results in mold or mildew, the loosening of paste or glue, weakening of paper and leather etc.

BIOLOGICAL FACTORS

The common biological agents for deteriorating papers are fungus, insects and rodents.

Fungus

Fungus attack paper materials. High humidity is helpful for the growth of fungus.

Insects

The most common insects, which attack library materials, are silver fish, book lice, cockroaches, termites, bookworm, Beatles, crickets etc.

PHYSICAL FACTORS

Light

The colours of pictures, photographs, writing ink are also faded and darkened by the ultraviolet rays.

Heat

Heat affects the binding materials and drive out adhesiveness.

Humidity

The increase of humidity accelerates bio-deterioration, weakens the adhesives and sizing materials.

Fire

Fire not only damages the books and manuscripts but also the whole stack room.

CHEMICAL FACTORS

Dust and impurities are the main chemical factors. The acidity makes the paper brittle and colour change. The acidity affects the ink and other color drawings.

HUMAN FACTORS

Damages caused by human beings are due to innocence and negligence. Books are teared and torned by rough handling. Ink and coffee stains may be caused by the careless handling. Mishandling of library materials are of many kinds:

a) While taking out a book from the rack.

b) While using/reading.

c) While reading in bed

d) While shelving the books.

Marking by pencil or ball pen also causes damage to the books.

CONTROL MEASURES FOR DOCUMENT PRESERVATION IN LIBRARIES

Librarians should know basic constituents of the library materials, its character, factors of deterioration, proper storage, preservation and restoration techniques.

CONTROL MEASURES FOR BIOLOGICAL FACTORS

Fungus and insects are controlled by maintaining the required humidity, proper lighting and ventilation facilities. The red colour acts as insect repellant. Library materials are treated with fungicide and insecticide by fumigation method to control fungus and insects.

CONTROL MEASURES FOR PHYSICAL FACTORS

Direct sunlight should be avoided on book stack and other storage area. Humidity can be controlled in winter season by using de-hydration agents. Much care should be taken for fire and flood damages.

CONTROL MEASURES FOR CHEMICAL FACTORS

The dust should be removed with fine brushes or vacuum cleaner. If the air pollution is controlled there will not be any external acidity in the paper materials.

METHODS OF PRESERVATION OF NON-BOOK MATERIALS

The present information centres have to preserve and conserve the information recorded on non- book materials also.

PALM LEAF MANUSCRIPTS

The palm leaf manuscripts face the following types of deterioration:

1. Stains

Distilled water can be used to remove the stains.

2. Discolouration

Warm distilled water with synpermic N wetting agent may be used.

3. Sticking together

This can be cured by dipping the leaves in a bath of acetone.

4. Insect attack

The preservation should be done by fumigating them.

5. Fungus

Ethanol can be used with a cotton swab to clean off the fungus from the surface of palm leaves.

6. Cracking

The leaves should not be allowed to bend. They may be stored in air-conditioned room.

7. Cleavages

Solution of Ethanol and water should be applied on such leaves.

8. Ink fading

Palm leaf should be cleaned first. Lemon grass oil should be smeared on the leaf using a soft cloth.

9. Brittleness

Lemon grass oil or camphor oil can be applied on the surface of the leaf. If the leaf is laminated using a solvent, the result will be better.

10. Edges

Coloured lacquer may be applied on the edges.

11. Covering

A bunch of palm leaves is protected between two wooden boards tied with a cord.

12. Storage

They are wrapped tightly in a piece of cloth and tied with a ribbon. Pigeon hole type cupboards are used to store palm leaves.

MICROFORMS

The storage of microform should be in a temperature between 15 and 22c and the Relative Humidity is to be 15 to 35%. Individual paper packets are advisable.

PHOTOGRAPHS

To clean photographs, a pad of cotton wool dampened with alcohol is to be used. Permanent storage in 40% R.H will be advisible.

GRAMAPHONE RECORDS

Before playing, records should be dusted with a soft damp cloth. After playing they should be put in their paper jackets. They should be stored vertically. They should be kept away from heat. The Gramaphone needle should be cleaned with alcohol using a soft brush.

AUDIO TAPES AND CASSETTES

It is advised to preserve them in air-conditioned room.

COMPUTER FLOPPY DISKETTES

They should not be used near any source of magnetic fields. Do not expose the diskettes to heat. They should not be bend. It is advised to store them in 10 to 52 c (or 50 to 125 F) temperature. Sunlight should not fall on the storage cabinet.

RESPONSIBILITIES OF THE LIBRARIANS

Librarians concentrate all the means to ensure the existence of document in storage or in use. The basic principle is professional ethics, civic duty and social responsibility. Any work in a library includes elements of preservation. The Librarian's task is to determine the method of document preservation. "Precaution is better than cure" is a common proverb in conservation. Preservation is an integral part of contemporary librarianship.

SUGGESTIONS FOR PROPER PRESERVATION OF LIBRARY MATERIALS

Pre-conservation work reduces the deterioration process of any reading material. The following are the suggestions for proper preservation of library materials.

1) Proper lighting and ventilation facilities should be provided in the stack room.

2) Periodic cleaning and dusting must be undertaken.
3) Library materials should be handled carefully.
4) Adequate provision must be made to control direct sunlight and humidity.
5) The affected reading materials should be kept separately.
6) The practice of keeping foodstuffs and other eatables in the stack room should be avoided.
7) Minor damages must be repaired immediately.
8) Spraying of insecticides must be undertaken every year.
9) Marking with pencil or ball pen on the reading materials may be avoided.
10) Books and manuscripts are to be cleaned with soft cloth or soft brushes.
11) Cassettes and floppy diskettes are to be kept on container boxes.

CONCLUSION

Preservation of reading materials is necessary and urgent. The contemporary preservation deals with conservation of old reading materials and currently added reading materials in any form and their survival into the future. As librarians and library users, we have a stake preserving the past for the future.

REFERENCES

1. Kathpalia, Y. P. - Conservation and preservation of Archives.
2. Nyuksha, Y U. P. - Conservation of library collections: a concept based on experience in the former societ union.
3. Perumal, P - Conservation of library materials.

17

Preservation of the Past for the Future in Indian Scenario

P. J. Nirmala,
Librarian,
Karunya Institute of Technology,
Coimbatore.

J. Dominic
Assistant Librarian,
Karunya Institute of Technology,
Coimbatore.

ABSTRACT

Preservation of library materials is most serious problem in today's librarianship. The modern libraries are more concentrating on dissemination of information than the preservation of library materials. Digital technology and increasing collaboration between libraries are likely to impact on how libraries see their preservation role, and how they try to fulfill that role.

Will digital technology overcome all of our preservation problems or will we still need to actively manage to accessibility of information? What do we need to do to prepare for the future? This paper discus these matters.

INTRODUCTION

Preservation means, as the process of keeping collections and the information they contain available for use for as long as they are needed. Preservation has played an important role in libraries. Because of the "things" that libraries have collected, preservation has developed with a strong focus on preserving physical material: understanding why materials deteriorate and what we can do about it. Our collections are made up of materials that are naturally subject to deterioration, caused or influenced by many things, including:

- the materials themselves – acidic papers, poor quality binding materials, unstable media such as cellulose nitrate and cellulose acetate photographic films, PVC – based audiotapes.
- the environmental conditions we store them in – the heat, moisture, light, pollutants they are exposed to
- mould, insects, mice, and other pests that live on them or in them
- the abuses, or just plain uses, of users and staff
- Sudden disasters such as floods, water leaks, fire, building collapse, vandalism acts of terrorism, war.

We all know that preservation is about protecting our collections from such threats, or salvaging and repairing them to compensate for their impact.

A range of good strategic for preventing damage.

- Reducing temperature and humidity levels will slow down deterioration
- Controlling storage environments to keep temperature and humidity levels consistent and at optimal settings that retard the natural processes of decay (such as photo oxidation and acids hydrolysis);
- Filter out air pollutants and control exposure to light and UV
- Pest control programs and disaster plan

- Train staff to how to store, package and handle collections
- Instructing patrons and staff on how to handle fragile materials in a way to minimize damage;
- Restricting access to fragile items (for example, by allowing only staff to photo copy)
- Developed national campaigns to eliminate the use of unstable materials such as highly acidic papers in publishing and cellulose acetate film in record photography
- Developed good micro filming techniques and standards.
- Removing items from service and providing surrogates to users (copy prints of photo graphs, digitized images, microforms, photocopies, and the like);
- Rehousing items in acid – free containers or inert Mylar sleeves; and, perhaps least visible of all,
- Implementing emergency preparedness strategies by equipping storage areas with water – damage protection and training staff in urgent response to catastrophes, man – made and natural, and by taking other similar steps.

CHANGES IN THE PRESERVATION CONTEXT

We are living in a digital world. The majority of current digital preservation efforts in libraries still operate as pilot projects. With the advent of the World Wide Web and the demand for effective user access on the Internet, this situation is gradually changing.

PRESERVATION AND DIGITAL INFORMATION

On the surface, digital technology appears to offer few preservation problems. Bits and bytes are easy to copy, so there should be no problems in developing an unending chain of copies in to the future, and having copies all over the world in care of disaster. But the reality is not so simple and that there are very significant technical and management problems.

The two main factors leading to in accessibility of digital

information. Changing technology platforms and media instability, are relentless, with the potential to render digital information useless. This becomes a critical preservation problem for libraries, because libraries unable to give access to information have no future.

PRESERVATION RESPONSES TO DIGITAL INFORMATION

The world of changing websites, unstable floppy disks and individual computers systems is not a place where any particular digital rescues are recovered for very long. Libraries that have a custodial function will need to bring preservation perspectives to bear on the ways they manage digital information from the beginning. The national library of Australia has suggest some useful practical things.

- building the technical infrastructure and procedures for archiving
- establishing mechanisms for recording the metadata we will need so we can manage preservation
- developing persistent naming conventions for digital resources so they remain visible and findable.
- moving digital resources from less stable carrier like floppy disks to more stable carriers like CD (knowing that we will have to move from CD within a few years as well).
- identifying formats that we should be able to migrate easily and formats that will cause problems
- setting up registers of existing emulation software that we may need to use.
- identifying when we need to take action so that we wont lose access to the digital resources in our collections.

The preservation problems applying to digital information will not be solved easily, but will remain a very significant challenge to libraries for a long time to come. With great optimism, dedicated research and availability of funds might make it possible to develop software tools that would solve the preservation problem automatically: a system that would accept digital information resources in one format and automatically convert them to different formats, again and again, without loss.

NEED FOR DIGITIZATION IN INDIAN LIBRARY MATERIALS

Most of India's ancient manuscripts were written in bhurj patras. Ancient India was well developed in the subjects like Astronomy, Mathematics, Space Science, Medicine (Ayurveda), Defense, Political system, Economics etc. Unfortunately many of these valuable manuscripts were lost due to improper care. Some of them were destroyed due to water; fungus, fire and some were purposely destroyed by foreign invaders. Books is one of the medium which deals with comprehensive knowledge and information. Preserving the books and other reading materials is a burning question which the Indian librarians of past and present are facing.

INDIAN SCENARIO

India's most valuable and precious gift to humanity is its profound and timeless heritage. This heritage encompasses almost every aspect of human enquiry, ranging from philosophy and religion, language and literature, meta physics and science, polity and social living, habitat and architecture, dance and music, to art and craft.

The former Prime Minister of India, Jawaharlal Nehru has stated the impotence of Indian heritage in his famous book discovery of India. "The past is ever with us, and all that we are and that we have comes from the past. We are its products and we live immersed in it. Not to understand the present. To combine it with the present and extend it to the future to break from it where it cannot be united, to make all this the pulsating and vibrating materials for though and action that is life. All the long past of the individual, moments of action All the racial memories, influences of heredity and environment and training subconscious urges, thoughts and dreams and action from infancy and childhood onwards, in their curious and tremendous mix-up inevitably drive to that new action which again becomes yet another factor in influencing the future".

Much of India's heritage, in its physical form, has unfortunately got mutilated and destroyed through successive invasions, some of which is still being stolen; books and manuscripts are decaying and oral and disciples traditions are slowly vanishing. The preservation of "Indian Heritage" presents a great challenge. Fortunately indeed, the emerging information technology can offer a solution not only for preservation but also for enhancement and for its wide scale access.

Today Internet has emerged as a new medium of communication. Its impact is far-reaching and per fund for the future of civilization. One of the greatest contributions of Indian libraries could be to bring the previous, oriented and timeless Indian Heritage on the Internet, so that any one in any part of the world, could access it and derive benefits depending on one's own curiosity, aspirations and seriousness.

C-DAC has under taken some projects of digitization of rare and valuable works like Vedas and Upanishads. Its team has already converted the text of well-known Marathi treatise "Dnaneshwari" into digital form which is available on compact disk. Similarly Bhandarkar Oriental Research Institute, Pune, has also undertaken the digitization of the great epic called "Mahabharata". In addition to these major projects some private concerns have entered in to this new trends and are offering attractive schemes and packages to librarians to help them to convert their valuable library material into digital form.

CONCLUSION

There is a great hope that digital technology can help to preserve and make more accessible many rare and fragile items, because the quality of digital image is high and the use of electronic surrogates is easier than that of microforms. Even though the problems of digital preservation have yet to be solved in a cost effective manner, all major libraries are devoting scarce resources to the development of an infrastructure that will support the creation of and access to digital information. Preservation is the art of managing risk to the intellectual and physical heritage of a community and all members of that community have a stake in it. A collaboration between scholars, who can advise about the intellectual value of collection items, and librarians, who can make judgments about the physical risk that the threatens collections, is the best and most responsible way to ensure that the legacy we have inherited, and to which we contribute, will survive into the future.

REFERENCES

1. The future of the past: Preservation in American Research Libraries by Abby Smith, April 1999.
2. The role of preservation and the library of the future, Collin Web, 11th congress of southeast Asian Librarians conference, Singapore, 26th – 28th April 2000.
3. Digitization of library materials, N.J.Deshpande, B.M.Panage, University News, 37 (38), September 20, 1999.
4. http://www.nla.gov.au/ferg.

Digital Archiving of Manuscripts: A Case Study of Karnatak University Library

R. M. Vatnal,
Assistant Librarian,
University Library,
Karnatak University,
Dharwad.

Ramesha,
Assistant Librarian,
University Library,
Karnatak University,
Dharwad.

ABSTRACT

India is very rich in age-old manuscript collection. Very important and precious information is stored in these documents. Preservation of manuscripts is very difficult even under the best conditions available in the country. Currently microfilming is the accepted method in a situation where it can be afforded. But many libraries and archives just do not have funding to go for microfilming due to several reasons. Emerging technologies becoming cost effective and planned efforts in transferring the knowledge embodied in the manuscripts and rare books may help to considerable extent to preserve the old thoughts and use them as and when necessary. This paper discusses the efforts made in Karnatak University Library in the process of digitization and creating the digital resources. This new approach to manuscript copying and digital archiving into computer databases might revolutionize electronic archiving efforts because of the savings in cost and human labour. Another advantage of this method is easy and effective access via Word Wide Web.

INTRODUCTION

In the past, Librarians, Museum Curators and Archivists have responded to Information and Communications Technologies developments by adapting them to traditional working practices such as Classification, Cataloguing...etc. Recent developments are creating new pressures, however, and the expectations on information professionals are changing. The most radical innovation is that of the Internet and it may no longer be appropriate to think in traditional terms to exploit this new medium to the full. The Internet offers remote access and digitization programmes but, so far, these programmes have concentrated on the digitization of findings aids or of selected primary source materials and there is also a need for other programmes (digital exhibitions) to be developed with a greater emphasis on collaboration and interpretation, aimed at the non-academic or casual user. However, conversion to digital form from existing media, is of particular concern to established the fair image of the libraries to fulfill their responsibilities in the areas of collection management, storage, preservation, and access.

The Karnatak University Library is just 5 decades old. The University is having a valuable collection of rare book materials and manuscripts scattered in Kannada Research Institute, Department of Kannada Studies and Folklore. The shrinking budget, lack of space, poor maintenance, and inadequate infrastructure are some of the hurdles faced in the library by building the organised collection and utilization of manuscripts.

It has been seriously discussed by the authorities to explore the possibilities of networking and utilization of available Information Technology in the process of Collection Management giving an emphasis on caring and preserving manuscript collection. Systematic efforts are made to follow the procedures and guidelines in the collection management. New approaches to manuscripts copying and digital archiving into computer databases with the realization of cost effectiveness are in the process. A serious thought was given to set digitize the rare and valuable manuscripts and store them on CD was made by the Library Advisory Board (LAB) in one of its meeting.

Prof. S. S. Basavanal Library, the Karnataka University Library was established along with the University. It started functioning from the same year i.e., from 1950. The library was housed in the main building of the Government Training College for Men where the university offices were also working in the same building. The Library was shifted to its new home in the main educational building in the year 1959.

Karnataka University Library has established a separate Manuscripts Library. This is attached to Dr. R C Hiremath Institute of Kannada Studies. It has rich collection of palm leaf manuscripts, Kore paper and common paper manuscripts in different languages and scripts. However, a majority of the manuscripts are in Kannada Language. Some of the outstanding manuscripts have been the main source for the publication of many learned books as a part of research studies. Moreover outside scholars have been greatly benefited by consulting these manuscripts of the Library. So far around 6000 manuscripts have been collected at this Library. These manuscripts cover the areas like Philosophy, Religion, Art, History, Medicine, Theology, Science and Literature.

IMPORTANCE OF PRESERVATION OF MANUSCRIPTS AND ACCESS

Digital information forms an increasingly large part of our cultural and intellectual heritage and offers significant benefits to users. At the same time preservation and access to this information is dependent on impermanent media and technologies; retaining metadata on the provenance and context; and retaining the authenticity and content of the resource. To assess and retain the content of digital information over time remains a substantial challenge.

Converting the digital content to analogue format with known long-term preservation qualities can be a potential solution in some cases and "hybrid" microfilm storage/digital access solutions for some digital information have been explored. Similarly organisations have often used a paper print-out to provide elementary back-up. However with the increasing complexity of electronic information such strategies can be limited and electronic content and functionality can be lost. Increasingly it is necessary to preserve the information in electronic form. Although experience in creating and managing specific forms of digital data has been built up over a number of decades in the sciences and social sciences, in many areas it is a relatively new medium where much of the future life cycle, activities and cost models are currently unknown. These factors have led to increasing concern about the potential loss of our "collective memory" in the Digital Age and have prompted further research into the long-term preservation of digital information and maintaining future access to it.

Physical preservation of manuscripts is very difficult even under the best conditions where in Indian manuscripts and books may last under the best of the conditions. Many of the ancient manuscripts are now found very important and needs to be copied. In the past, the scribes would have been meticulously copied them (Perhaps adding scribal mistakes to those that might already be there). Currently microfilming is the accepted method-when and where it can be afforded. But many archives just do not have funding to repeat microfilming even after thirty or forty years of the existence of microfilm. It is a expensive method and capable of full colour, faster and experienceble method.

METHODS OF PRESERVATION OF MANUSCRIPTS

Reprography such as photocopying (Xeroxing) are the some methods of preservation. But the life span of these documents are few years. Scanners may be used but are relatively slow and can damage the manuscripts especially for those are in deteriorating condition. Microfilming is very costly method. Microfilm the manuscripts and then use high definition scanner to digitize the manuscript the image.

DIGITISATION

Earlier rejected method was use digital still cameras which were both expensive could copy a few page before their images has to be to be downloaded into computer. Their flash card memory was much expensive and limiting for copying for days at a time. But in the year 2000 a new generation of digital camera introduced to meet the needs of in-house digital copying. The technology is cheaper and than conventional methods and learning time is very minimal. But there are some expensive mistakes that can be avoided.

The following table provides the comparative picture of the conventional copying and the digitization.

Sl. No	Item	Conventional	Digitizing
1	For recording (Filming)	To be photographed through micro film camera using the B&W films and dark room processing is essential	No exposing through camera No developing or processing but only scanning through computer scanner
2	Viewing	Can be only viewed through microfilm viewer (reader)	No extra equipment is required to view the image
3	Modification	No modification or correction of the image is possible	It is easily possible to modify the image such as contrast, brightness and colour
4	Colour	Only black and white is possible (to view)	Either colour or B&W is possible
5	Printing	Only black and white (to print)	Either colour or black and white is possible
6	Printing (time)	Bromide paper printing will take 30 minutes per print, in the dark room only	Computer print out can be had within less that 3 minutes either colour or B&W

7	Total time	Micro film exposing, developing, drying and printing will take atleast 2 hours to get a printout	It is possible to get an image within 1 minute
8	Printing cost	Minimum of Rs.30/- is required to expose and print an a-4 size image with lot of labour	Less than Rs.2/- is required to print an image with very little labour without a darkroom
9	Storage	300 pages book can only be stored in 10 rolls of films, say about 5 cubic inches	3,000 pages can be stored in a single 3 1/2" floppy and3,50,000 pages can be stored on a a Compact Disc (CD)
10	Transportation	Films and prints should be transported through post with proper packing and postage	No packing or postage is required for sending the images, but 1/25 of the amount is enough to transport to a distant country
11	Transporting time	15 to 20 days required to reach outside country	1 minute is enough to serve the images through out the world
12	Outside seekers	Outsiders can request for their need only through postage which takes weeks of time	Can be accessed by an outsider within a minute all over the globe

DIGITIZATION ACTIVITIES AT KARNATAK UNIVERSITY LIBRARY

The University Library is just 5 decades old. The University has a valuable collection of manuscripts scattered in Kannada Research Institute, Department of Kannada Studies and folklore. The shrinking budget, lack of space, poor maintenance, inadequate are some of the hurdles faced by the library in building the organised collection and utalisation of manuscripts. It has been seriously discussed by the authorities. The author of this paper was sent to acquaint with the skills of digitization and Computerization of Manuscripts at National Institute of Advanced Studies (NIAS), Indian Institute of Science Campus, Bangalore. This has paved the way for building the necessary minimum infrastructure for starting the digitization process. Realising manuscripts and rare collections of the library, the authorities made the facilities for digitization.

INITIAL EFFORTS

A HP5200'C A4 scanner was installed and employed to digitize these documents. Since these are available in Devanagari lipi, Halaganavada lipi etc., it can be only store in the GIF format, each page of the document scanned and indexed through Adobe Acrobat PhotoShop. After final touch up these are written in the CD. The CD writer has helped to preserve these manuscripts of high demand, which were in worst condition (in the original form).

A sample manuscript from Manuscript collection

THE KARNATAK UNIVERSITY DIGITAL ARCHIVING COMPUTERIZATION PROCEDURE(KUDAC)

Looking at the financial status of the University, it needs essentially less expensive method, more permanent, capable of full colour, faster, in-house and extensible(capable of being used to master books, CDs, databases and share over the internet). The following KUDAC procedure can easily promote the sharing of rare books and manuscripts with others as freely and widely as possible. Manuscripts can still be copyrighted by the archive or library that owns them so that others cannot publish or exploit them commercially. Their use can be licensed (especially manuscript graphics), and they can be shared via the Internet or by CDs of the books and manuscripts. The philosophy of sharing information is as important as any archiving and computerization technique.

The digital 'image' can be manipulated as a graphic or converted into alphanumeric (text). Images before compression are quite large but, when compressed into image formats like JPEG, become quite tiny files (say about 40k depending on quality and details required, and if need be only black and white also). Computerization is completed with various forms of storage (re-writable media like hard drives are quite fragile but CDs have at least a half-century life rather than a few decades like microfilm).

In the second method is to use a D-Link Dual mode Digital camera with a extra large storage capacity(200 MB). This camera can be interfaced with computer and images may downloaded within a second. This will also work for extended field trips to archives. The downloaded image may be instantly manulable for storage and distribution. This method is far superior to the digitization where the work out side the computer room.

This procedure includes direct copying of manuscripts and digitizes reducing great expense of current methods.

LEGAL AND ECONOMIC ENVIRONMENT

Legal issues may include; intellectual property rights in the resource or integral software supplied with it; contractual terms attached to a resource or the hardware and software needed to access it; protecting the confidentiality of individuals and institutions; protecting the integrity and reputation of data creators or other stakeholders in the resource; or any legal obligation to select and preserve the authenticity and content of categories of records or individual resources. What rights are vested in a resource will impinge on how and whether it may be represented in machine-readable form; how, by whom, and under what conditions it may be used; how it can and should be documented and even stored (e.g. where 'sensitive' information requires encryption or access restrictions); and how, whether, and by whom it can legally be preserved.

Similarly the business environment(s) in which a resource is created, managed, preserved and used will have a bearing on the application of the framework. Resources created in a commercial environment may have a commercial life cycle which can impinge on data management, preservation, and use. Some organisations may also be subject to more sudden and abrupt changes in ownership and rights, or location and data management than others.

The returns required on investment in resources may also require physical control of storage and access, and/or systems and procedures for encrypting, marking or locking the resource, user registration and authentication, charging, and rights management. All of these can affect and in some cases can mitigate against long-term preservation unless they are specifically addressed as issues and the requirements of different stakeholders can be met.

CONCLUSION

Digital libraries have been carried out in a wide variety of contexts. These range from the large scale that assume the creation of a wholly digital collection supported by a seamless digital meta information framework, to small projects that involve selective digitization of individual media. The smaller projects may involve simultaneous creation of finding aids that are independent from existing metadata.

The priorities and objectives of funding, and the funding agencies, for the resource through the life cycle can also vary and impact in a number of different ways. This is particularly important for documentation and metadata on the context and content of the resource which are most easily developed or captured when the resource are created and can only be re-constructed at greater expense, if at all, at a later stage of management and preservation. The cost-effectiveness over the life cycle of the resource of completing data documentation and metadata when the resource is created (and often its immediate benefits to the data creator) needs to be recognised and its practice encouraged. Librarians and archivists should know that these methods might pose a threat to their holdings.

Karnatak University Library is making a small beginning in the digitization process. It is the active participation and growing demand that initiates the authorities to promote the project with additional funds. Well planned user education programmes, active participation of the professionals in the professional forums may help the users to make use of the digitized resources and create a new wave in the library use.

REFERENCE

1. Course Material: Workshop on Digitization and Computerization of Manuscripts held on April 5-7, 1999 at National Institute of Advanced Studies, Indian Institute of Science Campus, Bangalore - 560 012.

2. Day, M. Matadata for Digital Preservation: an update. Ariadne, (22) December 1999, <http://www.ariadne.ac.uk/issue22/metadata/>.

3. Lee, S. Digitizing intellectual Property: the Oxford Scoping Study. Ariadne, (22) December 1999. (the full text of this article is available at <http://www.ariadne.ac.uk/issue22/oxford-mellonl/>

4. Pace A.K., Digital Preservation: Everything new is old again. Computer in Libraries, 20(2) February 2000, p.55-6, 58.(the full text of this article is available at *http://www.infotoday.com/cilmag/feboo/pace.htm*

5. Parkes, M., A review of the preservation issues associated with digital documents. Australian Library Journal, 48(4) November 1999, P.358-77.

6. Rajashekar, T.B., Digital Libraries: Attributes and Architectures. Digital Libraries : Dynamic Storehouse of Digitized Information. Eds. M.N. Malwad and others Pp.192-206.

7. Stephen, Ferguson: Rare books in University Libraries, Library Trends, Vol.36 (1) Summer 1987.

19

Preservation of Video Programmes for Future Use: Analog to Digital Media

P.Rajendran,
Librarian,
S.R.M. Engineering College,
Kattankulathur.

K.P. Yesudoss,
Assistant Librarian,
S.R.M. Engineering College,
Kattankulathur.

ABSTRACT

At present the educational video programs of all the academic and as well as other applications are available in the videotape format VHS (Video Home Services). Over a period of time, these videotapes are spoiled due to repeated viewing and natural calamities like dust, fungus etc., The quality of audio and video is affected.

The VHS (Video Home Service) is in analogue format and this is converted into Digital format and stored in the recordable CD's or DVD's. CD has long life and it requires less space.

INTRODUCTION

The main objective of this paper is to preserve the important and rare collection of educational video programs for future use of the members. At present the educational video programs of academic and as well as other applications are available in the videotape format VHS (Video Home Services). Over a period of time, these videotapes are spoiled due to repeated viewing forming of dust; fungus etc., Due to this reason the quality of audio and video is spoils after few years, the output of the audio and video is not visible and clear.

To prevent the videotapes for the above reasons the data or information stored in the videotapes may be converted into other reliable format. The format, which we are going to convert, may be latest and the life of the source will be higher than the videotape. The most reliable format is that the VHS (Video Home Service) is an analogue format and this analogue format is converted into Digital format and stored in the recordable CD's or DVD's. They have a self life of more than 100 years and occupies very little space as compared to VHS. About an hour of best TV-quality video on single CD may be stored, and this can be played in computer with a CD-ROM drive or in VCD player.

As a multi media producer or developer, may be need to convert video source material from its still common analog form (videotape) to digital form manageable by the end users application. Computer system an analog to digital conversion of video can be accomplished using the video overlay hardware described as follows.

In an analog system, the video signal from the camera is delivered to the video in connectors of a VCR, where it is recorded on magnetic videotape. The video signals is written to tape by a spinning recording head that changes the local magnetic properties of the tapes surface in a series of long diagonal strips. A single video frame is made up of two fields that are interlaced. Audio is recorded on a separate straight-line track at the top of the videotape, at the bottom of the tape is control track containing the pulses used to regulate speed. Tracking is fine adjustment of the tape so that the tracks are properly aligned as the tape move across the play back head.

VIDEO TAPE

[* Filter does not support this file format | In-line.TIF *]

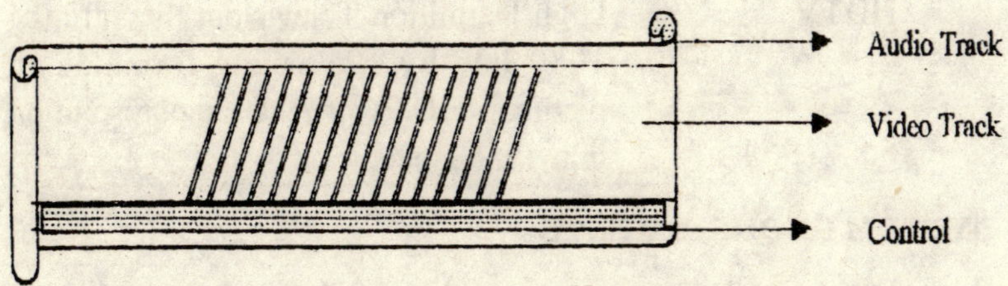

Figure 1.1

KINDS OF VIDEO STANDARDS

There are four types of broadcast and video standards and recording formats are commonly in use around the world: they are NTSC, PAL, SECAM and HDTV

PAL	Phase Alternate Line (PAL) system used in the UK, Europe, Australia, and South Africa. PAL is an integrated method of adding color to black and white Television signal that paints 625 lines at a frame rate of 25 frames per second.
NTSC	National Television Standards Committee. This standard defines a method for encoding information into the electronic signal that ultimately create the television picture. In NTSC standard a single frame of video is made up of 525 horizontal scan lines drawn on to the inside

	face of a phosphor-coated.
SECAM	Sequential Color and Memory (SECAM) system is used in France, Russia and few other countries. SCAM is 625 lines, 50Hz system it differs greatly from both the PAL and NTSC color systems in its basic technology and broadcast method.
HDTV	High Definition Television, they are the 1080 line by 1920 pixel formatat all pictures. HDTV provides high resolution in a 16:9 aspect ratio.

SYSTEM REQUIREMENTS

For doing this conversion work the following equipment are required.

1. Computer P-III 850 Mhz, Intel 815 IEE Motherboard
   128 MB SD RAM, 10 GB HDD, 1.44 MB
   FDD, Key Board, Mouse, Multimedia card
   with Snazzi Video Creator card – DVC –II.
2. CD Writer HP CD writer 9140 (4x8x32x) with Video
   Pack CD Burning Software.
3. VCR Any branded good VCR can play the video
   Tape. (PAL/SECAM)

There are number of external and internal conversion cards are available in the market. Based on our application we can select the conversion card and install in to the computer. The cards like RT-5, Yamaha, Dazzil DVC-II (Snazzi), Studio MP10 or Studio MP20 are also used for this same purpose. RT-5 and Yamaha internal cards are used in the field of highly professional moviemakers, and other editing orientation works may be carried out. For converting the videotape to CD (i.e. analog to digital) Snazzi DVC-II conversion card is sufficient to fulfil the work.

SOFTWARE SETTING OPTIONS

There are many preference settings, or options, that can be set in Movie Star for audio, video and still images. To access the options, click the options tab on the upper left side of the main Interface. (as per the direction mentioned in the figure

Fig. 1.2

This windows shows

1. Configuration
2. Adjust
3. Picture
4. Recording

1. Configuration

There are four categories of configuration options that can be set. Video, Audio & preference. Clicking once any of these buttons will reveal a panel with more buttons for each configuration option called pull down menu.

Main option a. Video configuration

b. Audio configuration

c. Preference configuration

a. Video Configuration

There are three types of video configuration options that can be set:

Video Input, Video Source and Video Standard

Video input Shows Camcorder, VCR, and TV select *VCR*

There are four choices: PC Camera, Camcorder, TV or DVD or LD And VCR.. Select the setting, which most closely matches our video Source's (example if we can using a VHS video Tape deck *Select VCR)*

Video Sources Shows S-Video, Composite select *Composite*

Select the source S-video or Composite that matches our type of input Jack we are using with DVC –II (if we use only one input, MovieStar. Select the *auto detect* the one we use).

Video Standard Shows NTSC, PAL, select *PAL*

Choose the video format of our video sources. MovieStar supports Two formats. One NTSC and PAL. NTSC is the format used in USA Canada, and Japan and PAL is the standard used in England and Europe & Australia.

PRESS OK

b. Audio

There are three settings in the Audio configurations:

Configuration	Source, Volume, And Input gain
Source	Automatically selects the settings from Device Line
Device	Line is currently the only audio source option
Volume	We select maximum i.e. 100

The volume slider shows, in percent, the output sound level. Moving. This slider is the same as adjusting the volume with the Thumbwheel. If the input gains slider to too low we won't hear any sound. If it is too high there will be distortion.

Input Gain up to 80.

The Input gain controls the sound input level of our recordings. The Level is shown as a percentage 0 to 100.

Press OK

c. Preference

Click the Preference configuration button and select the language we prefer (Select English).

2. Adjust

Usually, video images in MovieStar look very good as soon as start the program. But, if any changes require on screen, the software gives you an easy way to do it.

Adjust panel controls shows seven adjustments: Brightness, Contrast, Saturation, Tint, Sharpness, Horizontal Alignment, and Vertical Alignment. Click and hold on any slider to move left or right, immediately see the changes in the Video window. As per the requirement the Adjustment will be made.

3. Picture

The picture options panel is used to set the Capture Options and save options for images.

CAPTURE OPTIONS

Framethe frame option allows us to choose between single, multiple, and periodic frame Capture, Playback delay (in seconds) for slide show can also be set.

Single capture a single frame from the video source

Select *Single capture*.

Size The frame size is the dimensions

	measured in pixels, for example a typical 15" computer monitors displays 800 pixels across and 600 pixels up and down (this is the resolution of the monitor). The default size is 320 x 240.
Quality	Quality refers to video source most videos contain moving images. Moving scene is the default choice. Chose the option that most closely matches your input source and the type of image you want.

SAVE OPTIONS

Color	The default color option is True Color (16 bit true color). These means our Capture will be able to use up to 16.7 million colors to display your images.
Format	Format option determines the format in which still images will be saved. This is supports Bitmap (*.bmp), JPEG (*.jpg) and JPEG-TIF (*.jpg) etc., Select *Bitmap (*.bmp)*
4. Recording	Recording option contains various for audio and video recording

Audio/Video

Audio/video clip button sets the type of recording. Based on the type of recording the setup will be select. If we record only audio select audio, this will record only audio signals can be saved either wave(*.wav) or MPEG audio (*.mpg) file, if we record video and audio select audio/video, here the audio/video signals saved in one single file.

Current Template

Current template button selects and displays the name of the template is use and the names of all available templates. This will shows DVD (MPEG-2) SVCD, Video CD, DVD etc., Select *Video CD.*

Customize:This will show the following options like Image size, video Bitrate, preview while recording, Video format, Audio post process, audio channel, sample Rating, audio bitrate, Data rate etc.,

After complete the setting in the computer now the videotapes may be played in the VCR. Audio and Video out may be connected as per the figure 1.3

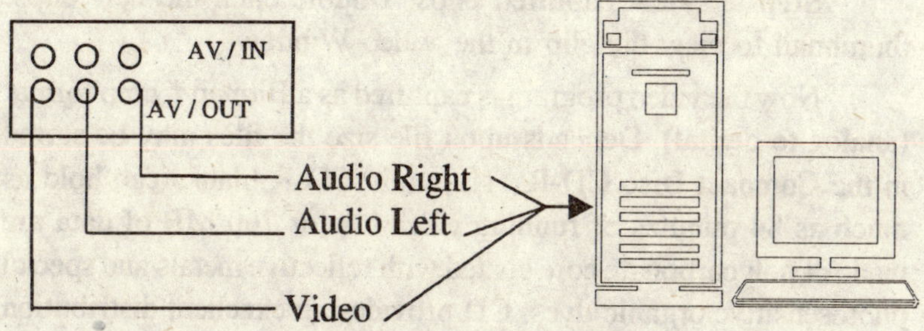

Figure 1.3

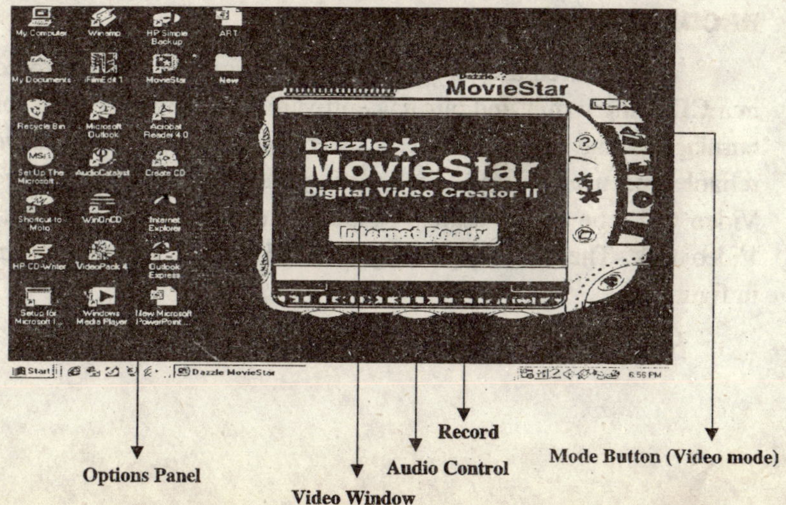

Figure 1.4

Step –1 Start your video sources make sure that your VCR playing a tape

Step- 2 Enter a Capture mode: Click on one Movie Star's three capture modes Video mode, still image mode, or audio mode.

Step-3 Select your Capture Options

Step-4 Capture a Video: Capture a video (mpeg1) click on the Record Button in the Control Buttons. Then click the stop button in the "Recording is over" the captured video clip will be displayed as thumbnail in the Work Space album in the media manager.

Step -5 View captured clips: Double click the new clips, thumbnail to view the clip in the Video Window.

Now the video program is captured as a Bitmap *.bmp format (analog to digital). Depends upon file size the files may be stored in the Compact Disc CD-R. Normally CD-R blanks can hold as much as 84 minutes of running video clip or 700 MB of data are made of polycarbonate core coated with reflective metals and special photosensitive organic dyes. CD provides an excellent distribution medium video program. CD players offer slow data transfer can be achieved by taking care to properly prepare digital video files.

RECORDING OF VIDEO CDS

The captured program of video files (bitmap) is to be stored in a CD using writer and burning software. The software used for burning (writing video files) CD is Videopack, this software package reliable and user friendly for creating Video CD. Click on the Video CD icon in the dialog window that opens after you start Video pack. The details of writing CDs and settings, options, shown in figure 1.5.

CD Burning Options in the Video pack Software

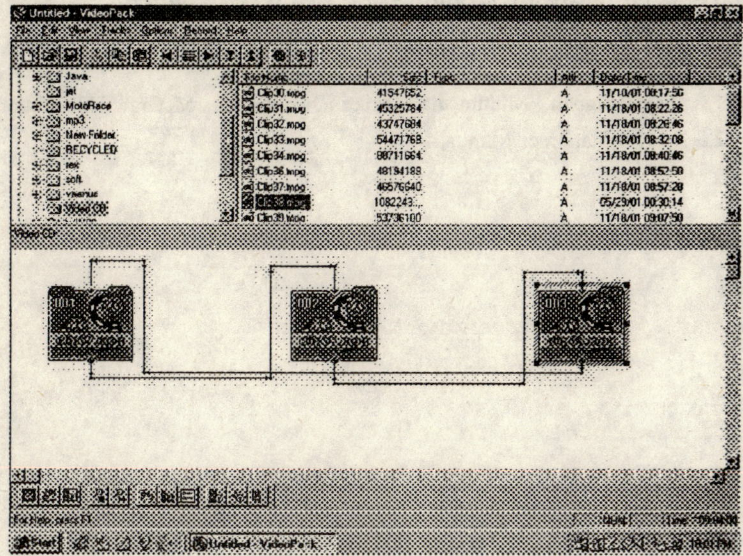

Figure 1.5

The above figure shows how to write the three (duration of the each programs is 20 minutes, 15 minutes & 30 minutes) different programs in single CD. Through this software we will create main menu and link to other programs for continues play in the VCD player. Before burning (writing) CDs always run the speed test and the simulation test in order to get the optimal speed. If don't do that, the maximum possible write speed of the recorder is kept as default, which may result in burning problems.

CONCLUSION

The importance of this study is to preserve the valuables to future use. As ultimate result that life of the converted (digital) programs is more comparatively video tape. And these programs may play any VCD Player or computer with CD-ROM Drive. To digitize full 1/30 second store it to disk or RAM severely taxes both Macintosh and PC processing capability. For compressing the full motion picture a massive amount of digital storage space and special hardware, compression firmware required.

REFERENCE

1. Tay Vaughan. Multimedia Making it work - Tata McGraw Hill Edition.
2. Movie Star User Manual.

20

Digital Subscriptions and Content Management in the Internet Era

M.G. Sreekumar,
Librarian,
Library and Information Center,
Indian Institute of Management,
Kozhikode.

T. Sunitha, P. Sreejaya, M. Gangatharan,
P.P. Noufal, R. Biju and K. Prasanna,
Library and Information Center,
Indian Institute of Management,
Kozhikode.

ABSTRACT

The Internet offers a wealth of opportunity for the library fraternity and the user community in terms of content enrichment, information access, dissemination, sharing, management and manipulation. The Information Super Highway, as it is rightly put, simultaneously act as a content publisher, content holder and a content disseminator. During the recent past there has been a considerably shift in the library acquisitions the world over, as the digital media dominates all its other counterparts in terms of its effectiveness, high-end flexibility, ease of access and dissemination. The plethora of formats, standards, protocols, and platforms of the Internet wonder world offer a wide spectrum of applications to the user community which undoubtedly empowers them in their smooth journey to value added and pin-pointed information at the stroke of a button or the click of a mouse. Today, the three predominant forms of information source/carrier are the print, CD/DVD/HDD and Web. The latter two are on an intense march forward with its reach, richness and robustness. With the information revolution coupled with media explosion, librarians are posed with multi-faceted problems of collection development issues, diminishing financial resources, and the spiraling cost of information. It has therefore become imperative on the part of librarians to learn the basics of digital subscriptions, digital collection development and its efficient management for one's own survival sake, leave alone the unprecedented user pressure. This paper discusses the variant forms of collection development and management through the Digital Media, with a view of support the "Access" Vs "Ownership" slogan. Also highlights the benefits of consortia approach to digital collection and elaborates the IPR, Copyright and related issues involved while arranging digital subscriptions. The tricks and catches in the digital subscription scenario, looking forward to exploiting the ignorance of the librarian is also discussed.

DIGITAL INFORMATION COLLECTION DEVELOPMENT

The information professional's never–ending challenges.

A Library's digital information collection development objective is nor far from its original mandate, i.e., to select those digital / electronic materials, which will support the current curricular and research needs of the parent institution or organization to which it is attached.

There is a paradigm shift, both from the approaches of the users as well as in their access facilities. In most of our endowed campuses and research centers, the user community have access to digital information using personal computers in their offices, libraries, computer centers, Net kiosks etc. Consequently, the Libraries provide (or rather forced to provide) access to a wide variety of materials using an equally wide variety of access mediums to meet the user needs.

ELECTRONIC SELECTION CRITERIA

Libraries today buy licenses for an ever-increasing number of information resources from a range of different publishers and providers, and use a diverse set of technologies for information delivery [1]. In addition, a wealth of relevant resources are freely available on the Web for libraries to incorporate into their e-collections and to make them readily available to their users. Materials may be in print and/or electronic form; formally and/or informally published; and stored locally, for access via an institution's intranet, or remotely and accessible via the Internet. A number of services are outside the library's control, but nonetheless libraries want to integrate their resources, presenting the information from any particular source within the context of the complete collection. Searching across repositories is only part of the solution. While not all subscriptions lend themselves to electronic delivery, electronic subscriptions offer a great potential for increased value to the entire organization. The move from atoms to bits complicates the jobs of information professionals, but the benefits - competitive advantage, access to information by a wide spectrum of the users, can be tremendous.

Like print materials, digital titles added to the collection need to match the needs of the clientele assuring appropriate scope, content, depth, and quality. The materials selected should be affordable, the content must be timely, bibliographically accessible and in the appropriate language, etc. It is also presumed that there are no technical reasons why the library cannot provide access, e.g., doesn't use a proprietary browser, permits printing, etc., and that their use by library user and librarians will not require an inordinate amount of training.

Similarly hyper-linking assumes major importance. The simplicity and ubiquity of the Web is such that users now have high expectations of their own digital library environments in terms of ease of navigation between the many and varied electronic information resources. They also expect minimum efforts for their information-seeking activities. It is the librarian, as information intermediary, who is in a better position to determine how resources should be interlinked to provide for ease of navigation, i.e. what should be linked to what, and how it should be linked. The librarian has traditionally applied a broader range of knowledge to packages of information and is now challenged in extending their skills to highly diverse and widely dispersed users wherever and whenever they need it. The Web is undoubtedly facilitating linking among digital items - and we see many excellent examples of this in current offerings from information providers - secondary and primary publishers, and from the aggregators.

ELECTRONIC JOURNALS : DIRECT, SECOND PARTY, AND AGGREGATORS

Electronic journals are the digital equivalent of their print counterparts. Whereas databases may contain only some full text or links to full text, electronic journals are literally the entire journal. For a good catalog of electronic journals currently available, see the World Wide Web Virtual Library: Electronic Journals [2]. An electronic journal is the whole journal, and libraries can subscribe to electronic journals from publishers or through a second party (e.g. vendors) just like they subscribe to print journals. This distinction between publishers and second parties is an important one, as these are the two ways libraries get electronic journals. Some companies create collections of entire journals and sell access to these collections. Second party electronic journal databases are different from other databases because in a second party electronic journal database, the entire journal is collected, as opposed to a full text database like "Academic Search Elite", where all, some, or none of any given journal may be included. Examples of second party electronic journal databases include:

1. JSTOR [3], which specializes in making back issues of a wide variety of humanities and social science journals available electronically; 2. Ingenta [4], the most appreciated journal portal, facilitates users to read, print, and email articles from 4,500 electronic journals from 140 publishers. Ingenta is the world's largest website

for the search and delivery of research articles and it offers access to article summaries from over 25,000 publications linked to the full text of over 5,200 titles. Full text access is set from over 170 publisher partners, but typically individual subscribers, or individuals within institutions that subscribe, can access the full text of their publications for free. For libraries and information professionals, Ingenta provides an extensive range of free and customized online services, from enabling authenticated campus-wide access to subscribed full text articles to creating branded library gateways incorporating management tools and deposit account facilities; 3. ProjectMUSE [5], which provides electronic access to journals in the fields of literature and criticism, history, the visual and performing arts, cultural studies, education, political science, gender studies, and many others; 4. Emerald Library [6], which contains over 140 electronic journal titles with full text articles published since 1994; 5. CatchWord [7], which provides access to hundreds of journals from approximately 44 publishers.

In India, J-Gate of M/s. Informatics Ltd. [8], is the best example for an E-journal gateway. The mission of J-Gate is to provide an e-content and e-commerce gateway for academic, research and corporate libraries in India to subscribe, access and manage their electronic journals. The vision for J-Gate is to act as:

- An electronic aggregator for several thousand scientific journals
- A common access and search interface for all the journals a library subscribes to
- An insured and dependable journal archive source for the libraries
- A large database for journal literature available, possibly free, to all Indian scientists, scholars, students and professionals for browsing table-of-content and abstracts
- An online e-journal subscription agent
- An online host for Indian journals

J-Gate is being implemented in a phased manner. Following are some of the features J-Gate will support when fully implemented:

- Browse and search a directory of e-journals
- Select a journal title in the directory and access TOCs and full text articles, from the Informatics journals archive or from the publisher's web site
- Search a bibliographic database of articles and access the full text from the Informatics archive or from the publisher's site
- Support archiving needs of clients for their e-journals
- Support online subscription, renewals and payment processing
- Support Indian journal publishers to host their journals
- Support copyright cleared article delivery to our subscribers for journals they do not subscribe.

Another category is aggregators. Aggregators use to buy the copyright of the journals in bulk and provide access to the journals through a single interface. Examples of aggregators include EBSCO Online [9] and PROQUEST [10]. EBSCO's Business Source Premier and Academic Search Elite are very popular services which attempt to provide management tools for full-text electronic journals. PROQUEST's ABI/Inform is yet another popular full-text journals service. There are advantages as well as drawbacks in each case. In the case of electronic journals, either sourced directly from the publisher or through a second party, the users have the advantage of accessing the journals direct. The disadvantage is that in the electronic journal services, search facilities are kept at a low profile. Whereas in the aggregated services, search facilities are fairly high, with low priority for content layout, get up etc.

THE GROWING PROMINENCE OF E-JOURNALS AND THE SWINGING PRICING MODELS

For want of brevity and focus, this paper will concentrate on the issues of "E-journals" and aggregated scholarly literature, primarily and originally appearing in E-journals. About 10 years ago when Electronic Journals first appeared the publishers didn't know how to sell them, nor librarians knew how to handle them. The technology scenario prevailing those days were entirely different too. Technology kept advancing and after 10 years, today the e-journals are sold as hot cakes in the developed world. The trends in the developing world also are equally encouraging, especially in India. This fast change in mindset has taken many publishers by surprise. Earlier, negotiations that involved expanded access to electronic text usually began with print subscriptions as the bottom line of the deal. During the past couple of years, especially in the West, a number of consortia demanded that print and online be negotiated separately. They wanted online access at the core of pricing negotiations because their users clearly preferred online. They wanted an online-plus-print model, rather than print-plus-online. This is called "flip pricing" [11]. As a model, flip pricing is not new. Academic Press introduced the concept with its first e-journal package. Few publishers adopted that model, however, and most libraries have continued to receive print and online more or less as a package deal. This has resulted as a real blessing to the Indian libraries. The reflections of the flip pricing has started crystallizing of late and most of the leading publishers have started offering flip price models to Indian libraries too, mostly under the consortia banner.

The evolution of the deeply discounted prices (DDP) model is yet another significant development in the journals pricing front in the recent past. As DDP has evolved, three models have emerged that govern the relationship between agents and publishers. First, the publisher requires the customer to place electronic orders directly with them; with the second version, customers may place their orders with agent or publisher, but customers are given an incentive to deal direct; and in the third scenario, customers are free to order either way.

In 2000, 75% of publishers offered online free with print, with the rest charging extra for online. But every year, publishers change their mind on this one issue, and last year the pendulum seemed to be swinging back in favor of charging extra for online with a print subscription. Of the 7,623 e-journals with set prices in EBSCO's reserve, 61% were offered free with a print subscription for this year (2001). The majority of major publishers still offer online "free" with print as a rule. The list includes Cambridge University Press, Elsevier, Emerald, Oxford, Routledge, Sage, Springer Verlag, and Taylor & Francis. Blackwell Science charges extra, but the other Blackwell imprints do not. University presses are split. Duke, Indiana, Johns Hopkins, and Penn State, charge; MIT, Chicago, and California do not. Society presses are also split, but the majority appear to charge for online with print. The list of STM publishers that charge extra include giants such as Academic, Wiley, Kluwer, Dekker, Nature, Plenum, and S. Karger.

COPYRIGHT AND IPR ISSUES

Issues of copyright, intellectual property, and fair use are important to libraries, but librarians are struggling to make sense of all the issues in the new Digital Age [12]. We need to learn a lot about the "tricks of the trade" so that our hands are not burnt in the process. The number of accessible electronic journals are fast growing steadily. Studies are in progress the world over towards determining the trends in copyright policies among scholarly electronic journals. There are a number of issues which the Librarian should be highly careful while entering into digital subscriptions. Catches can come in multiple forms with the vague yet meticulously manipulated term "licensing". The audit and accounts are to be amply briefed about the problems and features of digital subscriptions. Proper measures and back-up agreements are to be ensured from the publishers/vendors.

In the case of free electronic journals, according to literature, the policies are found to be quite generous in the area of fair use and encourage sharing of information. Some of the salient features of copyright issues of a select set of freely accessible electronic journals are as follows: (1) copyright policies are informal, (2) policies are common to print and electronic titles, (3) contributing authors generally retain copyright, (4) noncommercial uses permitted include browsing, printing personal copies, and downloading, and (5) republishing is not permitted. Several of these journals address library use.

ACCESS RELATED ISSUES

Access to E-Journals could be arranged from the respective publishers against UserID/Password or through IP authentication. For a wider audience, IP based access is mostly preferred, as the users need not have to bother about the UserID and Password every time. A useful alternative is to provide the UserID/Password in the library's portal / website so that users can pick them up during usage, and over a period of time, they also by-heart them. Libraries need to take care of the 'site license' aspects of content access, as some publishers lay stringent rules on this, making the life of the Librarian miserable. Before jumping into such services, the Librarian should ensure necessary Internet bandwidth also, failing which complaints will pile up, resulting in a growing aversion against the electronic services in general. For full-text access to E-Journals and datasets published online, usually non-exclusive, non-transferable right and licenses are provided by the publishers. Unlimited access is provided to Tables of Contents, article abstracts, chapter summaries and websites for other Electronic Products.

Another important aspect is the local administration of access management by the users. Users are to be properly oriented towards effective and efficient use of the Net as well as the journal sites. Unnecessary and unscrupulous hits, revisits and downloads can result in frequent choking of the Net connectivity, posing unwanted problems to the entire user community on campus, and also to LAN/Net system administration.

THE IIM CONSORTIA EXPERIENCE

The year 2000 was a landmark in the history of IIMs, with the formation of the IIM Consortia. IIMK took leadership in the formation of the IIM Consortia, and had the first meeting in Calicut.

The objective was to ensure among the IIMs, optimum utilization and enhancement of the resources, and to minimise the expenditure by consortia based subscriptions to the commonly subscribed databases and journals. The idea was to approach publishers of CD-ROM Databases to begin with, as a consortia, for better pricing and services. Eventually, other digital databases and journals were also planned to be covered by the programme. The meetings were proved to be very productive and successful. During the first meeting itself, a host of databases were jointly purchased at very competitive prices, and a number of others promised supply of their products at a nominal cost.

In the case of journals, all the six IIMs put together subscribes to over 2550 scholarly titles of which around 1200 are duplications (overlapping titles). Among these, 33 titles are being subscribed to by all the IIMs. Having convinced on the dire need for a journals consortia, major publishers such as Elsevier [13], Kluwer [14], Wiley [15], Blackwell [16] and MCB University Press were approached and they all represented in the second meet which was held at IIM Bangalore in 2001. The end result has been highly praiseworthy, that over 740 E-journals IIMs are able to get online access, across all the IIMs, by paying a nominal additional amount. The table below shows the salient features of the digital subscriptions at IIMK based on the IIM Consortia.

In the above table, the titles mentioned in column no.3 are the total number of print subscriptions from the respective publishers, made by all the IIMs, except the MCB University Press. The access fee to their electronic counterpart are worked out with the condition that all the IIMs shall retain their existing print subscriptions. In summary, 5% to 10% extra charges are only levied over and above the print subscription costs, for the electronic access, across all the titles. In the process, individually each IIM has a great saving while there is a substantial increase in the information resource base. This is a classic example of the flip pricing where libraries get the real benefit of both consortia and technology infrastructure. For example, the Internet connectivity and the broad bandwidth are

Table 1 : Features of the IIM Journals Consortia

Name of the Publisher	Web Site Address	No. of Titles accessed by IIMK	No. of print subscriptions by IIMK	Cost of the total titles Accessed	Cost paid by IIMK under the Consortia
Blackwell Publishers	www.blackwellpublis hing.co	268	17	US$ 149700.00 Rs.76,49,670.00	US$ 2495.00 Rs.1,27,494.50
Elsevier Science (Science Direct)	www.sciencedirect. com/web-editions	240	16	US$ 216430.00 Rs. 1,10,37,930.00	US$ 3607.16 Rs. 1,83,965.16
Kluwer Academic Publishers	www.kluweronline.Com	33	4	Euro $ 24,753.00 Rs.10,47,299.40	Euro $ 412.50 (Rs.17,453.00)
MCB University Press (Emerald Library)	www.ereraldinsight. com/ft	140	2	£11,999.00 Rs. 8,39,930.00	£1,650.00 Rs.1,14,658.50
John Wiley & Sons, Inc.	www.wiley.com	60	5	US$ 78110.85 Rs.39,05,542.50	US$ 1302.00 Rs. 67183.00

the prerequisites for this kind of a service delivery. Since all IIMs go together, the strength attracts the publishers to listen to our demands.

The MCB Press (Emerald Full-text Library) did the calculations in a different way, and they came out with a consortia model for the Indian higher learning institutions such as IITs and IIMs. In India, the Emerald Consortia is coordinated by M/s. Balani Infotech, New Delhi.

ELECTRONIC JOURNAL AGGREGATION PREFERENCES

The Libraries prefer a subject interface that permits the use of both a controlled vocabulary and keywords to search the full-text contents of electronic journals without giving up the ability to browse the contents of individual issues. It favors the following models of access:

a) Web-based indexing and abstracting services linked to full-text electronic journals, e.g., Institute for Scientific Information's (ISI) [17] ability in the near future to link between SCI/SSCI/AHCI and the contents of full-text journals.

b) Aggregated databases composed of a variety of media, e.g., newspapers, newsletters, government reports, monographs, reference works, etc., e.g., Business Source Premier, Academic Search Elite, Academic Universe, ProQuest Direct etc.

c) Aggregated collections of journals published by a variety of publishers but sharing a common searching interface, e.g., J-Gate or J-Stor.

d) Aggregated collections of journals published by a single publisher but sharing a common searching interface, e.g., Project Muse, Emerald Library etc.

CONCLUSION

It is becoming undoubtedly clear that the digital subscriptions are increasing in geometric proportions the world over, as technology gets absorbed by the library fraternity, and as digital materials dominate the domain of the information space. The comparatively reduced / affordable cost of the digital information as against their print counterparts give yet another boost to libraries to jump into the bandwagon, though there are a host of catches in the reserve. The user awareness coupled with the unprecedented demand-pull will even otherwise certainly compel librarians and the management to opt for more digital subscriptions in the coming years. Librarians may also feel proud that they are catching up with the trends in technology, by going digital. At the same token, it would be appreciated if licenses provide the libraries with permanent rights to the content that has been paid for. Publishers should permit "fair use" of the information, understood to mean to include the same sorts of curricular and research purposes that have been pursued with the print materials. They should allow the libraries to enhance the use of the data to make it more visible or convenient as needed. Provisions should be there to allow reciprocal rights to terminate the license agreements.

REFERENCES

1. Terry, Ana Arias (2000). *How today's technology affects libraries' collection choices.* Computers in Libraries Vol. 20, No. 6, pp. 51-55.
2. World Wide Web Virtual Library- Electronic Journals : www.edoc.com/ejournal
3. JSTOR : www.jstor.org
4. Ingenta : www.ingenta.com
5. ProjectMUSE : muse.jhu.edu
6. Emerald Library : www.ereraldinsight.com/ft
7. CatchWord : www.catchword.com
8. J-Gate : j-gate.informindia.com
9. EBSCO Publishing : www.epnet.com
10. Proquest Information & Learning : www.umi.com
11. Orsdel, Lee Van; Born, Kathleen, *Doing the Digital Flip.* Library Journal (2002) Vol. 127 Issue 7, pp.51-55.
12. Pavliscak, Pamela (1996). *Trends in copyright practices of scholarly electronic journals.* Serials Review 22 (3): 39-47.

13. Elsevier Science Direct : www.sciencedirect.com/web-editions
14. Kluwer Academic Publishing : www.kluweronline.com
15. John Wiley & Sons : www.wiley.com
16. Blackwell Scientific Publishing: www.blackwellpublishing.co
17. Institute for Scientific Information: www.isinet.com

21

Standards For Exchange of Bibliographic Data

M. Parameswaran,

Reader,

Dept. of Library & Information Science,

University of Calicut.

ABSTRACT

Explains the concept of exchange of bibliographic data in IT environment. Distinguishes between standard for bibliographic description and standards for exchange of bibliographic data. Briefly describes ISBD and its effect on the revision of Anglo-American cataloguing Rules (AACR). Explains MARC formats and other standards for exchange of electronic bibliographic data.

Describes the international developments and indicates the efforts in India in the field of bibliographic standards. Concludes that the bibliographic standards have made the exchange of bibliographic data easy but the developments in India are not keeping pace with the international developments.

BIBLIOGRAPHIC STANDARDS

Bibliography is a list of documents. It can appear either as separate publication or at the end of books or at the end of dissertations and research papers.

The purpose of a bibliography are (i) to give details of documents so as to identify it and procure it from available sources; (ii) to give authencity to the statement of an author. Bibliography consists of entries or descriptions on documents. A document description in a bibliography which is briefly referred to as an entry) consists of the name of the author of little of document, imprint collation etc. When a document is described in a bibliography it is desirable to have some standardisation. Standard is something that is established by authority or general consent as a model or example to be followed. If there is such an established pattern of description it is easy to distinguish the name of authors editors, publishes etc. without confusion.

Library catalogue is a list of documents available in the collection of a library. In this sense library catalogue is also a list of a bibliography. Therefore it should also follow some bibliographic standards. Conformity to the rules of a catalogue code automatically achieves standardisation in catalogue entries. However, in the context of electronic exchange of cataloguing data it is also essential that catalogue codes should frame the rules for description on conformity with the bibliographic standards. A bibliographic standard may be defined as a general frame work or structure prescribing an order for the elements of description in a bibliographic entry along with standard punctuation marks to indicate each of them.

BIBLIOGRAPHIC STANDARDS AND EXCHANGE FORMATS

Bibliographic data may be defined in the context of electronic recording of information as information related to the listing of books and other items containing recorded information. Bibliographic data should contain elements of information which help to identify a piece of recorded communication as a physical object.

Bibliographic data consists of a number of bibliographic records. Each bibliographic record pertains to a bibliographic item and consists of several elements such as author little etc. In the context of bibliographies and catalogues we may use the term entry to refer to a record of an item that a document, but in the context of automated systems bibliographic record is a more suitable term.

All data for computer handling must be converted to machine readable form. Each bibliographic record is divided into fields and sub fields when it is converted into machine readable form.

Bibliographic control has been defined as the mastery over written and published records through bibliographies. Information technology has not only provided sophisticated means of bibliographic control but also made possible the world wide exchange of bibliographic information.

The goals of Universal Bibliographic control is the creation of an international system for bibliographic information. UBC was adopted as a major programme by the International Federation of Library Associations and Institutions (IFLA) in 1974. An International MARC Network committee was set up by IFLA in 1983 and consequently an International MARC Programme (IMP) was set up at the Deietsche Bibliotheck at Frankfurt.

The aim of IMP is the promotion of an international network for the exchange of bibliographic data. Exchange of bibliographic data refers to the exchange of bibliographies or catalogues transferred into computer readable forms such as magnetic tapes CD-ROMS etc. In 1987 UBC was transfused with IMP to become UBCIM programme. Thus two aspects of the control of bibliographic records have been merged. 1) their creation is standardised from 2) their dissemination in standard MARC format. Thus we can see that bibliographic standardisation and exchange of bibliographic data are complementary to each other. Easy exchange of bibliographic information requires agreement on standards governing the medium of exchange, the ogranisation and representation of data and record definition and content. Therefore this paper examines the bibliographic standards and exchange formats in their mutual perspective.

IMPORTANT BIBLIOGRAPHIC STANDARDS

The following are the important bibliographic standards available.

i. International Standard Bibliographic Description (ISBD)

ii. MARC formats (Formats for Machine Readable catalogue)

iii. International Format of Bibliographic Information Exchange (ISO 2709).

iv. Common Communication Format (CCF).

The item (i) given above is meant for description of documents in bibliographies and catalogues while the other three standards are specifically meant for exchange of bibliographic or cataloguing data in computer readable form such as magnetic tapes or CD-ROM. Since ISBD prescribes the order in which bibliographic elements are to be stated in an entry conformity to this standard is a basic requirement for both manual and machine readable or online catalogues.

INTERNATIONAL STANDARD NIBLIOGRAPHIC DESCRIPTION (ISBD)

ISBD was prepared and adopted by the IFLA committee on cataloguing in 1971. First standard edition of ISBD (M) that is International Standard Bibliographic Description for monographs was brought out in 1974. This standard has been adopted by more than 20 national bibliographies and translated into over 14 languages.

International standard Bbliographic Description for Monographic Publications i.e. (ISBD (M) specifies the description of printed monographs. ISBD (M) has identified 7 special areas (parts) in the bibliographic description of a monographi and each area has been demarkalated into several elements. Following the ISB (M) a general standard for the description of all kind of library material known as ISBD (G) has been brought out. A special feature of this standard is the provision for an area of details which are special to particular material or type of publication.

The different areas of ISBD (M) and ISBD (G) are given below:

	ISBD (M)	ISB (G)
1.	Title and Statement of authorship area	Title and statement of responsibility area
2.	Edition area	Edition area
3.	———	Material (type of publication) specific details area
4.	Imprint area	Publication, distribution etc. area
5.	Collation area	Physical description area
6.	Series area	Series area
7.	Notes area	Notes area
8.	International Standard Book Number and Price area	Standard Number and Terms of availability area

ISBD (G) is supposed to serve as a model for specific ISBDS of other materials. IFLA has brought and ISBDS for serials, old books, manuscripts, cartographic materials printed music, computer files, electronic resources etc.

Anglo-American cataloguing Rules 2nd edition 1978 (AACR2) and its revisions (1988 revision and 19998 revision) have based on various ISBDs for the preparation of rules for descriptive cataloguing in Part I. IFLA and the Joint committee for Revision of AACR agreed that the revision of AACR will follow the framework of ISBD and their punctuations. Since LC MARC and BNB MARC follow AARC2 rules for descriptive cataloguing we can say that these MARC formats are in conformity with ISBD. Classified catalogue code is becoming out dated in this era of electronic library even in India because it has failed to revise itself in conformity to ISBDs.

MARC FORMATS

MARC is an acronym for Machine Readable Catalogue. MARC actually refers to a group of formats using a particular set of conversions for the identification and arrangement of bibliographic data for handling by computer.

Marc I Format

The original MARC format was developed by Library of Congress in 1965-66 with the financial aid from the Council of Library Resources. In 1966, the MARC Pilot project was initiated. Bibliographic data was distributed to selected libraries as magnetic tape for use on an experimental basis. These early MAR records were for English language monographs published in United States. The pilot project format was subsequently called MARCI to distinguish it from its successor. The distribution of MARCI format contained a fixed field of 108 characters holding considerable amount of coded data for record length LC card number, language, date of publication and other data useful for machine search. However this format allowed only 20 variable fields all designed with the requirements of monographs. There was also a limited character set and the project indicated that further work was needed to develop an extended character set for Roman alphabet languages.

Marc II Format

In the United Kingdom the Council of British National Bibliography observed the progress of the MARC Pilot Project. BNB conducted its feasibility study on the use of machine readable data for production of BNB in print. BNB MARC project was officially started in September 1967. The British interest coincided with the appraisal of the MARCI pilot format by LC. MARC II format developed in 1968 was the result of cooperation between Library of Congress and the Council of the British National Bibliography. MARC II is the archetype of all subsequent MARC formats. There were two versions of MARC II – LC MARC II and BNB MAR II. Library of Congress developed separate formats for different types of materials but the British format remained the same. The structure of these formats was as follows:

Leader Directory Control fields
Bibliographic data fields Record separator

This structure was later adopted by American National Standard Institute (ANSI). British Standard Institution (BSI) and the International Organisation for Standardisation (ISO).

The variable data fields contained the bibliographic data and the arrangement of elements in both formats followed the order of the traditional entry resulting in data grouped by bibliographic function.

Tag 01-109-Bibliographic control numbers and knowledge (ie class) number

Tag 1-	Main Entry Headings
Tag 2-	Title Edition Imprint
Tag 3-	Collation including price
Tag 4-	Series statement
Tag 5-	Bibliographic notes
Tag 6-	Subject entries including personal and corporate name subject entries
Tag 7 -	Added entries for persons, bodies and titles.
Tag 8 -	Series added entries (LC MARC only)
Tag 9 -	Cross Reference (BNB MARC Only) Number for local use

U S Marc

In 1980 LC MARC was changed to US MARC. At present there are three US MARC communication formats (i) for bibliographic data (ii) for authority data (iii) for holding and locations. For convenience and brevity these USMARC formats are referred to as UFBD, UFAD and UFHL. The physical structure for all US MARC formats is described in US MARC specification for record structure character sets and tapes. It may be indicated as follows:

LEADER DIRECTORY VARIABLE FIELDS

CONTROL DATA

a) Leader

The leader is a fixed field of 24 characters with positions counted from 0-23.

b) Directory

The directory begins in character position 24.

c) Variables fields

Following the directory are the variable fields comprising control fields and data fields.

UK Marc

The UK MARC manual (Ist standard ed,) was published in 1975 which consolidated earlier format documentation with minimal change. It presented the UK MARC format in a comprehensive manner with information for all types of users: librarians, system analysts, and local cataloguers. The change from BNB to UK MARC was an indication that MARC was firmly established at national level in Britain. The format complied in structure with ISO 2709 and British standard (BS 4748). The structure of this format may be indicated as follows.

Record level Directory Control fields Variable field

Marc 21

In 1987 Library of congress issued the first edition of the document MARC 21 specifications to aid libraries and other organizations who create or acquire MARC 21 records. Subsequent editions were published in 1990 and 1994. This document provides technical information on the structure of MARC records.

With the proliferation of microcomputer systems in libraries a standard was needed for the exchange of MARC records on floppy diskette. By making necessary changes and additions in the original MARC 21 format, a format for record transfer using diskettes was evolved. More recently specifications have been developed for the distribution of MARC records via file transfer (FTP). The diskette and FTP distribution specification first appeared in 1994 edition of MARC 21.

In general MARC 21 available in five formats as given below:

i. MARC 21 format for Bibliographic Data

ii. MARC 21 format for Authority Data

iii. MARC 21 format for Classification Data

iv. MARC 21 format for Community Information

v. MARC 21 Format for Holding Data

The different fields of MARC 21 indicated by tags are as follows:

010	LC control No.
020	ISBN
100	Personal name main entry (Author)
245	Title information (Title, Other title information and statement of responsibility)
250	Edition
260	Publication information
300	Physical description
440	Series statement
520	Contents note
650	Subject heading
700	Personal name added entry.

These fields are further divided into subfields. Sub fields are marked by subfileds codes and delimiters.

Example

300 # # $ a 675 p: $ b ill, $ c 24 cm 300 is the fields for physical description where $a is the subfield code for pagination $b for other physical details (illustration) and $ c for dimensions. $ dollar sign is called the delimiter code.

MARC formats provides a standard format for bibliographic data and therefore these are helpful for exchange of bibliographic data.

Unimarc

The differences in MARC formats paved way for the formation of UNIMARC: The standard International MARC Network exchange format. In 1972 working Group on Content Designators was set up. The working group had the task of exploring the reasons for the differences between the different MARC formats and arriving at a standard for the international exchange of data in machine readable form. It was necessary that each country needed to retain or establish its own format because of differences between national requirements. This was established in the IFLA General Conference in Budapest in 1972. It was decided that each national agency would also arrange for the development of conversion programmes to convert the data in its own national format into that of the international format. It was agreed that ISBD should be the basis of the data elements relating to the descriptive cataloguing in the records. Thus UNIMARC was published in 1977. This was followed by the publication of the second edition of UNI MARC in 1980.

National libraries had generally agreed to use UNIMARC as their exchange format. As agreed in the Conference of Directors of National Libraries in 1981 a test was conducted to ascertain the potential effectiveness of UNIMARC format. The test was conducted by obtaining photocopies of title pages from national agencies and converting them to UNIMARC format. Problems were identified and solutions were suggested by catalogue experts. Towards the end of 1983 UNIMARC hand book was published. The revised handbook was published in 1987 under the title of UNIMARC manual which had taken into account the developments of various ISBDs.

The main feature of UNIMARC is that it should have one set of tag or subfield identifier covering all materials. There would be no order of subfields so that they could be placed in the order required by the catalogue codes. The advantages of accepting UNIMARC as an exchange format is that the national agency will need to write only two software programmes one to convert from any national MARC format to UNIMARC and the other to convert from UNIMARC to any national MARC format.

Indimarc

The Bureau of Indian standards published Indian MARC which was based on UKMARC in 1985. As a need for revision was felt soon after the formulation of Indian MARC National Information system for Science and Technology (NISSAT) developed. INDIMARC on a framework prescribed by the CCF.

Common Communication Format (CCF)

Unesco sponsored Symposium on Bibliographic Exchange Formats was held in 1978. As a result of the resolutions passed in the symposium Unesco set up an Adhoc Group for the establishment of CCF. The group decided that the record structure should be that specified in the ISO 2709 standard. A data elementary directory was prepared in 1979. CCF is a bibliographic exchange format developed under the PGI programme of Unesco. It is intended for use by agencies having records of monographs, serials, journals, articles etc. which wish to exchange bibliographic records with one another. It follows ISO 2709 in full for its structure but it does not follow any particular catalogue code. One of the specific features of CCF is that it has special techniques to indicate the vertical relationship (ie. a monograph with its chapters) and the horizontal relationship (a work with its various versions in different languages)

CCF record structure consists of four major sections or parts.

i. Record label
ii. Directory
iii. Data fields
iv. Records separator

CCF has a number of vacant fields. Therefore it is not difficult for the institution following CCF to add information for which there is no provision. Since CCF does not follow any catalogue code Indian libraries which follow classified catalogue code will find it suitable for their use.

FORMATS FOR BIBLIOGRAPHIC INFORMATION INTERCHANGE (ISO 2709)

ISO 2709 is an international standard that specifies the requirements for a generalized machine readable format that will hold any type of bibliographic record. It was developed from the record structure of LC MARC. The first version of ISO 2709 was dated 1973. It was reviewed and a second edition was published in 1977.

It may be noted that ISO 2709 does not define the contents of individual records or the meanings assigned to tag indicators or identifiers. Rather it only prescribes a generalized structure and can be used to transmit records describing all forms of material capable of bibliographic description between the processing systems. According to ISO 2709 the general structure of a bibliographic record can be schematically shown as given below.

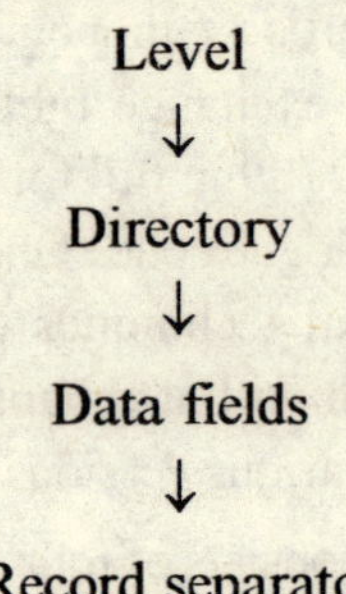

As per ISO 2709 a bibliographic record should include the following fixed and variable length fields.

(i) a record label

(ii) a directory

(iii) a record identifier

(iv) reserved field

(v) Bibliographic data fields

(vi) field separator

The second edition of ISO 2709 permitted the use of alpharnumeric tags and in this edition each entry in the record directory can be extended by up to nine characters. CCF has made use of this extended directory to identify repeated fields. ISO 2709 has influenced soft ware packages like MINISIS and CDS/ISIS used in microcomputers. ISO 2709 has been universally accepted for the exchange of bibliographic data on magnetic tapes. It is also used for the formatting of bibliographic data sent online and stored on other media such as flopy disk and CD-ROM.

CONCLUSION

A number of International Standards for Bibliographic Description (ISBDs) were created by IFLA. These standard have been accepted by all cataloguing and bibliographic agencies. MARC formats developed by Unesco/PGI and ISO 2709 developed by International standards Organisation are also general formats for electronic exchange of bibliographic information.. India has developed INDI MARC under NISSAT. India has also started developing Standard numbers viz., ISBN for monographs and ISSN for serials. But these have not been made compulsory. Thus it can be seen that the developments in India with reference to bibliographic standards are not keeping pace with the work an progress at international level.

However it can be said that the standards for exchange of electronic bibliographic data are efforts to make Universal Bibliographic control a reality.

REFERENCES

1. Guha, B. Documentation and Information: Services, techniques and systems. 2nd ed. Calcutta: World Press, 1983, Chap. 16.
2. Gredley, Ellen and Hopkins, Alan. Exchanging bibliographic data: MARC and other international formats. London: Library Association, 1990.

3. Govind, Vijay. Implementation of International Standard Book Number System in India: Perspectives and Prospects. ILA Bulletin, 35(3&4): Oct. 1999 – Mar. 2000, p.67-73.

4. INFLIBNET Regional Training Programme on Library Automation. Course Material. Ahmedabad: INFLIBNET Centre, 2002. p.31-57.

5. Varun, Vimal Kumar. Document description. Information Today & Tomorrow. Vol. 20(3): 2001. p.18-20.

22

Managing the Impact of Electronic Publishing

A.C. Ganesh
Chief Web Writer,
Express Network Private Limited,
Express Internet Division,
Chennai.

M. Tamizhchelvan
Librarian,
The New Indian Express,
Mount Road,
Chennai.

ABSTRACT

With the widespread implementation of Information, Communication and Technology (ICT), any individual with a PC along with a modem and subject knowledge has started harnessing information and hosts it on the Internet. The major question in information management is what, where and why does one need to store. These are the issues that an information management system needs to address.

In an era of information, with the growth of e-publishing, one of the biggest advantages of e-publishing is the speedy process, retrieval and dissemination of information and also the development of networking model across library and information centres. Access and exchange of information has been made simple through the network for end users.

This paper looks at the impact of Planning, Organisation, Staffing, Directing, Controlling, Regulating and Budgeting (POSDCORB) of e-publishing and some of its impact.

INTRODUCTION

The impact of information technology (IT) is seen as a industrial revolution. The impact of IT has been so dominant that it has affected everyone – be it economy, political, social and individuals at large. It has been a chief determinant of the growth of nations and individuals worldwide. For any country to develop, there should be a correlation between knowledge and idea, which form the heart and soul of any development process. India, over the years has invested in human capital providing quality education, acquiring and adapting to global knowledge, going techno savvy and working as a team.

In early days, for one to get a piece of information or knowledge had to read books which came in print format. In developing countries, one had to wait for a long period of time to procure the print material. This is where libraries came into picture as they placed orders and acquired the printed matter.

But, with the convergence of information, communication and technology, "a piece of information" which is seen as the soul of knowledge, which if organized, becomes a set of information. This information can be converted into bits or bytes and comes in packets over the network. This is how electronic publishing is born. This information if transferred into books or educational/ instructional courses becomes knowledge. This knowledge still comes in the form of reading books and through sheer experience. Though information can be received in a few minutes or hours, knowledge is acquired over a period of days or months.

Libraries play a vital role, where they acquire, organise through abstracting, cataloguing, indexing for easy retrieval and store the information so that it can become knowledge. This helps in easy access of to information at all levels and aids effective public policy, governance, and reduction in transaction costs and also results in high productivity and more opportunities.

The transition from print to e-publishing has been happening over the last few years with libraries either acquiring or providing connectivity or access to the materials in electronic/online form.

There was a time when librarians/ information professionals were seen as dead. But that has not happened and will never happen as the have bounced back strongly. Though there were fears initially, information professionals over the years have welcomed the technology with open arms. They have realised the benefit of ICT and have added them along with their earlier services. Apart from that, electronic publishing has helped in creating a dialogue between the publishers, libraries and end-users.

DEFINITION OF E-PUBLISHING

Essentially, "e-publishing" is when you have your book online to be downloaded onto a user's computer. These books are stored online and the reader's download the book or article to read in leisure. An "e-book" on the other hand, is an electronic book that can be read with a computer.

When Johann Gutenberg invented the printing press, people of his times never appreciated him, though the generations after him had lavish praises for the invention. Similarly, book lovers and information scientists will take time to accustom to the change in adapting to electronic publishing or books over a period of time. In fact, future generations of book lovers would appreciate the arrival of the technologies, which has opened a new avenue of reading at convenience.

ADVANTAGES AND DISADVANTAGES OF E-PUBLISHING

E-publishing can be said as library at your finger tips as newspapers, magazines, books, journals, catalogues, indexes, abstracts etc., are available in electronic format like floppies, CD-ROMs, e-books, e-journals, intranet, World Wide Web and Internet. They are also available in the form of online libraries and are just a click away.

A comparison of Printed-paper materials vis-à-vis e-publishing

Paper/ Printed materials	**Electronic publishing**
The format of the paper book is basically paper	Electronic books are available in electronic format like floppies, CD-ROMs, text files, databases, HTML format etc
Paper books are expensive	Expensive the first time, updates are nominal
The features of paper books are: portable, light, matter depend on paper and photo quality. There is no need of special care for the books and can be handled with less care. Reading is very simple and easy.	Electronic books are portable and light. The quality of the content depends on the technology. One has to handle with care as the hardware and system is costly. Reading is not that easy.
The reach of the paper books are not restricted	The reach of the electronic books are restricted to those who have or can have access to computers and networks
The mode of delivery may vary and the time taken for delivery is slow and limited	The delivery mode is fast ranging from seconds to minutes through networks
Cost of archival is relatively less	Cost of archival is relatively expensive at the moment
No need of technical knowledge	Need technical knowledge to handle
Physical storage and can be organised	As of now e-books are unorganised at present.

The potential of electronic publications are immense and they are surely going to live up to the promise. Some of the other factor's one needs to take into consideration are they represent the end of the veritable death penalty on scholarly and specialized works. The other factor is updation is pretty easy and need not the publisher need not reprint the whole book, magazine or newspaper again just for a few lines of updation.

MANAGING E-PUBLISHING

With the advent of World Wide Web and Internet, there has been a dramatic rise in flow of information. With access to information becoming easy, the growth in end-users like students, business and scientific community have started increasing and managing information have become crucial. The community expects libraries not only provide information, but also wants them to provide high-speed connectivity to access the information irrespective of costs.

Modern tools allow what people write and send to each other to be stored, and that stored material becomes a rich base from which people can acquire knowledge. The current issue is that of information management rather than a knowledge management. Today's challenge is that with the advent of e-publishing, there are no boundaries and restrictions and this helps professionals to capture knowledge from what people say and do as part of their day-to-day work and to make it accessible to others in an organised manner.

BRINGING POSDCORB INTO E-PUBLISHING

Planning: A publisher has to plan which books, journals, newspaper, magazines, pictures, etc., need to be electronically published and know his target audience. The following steps are involved in electronic publishing namely, developing or organise the content, evaluation of content, editing the content, proofing, page layout and design, scanning pictures and other relevant materials, website design if ported on to the Internet, uploading and publishing on the web an providing contact-information. From an online newspaper perspective, since the volume of content is huge and the flow of information if high an informational professional plays varies from the traditional Librarian role to that of a project manager where he has to plan the choose, test and decide the hardware, server' for storing data, software's for easy access, retrieval and content management.

Organisation of content

Once the basic plan is ready, the next step is to organise the content so as to present it in a readable format be it text, document, PDF, HTML format. The end-user must have no difficulties in accessing the information that he desires to read. The classification and categorisation of the publication should be user-friendly. The navigation should be simple and user-friendly. A well organised content in electronic format benefits archival and easy retrieval. Apart from that it helps to accelerated business processes, improved decision support, documents can be accessed anytime from anywhere, direct integration adds benefit to resource planning systems, groupware, Web, email, and legacy applications and option to use advanced authorization policies.

Staffing

Human resources is vital for any organisation to grow and staff's need to be treated as capital. The best available talent should be chosen and trained constantly to keep themselves abreast to the latest technological developments especially in areas related to Internet and online media so that they perform their tasks efficiently and effectively.

Directing

The top management should give direction as and when required so that the staff and management do not deviate from the given assignments. Since electronic publishing and e-libraries are at a nascent stage in India, is vital for proper direction so that, there are no deviations from the set organisational goals.

Controlling and Coordination

Any successful venture needs proper control, which can be affected through coordination. Control with lack of co-ordination results in chaos. There need's to be coordination at all levels be it management, departments, staff's, vendors, distributors, etc. In case of e-libraries, coordination between networks of libraries is essential for better service and customer satisfaction.

Regulation

In the Internet age where copyright violation is high, regulation is a must. In this information era, with copyright violations, licensing agreements and intellectual property rights being violated; both the Government and organisations worldwide should ensure that the laws and agreements are protected. Apart from copyright, there is a need to standardize the presentation of the content as the content available on the Internet is in a haphazard manner and does not follow the library conventions.

Budgeting

Once an organisation decides on moving into an electronic format of publishing, be it newspapers, magazines, books, journals or deciding to have e-libraries, they should allocate adequate funds. Since the initial setting up cost is high, they should not restrict the fund for it may tamper with the growth of the organisation in the long run. They should make a feasibility study before going into such a venture. Since the professionals need to keep themselves abreast with ICT, they need to constantly upgrade themselves for providing quality service and speedy delivery. The management has to allocate funds not only for setting up the basic infrastructure, but they also need to identify the training needs and attend to individual needs.

FUTURE OF E-PUBLISHING

On the technological side, Microsoft is working closely on device, which supports digital publishing by coming out with a system that is light-weighted, low-cost and durable tablet-size device that displays text that is close in quality to a book. A similar idea has been kicked around at Sun Microsystems with the general theme - portability, multimedia and crisp text — echoed the one sounded by Microsoft.

The exciting news is that the industry is groping toward this still uncertain, intriguing future. Though in the last year or so, since the dotcom bust, several e-book-only imprints have closed up shop. First, At Random (Random House), then iPublish (AOL Time Warner) and MightyWords (BN.com-majority shareholder) bit the dust. But that doesn't mean e-books are a lost cause. In fact, e-book reading and sales are stronger than ever. In the past year, 1,600 titles were downloaded more than 3.1 million times at the Etext Library at the University of Virginia. That's 8,715 free e-books per day. Meanwhile, independent publishers and retailers such as Fictionwise.com, Booklocker.com, Hardshell Word Factory and Palm Digital Corp to name a few have reported sales increases in 2001 from between 100 and 400 percent over 2000. OCLC, which provides computer-based cataloguing, reference, resource sharing and preservation services to 40,000 libraries in 81 countries and territories are continuing their efforts to romp in more authors, libraries, publishers to provide access to users a on a wide variety of subjects and topics.

Course curriculum are being developed to teach students about the creation and use of PCs, e-books, e-book readers, using the e-library system, how to get e-books on the Internet, and even how to create their own e-books. Finally, according to Jay Jordan, president of OCLC, "Electronic books and other forms of electronic content are quickly becoming strategic drivers in the sharing and advancement of knowledge in the digital age."

REFERENCES

1. Cooper, Charles, (2000): E-books: An idea still ahead of its time, ZDNet News Issue dated August 9, 2000.
2. Reuka K, (2002): Electronic books and the future of libraries: LIST 2002, 27-28 January, 2002. (133 p)
3. Chuoksey SS (2002): On-line Library Services towards On-line education system, MANLIBNET 2002, 3-5 April 2002, (258 p)
4. Rose MJ (2001): E-Books Live On After Mighty Fall, Issue Wired News, Dec. 18, 2001.

23

Copyright Issues in Electronic Publishing : A Librarian's Perspective

Meena. V.,
Research Scholar,
Department of Library & Information Science,
University of Calicut.

Dr. Jalaja. V.,
Lecturer(Senior Scale),
Deptment of Library & Information Science,
University of Calicut.

ABSTRACT

The exponential growth in the volume of published information makes retrieval of information from libraries difficult. In the present world link to knowledge bases and information resources are essential for being well informed. Conventional publishing gave way to electronic publishing realizing the potential and unique features of electronic media. Electronic publishing offers enormous potential for information delivery. It provides search facilities and inclusion of hypertext links to external sources. It will act as data warehouse of navigable information.

The paper discusses the concept of electronic publishing, its advantages and disadvantages. Legal issues like copyright and factors relating to the electronic distribution of copyrighted works have also been considered. The paper attempts to study the role of a library in the digitised world where electronic publishing will be the buzzword. Issues related to the use of electronic publications, the role of publishers and the role of the librarian have been discussed.

INTRODUCTION

The world is passing through a revolution in information technology which has far-reaching impacts. As far as communication is concerned, the current era is as important for mankind as the 15th century that saw Gutenberg's invention of the movable-type printing process. The popularisation of hyper textual structures has also added new degrees of freedom. Information is becoming more digital and networked and less paper.

The need to control and provide access to the ever-increasing information is felt much due to literature seepage and scattering. The increase in the cost of raw materials used in publishing has necessitated increase in the cost of books and journals. Conventional printing took considerable time to bring out a book. Due to the delay in printing, by the time the material came out, its relevance was lost and the contents turned out to be less significant. It was at this juncture that the need to reduce the time required in conventional printing was realized. The potential and unique features of electronic media were identified and the emphasis shifted from conventional publishing to electronic publishing.

Electronic publishing is the emergence of a new technology that enables us to publish in a completely different way from the way we have published before. The term 'electronic publishing' is generally used to signify the use of computers in the production of printed publications and also in the sense of distribution of information using computers and telecommunication technologies. It includes on-line publishing, CD-ROM and related technologies such as CDI. Electronic publishing can be defined as the publication process where the manuscripts are submitted in electronic format, edited, printed, and even distributed to readers by employing computers and telecommunications. Electronic publishing is the dissemination of information in electronic form and its distribution to potential users is either on electronic networks such as Internet and local area networks or in stand alone formats such as CD-ROMs and diskettes. It is a form of publishing where the computer network becomes the primary medium of creation, storage and distribution of information. Many of the recent advances in electronic publishing is made possible due to the existence of a large population which owns computers. Though advances in hardware and publishing technologies have a major role, it is continuing advances in telecommunication, which have made possible much of the recent growth in electronic publishing. This includes both improvements in the public switched networks and the arrival of dedicated data networks.

The internet has existed for years and has been utilized by the research community for a variety of purposes with little dramatic effect, but now it seems possible that electronic publishing could potentially and drastically alter the dynamic among authors, publishers and consumers of scholarly works.

ELECTRONIC PUBLISHING TECHNOLOGIES

The technologies of electronic publishing are diverse and this is true for the products that result from their application. A combination of computing, communication and publishing technologies have been used over the years to generate products falling into one of the following four main categories :

- broadcast non-interactive services(eg. Teletext, cable television);
- interactive services(eg. Videotext, online, some cable television services);
- discrete products(eg. Video discs, video cassettes, computer software, database subsets on discs); and
- others(eg. The electronic journal, hybrid products like videopat search)

With the use of electronic publishing technologies it is possible to give easier access to people regarding the background information and related works of the author, and via hyperlinking the potentially overwhelming amounts of information on the Internet.

CHARACTERISTICS OF ELECTRONIC PUBLISHING

Electronic publishing has specific characteristics that distinguish it from print publication:

- electronic publications can be produced and disseminated very rapidly
- if correction is necessary, an electronic text can be updated or corrected with the same immediacy
- electronic publication can be made collaborative and interactive, involving either several "authors" or authors and readers
- electronic publications can be disseminated world-wide without the need for separate rights/negotiations for different countries and without the costs of distribution and reprinting
- where an electronic publication is charged for; the producer does not incur the costs associated with retail bookselling
- through effective electronic interaction with the buyer or user of an electronic publication, the publisher can collect valuable market research data cheaply.

ADVANTAGES OF ELECTRONIC PUBLISHING

The following are the advantages of electronic publishing :

- minimizes time and cost effective than publishing on paper
- streamlines update process and promotes availability of accurate documents instantaneously
- reduces distribution and storage overhead
- allows media enhancement of existing reference materials with sound, animation and video
- increases user effectiveness and productivity
- error reduction in production process

DISADVANTAGES OF ELECTRONIC PUBLISHING

- electronic publishing still reaches only a minority of potential users or customers even though this minority may constitute most of the market for some products, and much of the majority is in the developing world, where usage is likely to be slow to emerge

- electronic publishing demands access to relatively advanced technology on the part of both the producer and the consumer of information or entertainment - even the base level of provision is still expensive for the ordinary citizen
- the non-compatibility of hardware due to the absence of common standards
- mobile computers and notebooks, are either too big or have screens that are, too small, or otherwise inadequate, for use across the full range of environments in which a book can be read
- the technology is still, to a significant degree, user-unfriendly to many people
- the technology consumes a greater amount of energy in its use than the book

Even though there are many disadvantages for electronic publishing, the advantages outweigh them. The increasing ease of publication in the electronic world is causing many to question the traditional relationships between academics and publishers to whom authors often assign copyright. In the developing countries steps facilitate access to online information and promote digital publishing. The communication infrastructure and digital literacy have to be recognised as fundamental enabling tools. Electronic explosion encourages many who never thought to publish before to begin creating electronic resources.

COPYRIGHT

Copyright is a limited monopoly created for the purpose of providing people with a financial incentive to create copyrightable materials, to create works of literature, art and so on. The most fundamental right conferred by copyright is the right to exclude unauthorized reproduction of the copyrighted work. Once a work is created it immediately becomes the property of the author who created it, whether published or unpublished. The owner of copyright has exclusive rights to do and to authorize others to reproduce the copyrighted work, prepare derivative works, distribute copies, to perform the copyrighted work publicly, and to display it. Almost all things are copyrighted the moment they are written, and no copyright notice is required.

Copyright refers to "the exclusive legally secured right to publish and sell the substance and form of a literary, musical or artistic work". Copyright is a legal device designed to protect livelihood of creators and producers of literary, musical and artistic works.

Copyright law gives authors, composers, creators and others who create works of expression certain rights over their creation. It protects the rights of intellectual creators with respect to their original works. Unlike patents, the subject matter of copyright is literary and artistic works. All such works are protected as long as these are original expressions of an idea. Copyright laws recognize much wider limitations to the exclusive rights granted to the right holder than in any other category of Intellectual property rights.

Copyright law plays an important role in the complex world of modern communications. It is the legal recognition of rights to control and benefit from the works of authorship. It provides protection to works of authors and its laws are designed to encourage the creation and dissemination of original works. Good copyright law strikes a balance between the interest of the writer and that of the reader.

In the context of technological developments the 1994 amendment of the Indian Copyright Act extended protection to owners of copyright and related rights by bringing it with in the scope of digital technology. Copyright holders, publishers and booksellers insist on strengthened copyright protection of everything published on internet and they insist on pay per use. This is equal to demanding royalty or profit as that of getting from each printed copy sold. If this is the case then there is no point in investing huge amounts for this facility. Copyright law provides downloading of information for private use and research purpose.

Computer programmes and databases are included in the category of literary works. Given the advances in technology that allow for high quality, instantaneous and simultaneous enjoyment, copying and dissemination of works throughout the world, new problems have appeared on the protection of copyright. In this context copyright issues in electronic publishing has to be considered.

COPYRIGHT ISSUES IN ELECTRONIC PUBLISHING

At the moment efforts are being made to adjust electronic publishing to international and national copyright regulations. This is very important and crucial for libraries and its users as it decides the future of library services. The Berne Convention of 1886 and the WIPO Treaty are the remarkable achievements in this regard. The Berne Convention of 1886 is a basic agreement on the protection of literary and artistic works. Most of the developed countries have signed this agreement and it has been revised several times. The Berne Convention is nowadays interpreted so that its decisions can also be made to apply to new forms of publication.

The WIPO(World Intellectual Property Organisation) Treaty includes an international copyright agreement signed in Geneva in December 1996. It complements the Berne Convention and 160 members of the WIPO have signed it. It is the first agreement applying to electronic materials. It stipulates copyright at international level and leaves potential exceptions and limitations to be devised at the national level. The central points in the WIPO Copyright Treaty are reproduction right and the right of communication to the public is a new exclusive right of the right owners. The general principle is that a digital work has the same protection as a work in analogical form. The Follette Report identified the importance of copyright issues, noting that "unless progress is made in this area, the potential of information technology is unlikely to be realised".

In order to safeguard the rights of authors and for keeping a balance of interest of public access to information, a strenghtened copyright protection with new fair use provisions have become essential in the changing environment. As multiple copies of digital works can be made and transmitted very easily, the issues surrounding copyright protection and licensing of electronic information are very important.

Digital watermarks are thought to be the hottest new technology to "bind authorship to electronic works". The idea of a watermark or unique identifier to a work that cannot be removed, except by the author or publisher themselves, is a first step towards the digital rights protection. The current approach to the enforcement of copyright restrictions on intellectual properties to be distributed by electronic means(particularly, via the web) aims at blocking unauthorised duplication by means of increasingly sophisticated protection systems like encryption, watermarks and net-active software. Although technology is in place for publishers to exploit, it will remain unused until the legal issues surrounding copyright are decided. With the internet growing at approximately a rate of one million new users per month, publishers are not going to be able to hold off much longer.

Presently, it is not possible to insure whether the presented information is legitimate or not. By making adequate provisions in the copyright law, the integrity of publishers and authors' works will be protected allowing for one to know the authenticity of a work. Some assurance must be there for the publisher that they are the ones making the profit on a work. Publishers will need to determine a way in which they can recover costs and still work within the constraints of the electronic format. Because of the uncertainty of electronic rights, publishers and authors are attempting to resolve the issue on their own because the legal field has not resolved copyright issues.

ROLE OF PUBLISHERS

The publishing industry is based on the integrity of any work created or published and the willingness of the public to pay for such works. The publisher plays an integral role in the creation of a work - through editing, quality control and assurance, design, production, distribution, marketing and promotion. Electronic publishing does not necessarily deprive the publisher of the opportunity to create a visual identity in the mind of the reader. But to avoid being a faceless address on the Internet, the publishers will have to resort to new strategies for helping to create or preserve their identity.

In an electronic world, role of publishers will be greater in the electronic publishing of works. As time goes by what the publishers do will become increasingly important as their role in managing the peer-review process and collecting papers into reasonably coherent and stable journals has been of great benefit in paper publishing. Hence it seems likely that it will be important in electronic publishing. By electronic publishing the publishers can create a much more individualised product for their customers as there are more opportunities for learning about one's customer base, for getting feedback from readers, and for improving one's product without having to wait years for one's inventory of the first printing to be sold out.

In the digital age, when text and even images can be manipulated and altered seemlessly, and without a trace, authenticity becomes a paramount consideration for which the publishers can try to offer reliable source for the real thing. With the new digital technologies the opportunities for theft are so much greater that in fact the market for legitimate sales will shrink as the market of readers and users increases.

Publishers justify the assignment of copyright to them by the values that they add to publications and the services they offer. It is sometimes difficult to understand how their role would be compromised if they were just licensed to publish in specific ways;

if real, the value they add should ensure their prosperity. More and more innovative ways of producing, collecting and disseminating information are being invented in the digital world. Publishers, scientists and libraries will have to move with times and adapt themselves according to the need of the situation. The roles of the publisher in the digital age will certainly include many of these aspects with some changes and additions that will evolve.

ROLE OF LIBRARY IN AN ELECTRONIC ENVIRONMENT

Libraries and information centres are the beneficiaries of the electronic publishing revolution. Electronic publishing resources improved library services to their customers and made their internal operations more efficient. In the process of disseminating information, libraries used various digital formats such as online materials, materials in the hard disk, CDs, DVDs, DAT, etc. It may also have to permit the users to make copies if needed and facilitate exchange of materials between libraries. Since library is a non profit organisation and a social institution copyright law allows certain exception over its rights.

Presently libraries are to supply what the users need rather than store materials which are likely to be needed. Library and information centres must be treated as separate entity while framing copyright laws. Providing multiple user license is a must in a digitalised environment. Electronic publishing is forcing libraries to shift more and more financial resources from print publications to the acquisition of electronic resources. Such a financial shift will dramatically affect the publishing industry and the print industry may lose its viability. Another aspect which is worth considering is that, the publishers have relied on libraries to preserve the paper version of their products, but, without economic incentive, it seems likely that libraries will reliably undertake the preservation of the electronic versions.

Libraries play a significant role as information distributors, so we are expected to be knowledgeable and active when copyright issues are solved. In the present information society librarians have a crucial role in controlling and facilitating access to various electronic information sources. Information professional is the responsible intermediary between the users and various sources of information including digital.

Knowledge of computer technology, networking developments, library software packages, etc. is also necessary to cope with the changing environment. He must also have the ability to communicate with the library clientele. In order to provide a better service to the user, it is becoming necessary for all the library staff to specialise in particular subject areas and be more computer literate.

Access to information is the right of the public and no librarian can afford to deny it to the user on the question of copyright violation. Remote accesses to expensive and rare materials, solving massive storage problems and to support both formal and informal learning are some of the reasons why libraries choose to go digital. Librarians should be given some sort of a permission to copy digitally and store temporarily copyright works as part of an electronic document delivery systems. The staff of the library should be equipped with technical skills and capabilities to deal with the changing scenario. If the libraries are to acquire information in electronic form, they must address the technological needs of staff and users. The librarians face the problem of techno stress in that they are expected to learn about a large number of elctronic resources with their differing protocols, user interfaces and retrieval capabilities. The tasks librarians perform in identifying and organising materials are still needed for electronically published materials, and may be appreciated more, since the alternative is more visibly obvious.

CONCLUSION

The technology is racing ahead for a revolution to take place in the publising industry. But it is not possible to see the explosion of publishers on the net without putting the legal issues of copyright in the right place. Both the publishers and authors need protection from digital copying and distribution to preserve the authenticity of their work.

REFERENCES

1. Ahuja, Ashish A."Chaining the Unchained Books : Copyright as an Infringement on the Philosophy of the Library Science", DESIDOC Bulletin of Information Technology 16.6(1996):5-10
2. Aitufe, Thomas A."Preception of Copyright law decree and reprography in Nigerian Academic libraries", International Library Movement(1996):137-157
3. Aluri, Rao."Electronic Publishing : The Unfolding Revolution", DESIDOC Bulletin of Information Technology 16.1(1996):9-16
4. Hickey, Thomas B."The Impact of Electronic publishing on Academic Libraries", DESIDOC Bulletin of Information Technology 16.1(1996):9-16
5. Malavya, V C.Electronic libraries. New Delhi:Ess Ess publications, 1999
6. Nishat Fatima."Redefining copyright in an electronic era", Organisation of libraries and Information centres in 21st centrurty.Ed.M Bavakutty et al.New Delhi:EssEss Publications,2002,78-83
7. Sambasivan, K.Investigating Library resources.New Delhi: Ess Ess publications,2000
8. Sobhana Devi, A K and Al-Assankutty, C K."Copyright law : The Question of Ownership, Infringement and Fair use in a Digital environment". Organisation of libraries and Information centres in 21st centrurty.Ed.M Bavakutty et al.New Delhi:EssEss Publications,2002,61-73
9. Watal, Jayasree. Itellectual Property Rights in the WTO and Developing countries.New Delhi:Oxford University Press,2001
10. http://www.jisc.ac.uk.pub/copyright/intro.com
11. http://www.ifla.org/utsystem.edu/ogc/ip/1-schpub.htm
12. http://www.mvc.ac.uk/SIMA/WWW/legal.html
13. http://www.iyu.fi/library/yleista/henkilokunnan kotisivut/alhpuho.html
14. http://www.jisc.ac.uk/pub/copyright/start.htm
15. http://www.emory.edu/WHSCL/elec.p.html
16. http://www.press.umich.edu/jep/works/strong.copyright.html
17. http://www.firstmonday.dk/issues/issues2-11/zamparelli/index.html

24

Impact of E-Journals on User Community

P. Mounissamy,
Library Assistant,
Regional Engineering College,
Thiruchirappalli.

R. Gunalan,
Graduate Apprentice,
Regional Engineering College,
Thiruchirappalli.

ABSTRACT

Electronic and online journals have helped publishers and scholars to disseminate information much more quickly than was previous possible. The emergence of electronic and online journals and their attributes are explained. Impact of online and e-journals on users of academic community are discussed. Attempts are also made to explain various types of ongoing projects on e-journals.

INTRODUCTION

Publications of the network society are appearing with mixed digital media and increasingly in a completely electronic format and type have created new products and market places. Electronic publishing has led to a new era of communication and information sharing. Today a new electronic environment is challenging the scientific and technical publications. Electronic publications have helped publishers and scholars to disseminate information much more than ever. Emergence of electronic publications followed the widespread adoption and use of electronic mail, list serves and discussion groups to disseminate information quickly to large audiences.

ELECTRONIC JOURNALS

The term 'Electronic journal' is ambiguous, and it is not always clear whether the producers of a given title are referring to a distribution format for a print journal, an electronic archive of a print journal, or a journal published exclusively in an electronic format. Electronic journals come in a variety of styles and formats, much like their print counterparts. Early electronic journals were primitive with unattractive layouts and were difficult to read and down load.

Duranceau et al. (1996) describe early and contemporary version of electronic journals as 'first-generation' and 'second-generation' electronic journals. Each generation shares a set of common characteristics.

First-generation electronic journals often are:

- ASCII-text files
- Simply file structure (one file equals one article)
- Published by individuals or groups of scholars
- Disseminated by e-mail, and the complied audience is the individual subscriber.
- Copyright restrictions are usually waived to the extent that proper attribution is made.

Second-generation electronic journals are often:

- HTML-based or use the Web to disseminate.
- Include Graphics, multimedia or links to other Internet resource.
- File structures are less hierarchal and less uniformity in structurer.
- Users are notified by e-mail to retrieve from the server.

Franks (1993) describes electronic journals as database model and the software mode. Under the database model, articles reside in centralized database maintained by the publisher. The Service is similar to Lexis/Nexis and dialog and subscribers are given permission to access the data base and use search software on the central computer to locate and download articles. With the software on the model, subscriber gets a piece of software which runs on an Internet connected computer and connects to the database of the journal's central computer. But Electronic journals provide following archiving options:

- Networked-based journals may be acquired from the publisher as offline products, such as fiche or floppy disks.
- Publishers of electronic journals maintain archives of back files at network sites.
- Libraries provide access to back issues through Web pages and gopher sites.

Archiving is also being provided by groups like the CIC-EJC which was statea in 1992 as an archival project of the Committee on Institutional Cooperation (CIC), an academic consortium of 13 major research libraries.

ELECTRONIC JOURNALS AVAILABLE THROUGH INTERNET APPLICATION

Electronic journals have undergone a dramatic transformation in style and format since their initial appearance in the early 1990. Many now have full-color Web pages with an attractive and easy to use layout. Electronic journals available through Internet application are described as the 'classic electronic journals'. E.g. LIBRES, Mc-journal, PACS Review, and The Online Tree etc.,

The first three are now available on the Web and the announcements of new issues are distributed by e-mail or to list serves. The Online Tree was is now ceased publication. LIBRES, Mc-journal, and PACS Review are first generation electronic journal, and PACS Review are first generation electronic journals which have evolved into second generation electronic journals. Subscriptions and access to this category of electronic journal are free. Some other web site are given below

http://www.biomedcentral.com,

http://www.math-net.de/links,

http://www.icaap.org,

http://www.library.msu.ac.th/arec/e-journals/nid.html,

http://www.info.lib.uh.edu/wj/webjour.html

http://www.freemedicaljournals.com,

http://www.pscw.nva.nl/sociosite/journals.html/

http://www.uvm.edu/~bmaclenn,

http://www.hesinki.fi/WebEc/journals.html/

http://www.allacademic.co

http://www.clas.ufl.edu/users/gthusby/psi/journals.html

COMPARISON WITH PRINT JOURNALS

Evidence of the stability of electronic journals is reflected by the fact that many are now indexed in standard print sources such as Library Literature and Library and Information Science Abstracts (LISA). Although it may seem like an anomaly that an online publication is indexed in a print publication, it reflects the growing acceptance of electronic journals by the library profession and users as the provide

- searchable text
- hypertext links to other resources

- use of color graphics, photographs, video and audio
- the ability to provide unedited prepublication advance copies of articles

IMPACT OF E-JOURNALS

1. It is clear that the new online medium is not being exploited since many online journals are simply electronic editions of paper journals.
2. Production of an issue of a journal is accomplished much quickly since communications between the editorial board, reviews of submissions, and exchange if information can proceed much more quickly than through the channels typically used for print journals.
3. Personal computer and the Internet are advantages in electronic publishing with a personal computer and the Internet, it is now possible for even one person to take full responsibility for the output of a document up to, and production of the final copy. Although electronic journals can be produced more quickly than their print counterparts, the editorial work to support a journal published exclusively online can be substantial while the time lag for may processes associated with print publication has been removed, a good deal of time may be spent attracting potential contributors and readers reviewing and refereeing articles, producing and distributing issues and maintaining an online archive.
4. Electronic journals can reach a wide audience quickly, information can be distributed almost as soon as it is made available, and is stored once it is entered online.
5. Electronic journals are user friendly and more functional than a print journal, and copies of article from an electronic journal should be comparable in quality to a photocopy made from a print journal.

CONSISTENCY WITH PRINT VERSION

Electronic version of a journal can differ substantially from its print counterpart, for example, an electronic publication may omit articles, illustrations, or reviews found in print. Conversely, the electronic version may have more current content or contain content not found in its print counterpart. If an electronic publication has a print counterpart, the selector should compare the versions to determine whether they are consistent. Online access should include the complete articles, chapters or essays, with accompanying graphics, tables, references, and text plus an official citation. In practice the competition among publisher is forcing them to include full image and thereby eliminate the problems faced by the libraries in this regard.

CURRENCY

How quickly the most recent issue of an electronic journal becomes available in comparison with its print counterpart or vice-a versa. E-journals would be a viable product for academic use as an added functionality over print versions. This functionality may be as varied as inclusion of multi-media information, full text searching, markup citation formatting, reference linking, convenience, portability, interpretability on a variety of devices, viability in advance of print, sharing information.

CONCLUSION

Internet publishers are providing this service in all disciplines. However Elsevier science cover the area of Chemistry and Chemical Engineering, clinical Medicine, computer Science, Earth and Planetary Science, Economics, Business and Management Science, Engineering, energy and Technology, life Science, Material Science, Mathematics, Physics and Astronomy and Social Science. Chemweb, Emerald insight.com provide free access t full text journals, for a limited time and also offer free trail. The researchers find articles of their interest, can use other service like bibliographic, abstracting, full-length article delivery services. E-journal technology has a long way to go before it can equal the readability and richness of traditional journals. E-journals have enormous impact over users community, which is changing the searching and reading style of the users community. This has resulted advancement in research and developmental activities too.

REFERENCES

1. http://www.press.umich.edu/jep/06-02/sweeney.html
2. http://www.press.umich.edu/jep/04-02/steingerger.html
3. http://www.library.ucsb.edu/ist1/00-summer/refered.html
4. http://www.chemweb.com
5. http://www.emeraldinsight.com
6. Natarajan.M,(2001),User's Attitude towards E-journals, NACLIN 2001, 56-68.

25

Exchange of Electronic Catalogue Records of Composite Multimedia Works on CD.

Prof. A. Neelameghan,
Hon. Visiting Professor,
DRTC, ISI, 8th Mile,
Mysore Road,
Bangalore.

Dr. K. S. Raghavan,
Professor and Head,
Department of Library and Information Science,
Madras University,
Chepauk Building,
Chennai.

ABSTRACT

Exchange of databases of library catalogues of electronic / digital resources pose challenges. This paper discusses in particular exchange of digital catalogue records for composite multimedia works on compact disc (CD). Discusses with examples format conversions between catalogue entries for multimedia CD resources prepared according to (ISBD (ER)) and AACR2, 1998 rev., CCF (B), and MARC21. The generation of records in XML and HTML formats is also demonstrated.

INTRODUCTION

Abbreviations Used

ISBD(ER) = International Standard Bibliographical Description (Electronic Resources) [3]

AACR = Anglo American Cataloging Rules [2]

CCF(B) = Common Communication Format (Bibliographical Record)

MARC = Machine Readable Catalogue

Libraries and other information institutions have, for some time now, been providing access to digital resources in addition to the more conventional documentary materials. The digital resources could be in the form of CDs, increasingly being acquired by libraries. These may be in lieu of or in addition to the corresponding print versions, for instance, secondary sources including large databases or in the less tangible form of subscription and / or access to online resources including Web resources located on remote servers. Some of these resources hold traditional information sources (text, film, map, sound recording, etc.) in different formats (e.g. in gif, tif, wav, pdf, doc, and txt.). However, digital resources are not limited to presenting in an alternative format their more conventional counterparts. For instance, a record or a file in a CD can be linked to related digital resources on a remote server.

The issue of providing effective access to digital information resources is complicated by a variety of factors. These factors and the cataloguing of multimedia CD are discussed in a recent paper by the authors [1]. More specifically we discussed with examples, based on our experience, the applicability and adequacy of the rules and prescriptions of ISBD(ER) and AACR2 revision 1998 for cataloging of multimedia resources on CD, given the fact that the record medium, the physical form and format influence the effectiveness of accessing, retrieval and use of the information content of electronic resources.

DEFINITION

General

According to IFLA ISBD (ER): "Electronic resources consist of materials that are computer-controlled, including materials that require the use of a peripheral (e.g. a CD-ROM player) attached to a computer; the items may or may not be used in the interactive mode. Included are two types of resources: data (information in the form of numbers, letters, graphics, images, and sound, or a combination thereof) and programs (instructions or routines for performing certain tasks including the processing of data). In addition, they may be combined to include electronic data and programs (e.g. online services, interactive multimedia)".

A digital work may exist in two or more digitized forms. The whole or a part of a digital work may exist in a hard copy or printed version as well as in two or more digital forms

Composite Work

A work with two or more contributions, each with its own title, not forming a continuous exposition and often, though not necessarily, by different authors.

Ordinary Composite Work

Composite work provided with a single, generic or collective title to denote all the contributions collectively (Ranganathan [4]; AACR2, 1998 rev.)

Artificial Composite Work

Composite work without a generic title to denote all the contributions collectively.

Associated or Related Work

A Work X is deemed to be associated with another Work Y if work X is helpful in the use or understanding of Work Y. Work X may be an accompaniment to Work Y or Work X and Work Y may be linked to each other (e.g. hypertext link) or may be so indicated in the catalogue entry of Work X and/or Work Y (e.g. Note section). IFLA's UNIMARC format specifies three basic kinds of relations:

* *Horizontal relation*: Relation between two resources representing different versions of a resource: for example, the English and French versions of a resource;
* *Vertical relation:* Relation between a 'whole' and its parts; and
* *Chronological Relation:* Relation between a resource and its earlier/later versions

CATALOGUING OF DIGITAL MATERIALS: SOME ISSUES

For print and materials of similar format libraries have developed effective tools and techniques to support and carry out resource discovery, description, and delivery. Although a great deal of valuable information is available through the Internet, on CD and such other media, the digital world is relatively less stable, less well organized and lacks standards.

Integrating information about non-digital resources with that about digital resources available in a library and obtained through exchange or downloading via networks will ensure access to all forms of information resources.

Library catalogue records give descriptive information to help user identify and judge whether the works selected meet his or her need.

Multimedia resources on CD, for instance, though there are similarities to their printed versions, also present several differences, which need to be taken into account in cataloguing them.

Several rules for cataloging, formulated over 150 years ago, are applicable and can be the basis for designing or formulating efficient and effective means of organizing and providing access to digital resources. But these rules, codes, and standards developed need extension and rephrasing to cover the newer media.

Those who develop digital products (e.g. CD) do contribute value addition in terms of accessibility, retrieval facility and use of the embodied ideas. Thus, for instance, we can recognize two levels of Responsibility in the development of a CD resource: 1. The responsibility for creating the ideas embodied; and 2. the responsibility for creating the CD product adding value to the accessibility, retrieval, and use of the content of the CD.'

The value of the catalogue record will be enhanced by indicating therein the value additions made to the work(s) / items). Three types of value-additions to the work are:

Value Addition to the Work

* Means for better understanding the work, such as, illustrations, online glossary, etc.
* Translations and transliteration of the whole or portion of the work, addressed to multilingual audience.
* Commentaries, views, notes, evaluations, and analytical studies
* Links to descriptions of associated entities
* Text with image
* Text with audio
* Text with image and audio
* Image and audio
* Animation
* Combination of two or more of the above.

Facilitating Use of the Item

* Hypertext linking among the components within the item.
* Hypertext linking of some or all of the works in an item to other digital resources, for instance, a website.
* Organization and presentation.
* Providing indexes.
* Providing for user-interface mechanism, including voice querying.

* Special facilities for the physically challenged to use the system.
* Facility to print portions or whole of the work.

Facilitating Evaluation of the Product and Works

In addition to the 'Commentaries, Views, Analytical studies' mentioned under 4.1 information on the bodies or individuals who have in various ways contributed to the preparation of the work and/or the preparation of the product (e.g. CD) may be found in the acknowledgement or credit section of the product. Such information may be helpful to users in evaluating the work or the product or both. It is, therefore, useful to select and record the names of such contributors and their respective contributions in the bibliographic record (e.g. Note area). Of course, this is optional.

EXCHANGE OF CATALOGUE ENTRIES

Three factors need to be considered with respect to the exchange of databases of electronic resources:

1. The use of a set of widely accepted cataloguing rules considered adequate for the description of electronic resources. For example: ISBD(ER), MARC, CCF/B, AACR2 Re. 1998;
2. A set of fields and tags.
3. To use a methodology / program / software adequate for inter-conversion among the formats.

In our earlier paper [1] it was shown, with examples, that ISBD(ER) and AACR2 rev. 1998 do provide an adequate set of descriptive elements for cataloguing composite multimedia works on CD. These areas of description are:

- Title and statement of responsibility area
- Edition area
- Type and extent of resource area
- Publication, distribution, etc. area
- Physical description area

- Series area
- Note area
- Summary area
- Standard number (or alternative) and terms of availability area.

Obviously these areas of description relate to the attributes of both the work and its carrier. The question is whether these areas and the associated data elements (attributes) are detailed and flexible enough to accommodate digital resources. For example, the traditional focus on publication may not always be applicable to a digital resource. Further, the physical representation of the same digital resource may vary from one location to another (e.g. one site making available a resource in text format and another as a PDF file). New data elements may be required for encoding the location of the resource. The existing codes of cataloging and bibliographic record formats are rather description-oriented without giving much attention to access This may be because they have evolved in the context of cataloging resources that are physically located in a library or an institution. It is clear that while descriptive information is necessary, access information (information to logon, electronic addresses, etc.) is equally crucial. Data specifying the facilities required to use a digital resource (the system and software requirement to view a data file, or play an audio / video file) is an important element in the description of a digital resource, such as an optical disk (CD) recording. These questions have been discussed in our earlier paper [1].

Guidelines are given in ISBD (ER) and AACR2 rev. 1998 as to what type of information is to be given in each of these areas.

Therefore, we have used these areas as fields in the catalogue database for works in multimedia CD.

Corresponding Tags from the Common Communication Format (CCF/B) have been assigned to the fields.

The databases have been developed using Unesco's CDS/ISIS for Windows (WINISIS 1.4 Build 19, January 2001). The software provides facility for format conversion and database exchange, hypertext linking, and for generating entries in XML and HTML formats

THE DATABASES

CATCD Database

Database CATCD has, as fields, the nine description areas mentioned above. ISBD(ER) does not prescribe tags. In CATCD database the corresponding field tag of CCF(B) are used. Given below is the Field Definition Table of CATCD (CATCD.FDT).

Tag	Name	Type	Rep	Pattern/Subfield
60	Type / Extent of resource area	Alphanumeric	-	abcdefg
100	Standard no./Availability area	Alphanumeric	R	abcd
200	Title / Responsibility area	Alphanumeric	-	Abcd
260	Edition area	Alphanumeric		abcdefgh
460	Physical description area	Alphanumeric	-	abcdef
480	Series area	Alphanumeric	R	abcdef
500	Note area	Alphanumeric	R	abcdefgh
600	Content description/Summary	Alphanumeric	R	abcdefgh
620	Access points area	Alphanumeric	R	

The Fields and Tags of the MARC21.FDT given below more or less conforms to the MARC format actually used in a library:

7	Physical medium	Alphanumeric	-	a
20	ISBN	Alphanumeric	R	a
41	Language	Alphanumeric	R	a
82	Call number	Alphanumeric		ab
100	Personal name	Alphanumeric	R	a
110	Corporate name	Alphanumeric	R	abcd
111	Conference	Alphanumeric		acdn
245	Title	Alphanumeric		abc
250	Edition	Alphanumeric		a
260	Imprint	Alphanumeric	R	
300	Collation	Alphanumeric		abcd

440	Series	Alphanumeric	R	abc
500	Note	Alphanumeric	R	a
650	Subject descriptors	Alphanumeric	R	a
653	Keywords	Alphanumeric	R	a
655	Abstract	Alphanumeric	R	a

Comparison of CCF(B) and MARC21 fields and tags as per ISBD(ER) description areas applied to multimedia CD works given in the following table:

Fields/Description areas as per ISBD (ER), AACR2 rev. 1998.	**Tag**	**Rep**	**Sf**	**MARC21**	**Rep**	**Sf**
Title/Responsibility area	200		abcdef	245		abc
Edition area	260		abcdefg	250		a
Type/Extent of resource area	60		abcdefg	260	7	a
Publication, distribution etc. area	400	R	abcdefgh	300	R	a
Physical description area	460		abcdef	440		abc
Series area	480	R	abcdef	500	R	abc
Note area	500	R	abcdefgh	655	R	a
Content/Summary area	600	R	abcdefgh	20	R	a
Standard number (or alternative)	100	R	abcd	650	R	a
Access points area	620	R		653	R	a

Rep = Repeatable. Sf – Sub-field

EXAMPLES

Descriptions of three multimedia CDs have been entered in MARC21 database initially and then downloaded into CATCD database after format conversion.

For converting the records entered in the MARC21 database to CATCD format the following Field Select Table is adequate:

ID	IT	Data extraction format
60	0	v7
100	0	v20
200	0	v245
200	0	(v100/), (v110/), (v111/)
260	0	v250
400	0	v260
460	0	v300
480	0	v440
500	0	v500
600	0	(v655/)
620	0	(v650/), (v653/)

Brief descriptions and record output for the three CDs are given in Appendix.

XML AND HTML FORMATS

Record 1 (Tyagaraja) in XML and HTML formats have been generated. They are not, however, reproduced here because of the large size of the files.

CONCLUSION

It may be noted that for generating index in the ISBD(ER) format, the terms are collected in the Access Points Area. These may be entered in the Subject Descriptors and Keywords fields in other formats. In the ISBD(ER) there appears to be no separate field for Author, etc. but these names are entered in the Title / Responsibility area., whereas there are separate fields for authorship in MARC. However with a software such as WINISIS, any word or part of a word or a whole phrase or line in any of the fields can be indexed. Also, any desired print / display format can be generated. Different predefined formats can be called as desired.

REFERENCES

1. Composite multimedia works on CD: catalogue entry according to ISBD(ER) *and AACR2 revision 1998* / By K.S.Raghavan and A.Neelameghan

Cataloguing and Classification Quarterly, 2002 (in press)

2. *Anglo-American cataloguing rules* / Prepared under the direction of the Joint Steering Committee for Revision of AACR. 2nd ed., 1998 revision, Chicago: American Library Association, 1998.
3. *ISBD(ER): International standard bibliographic description for electronic resources.* http://www.ifla.org/VII/s13/pubs/isbd4.htm
4. *Classified catalogue code with additional rules for dictionary catalogue* / By S.R. Ranganathan; assisted by A. Neelameghan.- 5th ed..-Bombay: Asia Publishing House, 1964.

ANNEXURE 1

Catalogue Entries with Headings according to ISBD (ER) and AACR2 1998 rev. *(Does not attempt at exhaustive description and also in the enumeration of Access Points)*.

Example 1: Tyagaraja CD

Example 1 is a multimedia CD on the musical compositions and life of Saint Thyagaraja The product includes the music, meanings, commentaries, and text of 108 selected devotional *Kritis* (a form of composition in Carnatic Music) of Saint Thyagaraja. *Kritis* included represent different themes, art models, ragas, talas, etc., used by the Saint. Integrates the music, meanings, summaries, and text of the *Kritis* with special commentaries and images. The *Kritis* have been sung specially for the product by commissioned vocalists. Thirty-five *Kritis* have been rendered on the veena, violin, and flute. The database of *Kritis* can be browsed record by record and is searchable by several keys. The index to the *Kritis* can be sorted by title, raga, and tala. An index to deities featured in the *Kritis* is provided for searching. Index to the lyrical content, that is, words or phrases in Telugu in each of the 108 *Kritis* with their meanings in English. Text of the *Kritis* can be displayed in Telugu, Tamil, Devanagari, and Roman scripts. Index to common errors in rendering lyrical content with suggested correct rendering of such words or phrases. Specially commissioned articles in HTML format providing also links to other web-based resources on Carnatic music and Thyagaraja. Slide show on quantitative analysis of Thyagaraja compositions. Provision for continuous play of vocal and instrumental renderings.

The corresponding catalogue description with headings in given below.

TYGARAJA CD

Title/Responsibility area (200): Saint Tyagaraja, a multimedia presentation; a unique portrayal of 108 krithis of Tyagaraja. Electronic resource / Developed by B.R.C. Iyengar, T.N. Rajan, L.J. Haravu.

Type & extent of resource area(60): Electronic optical disc, Electronic text data, Electronic image data, Electronic sound, Electronic numeric data.

Publication/distribution area (400): Secunderabad, India, L.J.Haravu, cop.2001.

Physical description area (460): 1, Electronic optical disc (CD-ROM): sd., col.:, 12 cm., 1. User manual.

Note area (500): Music, music recording, special commentaries, and other music related matters: B.R.C. Iyengar. Database content, life and works of Tyagaraja, and specially commissioned articles: T.N.Rajan. User interface, software development: L.J. Haravu.,

System requirements: PC with a CPU of at least 166 Mhz, 32 MB RAM; Windows-95 or higher. Windows-NT; Sound card with speakers; at least 25 MB hard disc space; SVGA colour monitor; CD drive.

Content description / Summary (600): Features of the product: 108 selected Kritis (a form of composition in Carnatic Music) representing different themes, art models, ragas, talas, etc. used by Saint Tyagaraja. Integrates music, meanings, summaries, and text of the kritis (in Telugu, Devanagari, Tamil and Roman script) with special commentaries and images. The kritis have been sung by well known vocalists. 35 of the kritis rendered in veena, violin and flute. Database of kritis can be browsed record by record and also searchable by several keys (e.g. title, raga, theme, tala, name of deity). Facility for printed outputs provided. Specially commissioned articles on Tyagaraja and Carnatic music. Glossary of specialized terms. Slide show on Tyagaraja's life and works. Quantitative analytical data on Tyagaraja's compositions. Continuous play of vocal and instrumental renderings possible.

Access points area (620) : Tyagaraja, Saint; Thyagaraja, Saint; Iyengar, B.R.C,, dev.; Rajan, T.N., dev.; Haravu, L.J., dev.; Music; Carnatic music; Classical music; Devotional music; Deities; Hindu deities; Carnatic music - Learning aid.

Example 2: Swami Vivekananda CD

Example 2 is a multimedia CD on the Life, Works and Research about Swami Vivekananda. It consists of nine components, each of which can be opened by clicking on the respective icon: *Introduction* (in the opening screen); *Works*; *Life*, *Works & Thinkers* / edited by Swami Lokeswarananda; *Call to Humanity; Gallery, For Children; Quiz; Benediction; About Us; Centres.* Of these the last two are sort of associated files. Each screen offers options for moving forward and backward, up and down, return to main screen and to exit. Additionally, there are options (icons) for search using the index, link to a Glossary, and for play audio, if applicable, and printing. Selected terms from the text are hyperlinked to the glossary. Display of the transliteration into English of Sanskrit text is provided for. Display of the contents of volumes and facility to click on any of the content heading to display the related page(s) from any of the volumes is possible. For the Introduction, gallery of pictures, and life of Swami Vivekananda there is also voice narration in addition to the text and pictures. Soft background Indian classical devotional instrumental music is played while opening, using, and closing the CD.

The corresponding catalogue description with headings is given below:

SWAMI VIVEKANANDA CD

Title/Responsibility area (200): Swami Vivekananda, life, works & research, Electronic resource / Advaita Ashrama, Kolkata. (Calcutta), India.

Type & extent of resource area(60): Electronic optical disc, Electronic text data, Electronic image data, Electronic sound, Electronic numeric data.

Publication/distribution area (400): Kolkata, India, Advaita Ashrama, 2001.

Physical description area (460): 1, Electronic optical disc (CD-ROM): sd., col.:, 12 cm.

Note area (500):

System requirements: PC with a CPU of at least 100 Mhz, 32 MB.; RAM; Windows-95 or higher / Windows-NT; Sound card with speakers; at least 25 MB hard disc space; SVGA colour monitor; CD drive.

Content description / Summary (600): Features of the product: Nine volumes of 'The Complete Works of Swami Vivekananda;' two volumes of the 'Life of Swami Vivekananda by His Eastern and Western Disciples;' six volumes of the research work by Marie Louise Burke, namely. 'Swami Vivekananda in the West: New Discoveries;' Story of Swami Vivekananda for Children; world thinkers on Swami Vivekananda / ed. by Swami Lokeswarananda. A photo gallery of some 300 photographs of Swami Vivekananda and of people and places connected with him. Selected classified quotations from the works and speeches of Swami Vivekananda. Quiz on Swami Vivekananda. A benedictory address (text and audio) by Swami Ranganathananda, thirteenth President of the Ramakrishna Order. A glossary of about 600 terms hyperlinked in the Collected Works. Word search facility for the whole section with an additional index search facility for the Complete Works. Each screen offers options for moving forward and backward, up and down, return to main screen and to exit. Additionally there are options (icons) for search using the index, link to the Glossary, and for audio and printing.

Display of the transliteration into English of the Sanskrit text is provided for. Display of the contents of volumes and facility to click on any of the content heading to display the related page(s)from any of the volumes is possible. For the Introduction, Gallery of Pictures, and Life of Swami Vivekananda there is voice narration in addition to the text and pictures.

Soft background Indian classical, devotional instrumental music is played while opening, using, and closing the CD.

Associated files include brief information about the Advaita Ashrama and the centres of the Ramakrishna Order worldwide.

Standard number / Availability (100): Price: Rs. 700 + postage within India. US$20+US$15 for postage outside India.

Access points area (620): Vivekananda, Swami; Vivekananda, Swami – Biography; Vivekananda, Swami – Quotations; Vivekananda, Swami for children; Vivekananda, Swami - Quiz; Advaita Ashrama, Kolkata.

Example 3: S.R. Ranganathan CD

Example 3 is a multimedia CD containing several types of information in various formats relating to the life and works of Dr. S.R. Ranganathan (SRR) who has contributed significantly to formulating normative principles and theory of library science and service in general and information organization, subject classification and indexing in particular.

The product (Release 1.0) prepared by the Sarada Ranganathan Endowment for Library Science with financial support from the National Information System for Science and Technology (NISSAT) of the Department of Scientific and Industrial Research (DSIR), Government of India, includes: selected extracts from SRR's correspondence, (over 500 letters out of about 3800), compiled and edited by S. Parthasarathy and A. Neelameghan; bibliography of works by and on SRR (about 4,000); Memorabilia, that is, quotations from SRR's writings (c. 420); full text of five select papers on classification and subject heading; life-sketch; picture gallery (c. 30) of persons, institutions and events associated with SRR; video prepared during the birth centenary celebrations (1992) of SRR – appreciative speeches by close associates of SRR with their pictures and of institutions associated with him.

The corresponding catalogue description with headings in given below:

S.R. RANGANATHAN CD

Title/Responsibility area (200): Dr. S.R. Ranganathan: life and works. Electronic resource / Sarada Ranganathan Endowment for Library Science, Bangalore, India.

Type & extent of resource area (60): Electronic text data (10 files), Electronic image data (24 files), Electronic video file (1 file) Edition area (260): Release 1.0

Publication/distribution area (400): New Delhi, India, National Information System for Science and Technology, Department of Scientific and Industrial Research, New Delhi, India, 2002; Bangalore, India, Sarada Ranganathan Endowment for Library Science, Bangalore, 2002.

Physical description area (460): 1, Electronic optical disc (CD-ROM): sd., col.

Note area (500): User manual, System requirements: PC with a CPU of at least 100 Mhz, 32 MB RAM; Windows-95 or higher / Windows-NT; Sound card With speakers; at least 25 MB hard disc space; SVGA colour monitor; CD drive.

Content description / Summary (600): Databases of: Extracts of letters of and to Dr. S.R. Ranganathan; bibliography of works by and on Ranganathan; quotations from the writings of Ranganathan (Memorabilia); life sketch; selected writing of Ranganathan on classification and subject indexing; pictures of persons, places and events associated with Ranganathan; video (30 min) prepared by Randor Guy on the occasion of Ranganathan's birth centenary (1992).

Access points area (620): Ranganathan, Shiyali Ramamrita; Sarada Ranganathan Endowment for Library Science; National Information System for Science and Technology; NISSAT; Guy, Randor; Randor Guy; Library science; Information science; Information service; Documentation; Library service; Classification.

26

Electronic Publications and the Librarian

Jyoti Misra,
Assistant Librarian,
Tagore Library, Lucknow University,
Lucknow.

Prof. N.R. Satyanarayana,
Dept of Library and Information Science,
Lucknow University,
Lucknow.

ABSTRACT

The ever-changing scenario of information technology and its increasing influence in library and information centers are imposing tremendous stress for librarians. In the present technological age, libraries and information centers have started acquiring and maintaining new forms of information resources such as: CD ROMs, electronic journals, on-line databases, e-documents etc. along with printed forms. The very nature of these electronic publications put forward problems to librarians for their identification, selection, organization and retrieval. The present paper identifies and discusses some of the problems associated with these types of information sources. It concludes that librarians and information managers are now required to build their collection and organize information services accordingly in the new technological age for their survival.

INTRODUCTION

Electronic publishing has become a major topic in the world literature in recent years, particularly because of the developments in information technologies. Electronic publications are those publications that are in electronic or digital forms[1]. These electronic and on-line publications are making a forceful entry into the libraries, especially the academic and more affluent R & D institutions are slowly and steadily migrating towards the electronic publications including CD-ROM databases, electronic and on-line journals and e-documents. The very nature of these electronic publications put forward problems to librarians for their identification, selection, organization and retrieval. The present paper identifies and discusses some of the problems associated with these types of information sources.

PROBLEMS POSED BY ELECTRONIC PUBLICATIONS

The very nature of electronic publication poses difficulties for their selection, organization and retrieval. The organization of CDs is troublesome. If we remove the CDs that come along with the books from books and organize them separately on racks, librarian shall face problems in charging and discharging a book and face problems in selecting the right CD of the book which is being charged. On the other hand, if we keep the CD in the book itself, chances for its missing or damages are very high. It is an issue the librarians have to tackle in the near future.

Apart from this, there are some more issues that arise at the identification, selection and acquisition stages relate to the nature of electronic resources.

ACQUISITION

Identifying potential electronic resources for building collection often requires different processes and pathways than those established for print materials. These processes are complicated as electronic resources often come in several different packages. And indicating just what is in each package is not a completely straightforward process. Acquiring electronic resources poses yet another kind of challenge since one is not sure whether to buy them or get them on rent. E-documents differ from printed materials in the ways they arrive at the library as they tend to come through wires and cables rather than in boxes. A further consideration is that e-documents, in nearly all media, are not like printed things in that they refuse to stay in a fixed, permanent arrangement. Imagine the consequences of these differences[2].

Periodicals in printed form are usually selected basing on certain procedures such as asking for a sample issue, evaluation, reviews, etc. before they are actually acquired[3]. In electronic environment, there is a certain amount of 'try before you buy' in the form of trial subscriptions and access to a demonstration version of the resource, but the form of the resources tested may depend on the computer equipment available to the selector. It may differ substantially from the version that would be acquired[4]. Therefore, identification, evaluation, selection and organizing are the main issues to be addressed before resorting to subscription of e-journals and for the selection of e-documents.

ACCESSIBILITY

Another concern is the decision regarding the format and type of journals to be subscribed, i.e., whether to continue the print version or subscribe to electronic version only or both[5]. Accessibility as availability for use is one consideration. Typically, this question does not arise in the world of printed documents. An item, once catalogued and shelved, remains available and accessible for all those who can use the catalogue. Sharing resources through inter library borrowing is an established service in libraries, so the potential user need not to be a member of the library's user community to access the books or journals. With electronic documents, all these certainties disappear. Availability may be restricted to those of the immediate library user community. There may arise major restrictions on making the resource available to those who are not affiliated to the library. Another dimension of accessibility is how the electronic resources may be accessed. Access may depend on factors such as the library's technological infrastructure. It may need to be considered when deciding whether to acquire an electronic resource or not. With electronic resources, one is simultaneously expanding and contracting the user base, i.e., by expanding the number of users who can use a resource from home or office on one hand, but contracting by including only those members of the primary user community on the other hand.

In some cases, the quality of information in the resource may be of known value but for some it may be completely untested. Sometimes similar information is available through a different source with a different interface. Therefore, the question arises how does one weigh the relative merits of content and presentation of these documents. Librarians and information managers have had to answer these questions concerning accessibility in all its dimensions[6].

OWNERSHIP

If all the identification and selection issues had been resolved, then there is still a multitude of acquisition factors. First is the nature of acquisition, which commonly is understood as buying and owning. Nearly all the printed volumes survive in the hands of users or on the shelves until withdrawn or until doomsday. By contrast, electronic resources cannot be described in terms of ownership but frequently described in terms of access and use. One acquires rights or licenses to access to electronic resources[7]. As back-files are maintained on networks, libraries have to pay extra charges for accessing back volumes (subscribed earlier) after the expiry or cancellation of subscription by way of access fee, password fee or renewal fee. This is not the case with printed journals. It means that, even after paying subscription charges to electronic (on-line) journals and documents, the library may not possess (own) them; they merely provide access to information contained in them even during the subscription period[8].

PERMANENCY

While discussing any electronic resource, its fluid nature

makes it difficult to say what it is being described. CD-ROMs even though seems permanent in format vary when they are replaced with an updated disc or have an upgraded interface. This creates some thorny issues when one imagines cataloguing these resources[9].

PROCESSING

Electronic data differ from printed materials in the ways they arrive at the library as well, since electrons have only a negligible physical presence. They tend to arrive through an electronic 'pipe' with a computer for a faucet. When they are not being used, they exist in a state of potential, rather than reality. The reality that exists for any user will very likely differ in appearance and capabilities depending on the size of the pipe and the type of faucet being used to access the resource. There may be an all text option, or a low graphics version of a resource. The version one finds on the World Wide Web may differ in substantive as well as graphical ways from the version reached through Telnet. In creating a permanent record for these resources the cataloguer cannot reflect the variations in any way. Can he catalogue the documents as presented through the computer screen available at the cataloguer's workstation, or does the cataloguer travel from version to version to discover the common elements. If the resource has different names in its different incarnations how is that to be reflected in the records. To put it another way, one may not know a book by its cover, but at least it has one. Then what is the equivalent of an electronic resource's cover? Another question is what kind of record is being created for the electronic resource, and its corollary, where will the record reside? Devising unambiguous, durable, robust, and accurate locating schedules for these resources is another challenge[10].

READABILITY

Even computers with the best resolution cannot match the print equivalent for reading. Furthermore, conventional publications allow continuous, uninterrupted reading. Computers cannot hold a full page at a time and need scrolling of screen every few minutes for browsing which may detract the attention of the readers. The quality of figures in the computer printed output even using laser printers, cannot match that of print publications because of resolution. This is in addition to the lack of pagination, ease of usage, and the transportability of publication for a leisurely reading at a convenient place and time still make the printed journal preferable over the electronic journal.

STANDARDIZATION

At present the e-journals are available in various forms, formats and through different access points. This is a problem for the reader for accessing. Some of the e-journals do not include page numbers as the size of the page in different computers(VDUs) is different. This raises citation problems when the same material to be cited can appear in different pages. The hardware and software also need to be standardized to enable the end-user to retrieve information irrespective of the make of the machine and the required retrieval software. At present a user has to get familiarized with a plethora of retrieval software associated with the various CD-ROM databases. A common command information retrieval language which can work with any computer and retrieval software may be useful in such situations.

CONCLUSION

In the present technological age, library's organization may need to be revised to better support the growing number of electronic resources in its collection. If all the records that identify the resources available to the users' community were integrated with the necessary access guides and suggestions for its use, they would provide the user an opportunity to get the maximum utility from each resource. This would make the resources even more cost effective for the library acquiring them.

As on today, where business enterprises are increasing their marketing efforts to sell information directly to users over the WWW and the Internet, libraries that do not meet users' expectations may not thrive or even survive. Redesigning the library's organization is one step in ensuring a dynamic and vital future for librarians, libraries and the users who rely on them. Electronic forms of information in libraries and information centers are making the job of librarian tough as far as their identification, selection, organization and retrieval is concerned. It is the responsibility of librarians to accept the challenge and organize the library accordingly. Though electronic publication involves certain problems due to its very nature, its increasing use in library proves its popularity with users. In ever changing scenario, librarians are required to reorganize their services and collections in an entirely new perspective that should exactly match the interest of users.

REFERENCES

1. Ravichandra Rao, I.K. Sources of information with emphasis on electronic resources. Annual seminar on electronic sources of information. 1-3 March, 2000, DRTC, Bangalore, P. 7.
2. *www.ala.org*
3. Lakshmana Moorthy, A. Electronic publications: issues and concerns. Annual seminar on electronic sources of information. 1-3 March, 2000, DRTC, Bangalore, p.9
4. *www.ala.org.*
5. Lakshmana Moorthy, A. op. cit., p.9
6. *www.ala.org*
7. Ibid.
8. Lakshmana Moorthy, A. op. cit., p.9
9. *www.ala.org.*
10. Ibid

27

Need and Perspectives of Electronic Publishing in the Present Century

Dr. Rabinarayan Mishra,
Workshop Instructor,
P.G. Dept. of Lib. & Inf. Science,
Sambalpur University,
Jyoti Vihar – (ORISSA).

ABSTRACT

The varied tastes of the user communities along with their steady claim, pin-pointed and instant information obligated the Librarians and Information Scientists to transform the dimension of dissemination of information from customary to electronic form so as to persuade the need of the users at any point of time, for which the electronic publishing became a positive modus operandi to unravel the problems of the users. In electronic era, electronic publishing is a decisive constituent to prove the validity and the validity of technological efficacy of information sources in the most appropriate and effectual manner. In the present century, the only option left out for the Libraries and Information Centers to espouse the devices of accumulating the electronic information in various forms and the creation of different databases of their own excluding the databases available in Internet will certainly bring a positive accomplishment of the goal and aspiration of the user communities as the e-publishing is more efficient, cost effectiveness, greater educational collision, better reach, providing customization at the student level, improved student exposure, enhancement of research value. The paper deals with various aspects of electronic publishing.

INTRODUCTION

The Libraries and Information Centers in the rudder of present information technology age no longer reckoned on the traditional shape of meeting the requirements of the users rather, they adopted new technological devices to satisfy the assorted tastes of information requirements of the user community. The recorded form of information in the ditised bits could able to reach the user's personal computer through the trail of information technology. The enlargement of Communication Technology with the landmark development more particularly in Computer Technology could unravel the problems of the libraries and Information Centers.

Increased availability of electronic information has led the libraries, particularly in universities and research organizations and the information centers to maintain intensive interaction with the computer centers. In some places the computer center is the place responsible for electronic information and the library is responsible for print information. In some educational institutions librarians have assumed responsibility for both the library collection and computer services as well. As the technology has altered and allowed ever-new ways of creating, storing, organizing, and providing information, user's expectation of the role of libraries has increased. In the age of advanced technology the Libraries as well as the Information Centers have responded by developing more sophisticated on-line catalogues through Internet, which has allowed the users to find out the required information pertaining to their research with in affordable price.

While the quantum of information issued in the form of printed matter continues unabated, the *electronic publishing* industry has begun to disseminate information in digital form through many electronic storage devices such as CD-ROM, Floppy, and DVD etc, which have been discussed threadbare. The digital *optical* disc is developing as an increasingly popular means of issuing large bodies of archival information—for example, legislation, court and hospital records, encyclopaedias and other reference works, referral databases, and libraries of computer software. Full-text databases, each containing digital page images of the complete text of some 400 periodicals stored on *CD-ROM*, entered the market in 1990. The optical disc provides the mass production technology for publication in machine-readable form. It offers the prospect of having large libraries of information available in virtually every school and at many professional workstations[1].

The coupling of computers and digital *telecommunications* is also changing the modes of information dissemination. high-speed digital satellite communications facilitate electronic printing at remote sites; for example, the world's major newspapers and magazines transmit electronic page copies to different geographic locations for local printing and distribution. Updates of catalogues, computer software, and archival databases are distributed through *electronic* devices, an intensive method of rapidly forwarding and storing bodies of digital information between remote computers.

ELECTRONIC PUBLISHING: THE NOTION

The concept of Electronic Publishing was originally originated in 1960 as the application of computers to primarily the 'front-end' that entailed the use of word processing capabilities and called computerized photocomposition or typesetting. The dimension of electronic publishing (E-publishing) changed more specifically when the dissemination of information started flowing through computers and e-publishing came to encompass all aspects of publishing from initial to final access by the user communities to promote their research and other purpose.

Lancaster[2] has more pertinently revealed the evolution of electronic publishing with the following manifestations:

* Use of computers to generate conventional print-on-paper publications;

* The distribution of text in electronic form, where the electronic version is the exact equivalent of a paper version;
* Distribution in electronic form only, but with the publication being little more than print on paper which are displayed electronically and act as a value added features such as searching through electronically form, data manipulation through profile matching etc., and
* Generation of completely new publications that exploit the true capabilities of electronics i.e, hypertext, hypermedia, electronic analog models, motion sound etc.

With the surfacing of Internet, the WWW (World Wide Web), which is a hypertext, the whole scenario of publishing received a avant-garde change. With this technology, the Libraries, Information Centers including the leading Publishers changed their notion of publishing rather, they adopted the electronic devices to record and publish the document irrespective of types so as to access them by the users though Internet. Before the Internet, three kinds of electronic publications were on record and they are (i) On-line publication, (ii) CD-ROM Publication, and (iii) Networked publication. Now, the Internet has changed the whole world into a global village in regard to access of information.

Indeed, a large-scale transformation is taking place in modes of formal as well as informal communication. For more than three centuries, formal communication in the scientific community has relied on the *scholarly* and professional periodical, widely distributed to tens of thousands of libraries and to tens of millions of individual subscribers. In 1992 a major international publisher announced that its journals would gradually be available for computer storage in digital form; and in that same year the State University of New York at Buffalo began building a completely electronic, paperless library. The scholarly article, rather than the journal, is likely to become the basic unit of formal communication in scientific disciplines; digital copies of such an article will be transmitted electronically to subscribers or, more likely, on demand to individuals and organizations who learn of its existence through referral databases and new types of alerting information services. The Internet already offers instantaneous public access to vast resources of noncommercial information stored in computers around the world.

Similarly, the traditional modes of informal communications—various types of face-to-face encounters such as meetings, conferences, seminars, workshops, and classroom lectures—are being supplemented and in some cases replaced by electronic mail, electronic bulletin boards (a technique of broadcasting newsworthy textual and multimedia messages between computer users), and electronic teleconferencing and distributed problem-solving (a method of linking remote persons in real time by voice-and-image communication and special software called "groupware"). These technologies are forging virtual societal networks—communities of geographically dispersed individuals who have common professional or social interests.

ELECTRONIC DOCUMENT DELIVERY SYSTEM

The Internet plays a high-flying role in dissemination of information in a networked world through the Internet Service Provider in the electronic environment where the documents are delivered in the electronic form either in the coded form of information or computer decipherable media. The distribution of documents on paper is aided by the recent generation of fast, high quality printers which incorporate the laser printers and refinements of the more conventional methods of printing through ink-jet printers, electrostatic printers etc.

Internet has brought about a new breed of journalists who are technogically confident and want to disseminate news items in an enhanced mode. With the initiation of databases in electronic form, the journalists are publishing newspaper officiating from different places of the world. Network resources have also caused a significant increase in informal communication- 'informal' journals now exist within electronic mail and computer conferencing facilities and such resources diminish the role of the conventional printed journal as a vehicle for the dissemination of research results;

increasingly it exists solely to satisfy social and archival requirements[3]. Added to it, the experts and creative writers also have joined hands together by exchanging their view and innovative thoughts by providing new to the society at large.

The storing of information including electronic publishing are available in this technological scenario in various forms include[4].

Magnetic Tape Disk

Magnetic Disk

Winchester Disk

Floppy Disk

Compact Disk Read-only-Memory (CD-ROM)

Digital Versatile Disk Read Only Memory (DVDROM)

Thus, there lies a tremendous impact of optical storage technologies resting on electronic publishing through different modes.

MODELS OF ELECTRONIC PUBLISHING

With the augmentation of Internet, the spectrum of electronic publishing has increased which are available in different models so as to facilitate the user community to take the best use of information in electronic form through various devices and the publishers at large in advanced countries have exposed their awareness for electronic publishing of their documents irrespective of the types. The different models available clannishly embody the following:

a) Electronic Book:

The Electronic Book is an allegory for management and structuring large amount of computer based information, which are available in text, picture, and sound forms. Many factors are responsible for enhancing the stream of development of electronic book. They may be categorized as follows:

Growing demand and acceptance of paperless publishing;

Availability of Desktop publishing;

Easy creation of electronic information, sharing of information, distributed texts in various forms, easy searching of information;

Cost-effectiveness;

Reliability, authenticity, easy accessibility of information;

Awareness of computer;

Wide spread of LAN and WAN technologies;

Availability of different databases on net; and

Incipient on set of the electronic information explosion.

b) Electronic Databases:

The collection of interrelated information in computerized system is called electronic database which is available in structured form where data/ items are stored, controlled and easily accessed through a computer based on predefined relationship between predefined types of data /items related to a particular situation or problem. The scholars, engineers, doctors, professionals, librarians, information officers and students at large access the required information relating to their respective fields through the electronic databases through various networking.

ROLE OF ELECTRONIC PUBLISHING IN LIBRARY AND INFORMATION CENTRE

The varied tastes of the user communities along with their steady claim, pin-pointed and instant information obligated the Librarians and Information Scientists to transform the dimension of dissemination of information from customary to electronic form so as to persuade the need of the users at any point of time, for which the electronic publishing became a positive modus operandi to unravel the problems of the users. In the words of Lancaster and Sandore[5], the electronic publishing has a tremendous brunt in Libraries and Information Centers as the future of the library range from one extreme to the other along with a kind of gamut where the:

Libraries will not be needed at all;

Libraries will become nothing more than switching centers;

Libraries will be switching centers but will build indexes and other tools to facilitate access to network resources;

Libraries will take on important new riles in building databases, creating new information composites in shape of electronic publishing activities; and

Libraries will remain important as places that people visit at least in the foreseeable future.

The information available in different databases are prepared on CD-ROM for quick access of information by scanning the respective databases by the Scholars, Students, Teachers, Librarians, Information Officers etc. The CD-ROM databases available include:

Brook man's Price Index;

Chemical Abstracts;

Encyclopedia Britannica;

Directory of Special Libraries & Information Centers;

Oxford English Dictionary;

Publisher's Directory;

Ulrich International Periodical Directory, etc.

Further, the international databases available in Internet have proved to be a positive impact for flourishing research and development in different areas irrespective of the disciplines.

CONCLUSION

The changing concept of technology in electronic era made a substantive availability of information including the electronic products in various forms in Libraries and Information Centers. The Librarians including the Information Officer could spawn scope to satisfy the varied interest of the user communities by providing the information in electronic form through Internet, CD-ROM, Floppy, etc. Electronic publishing is a process for production of typeset-quality document containing text, graphics, pictures, equations, tables etc that is used to mean any information source published in electronic form[6]. Further, the electronic publication includes sources like magnetic tapes, videodiscs, image. It may be mentioned here that, the first electronic book was published in 1985 in Germany (Ibid).

In electronic era, electronic publishing is a decisive constituent to prove the validity and the validity of technological efficacy of information sources in the most appropriate and effectual manner. In the present century, the only option left out for the Libraries and Information Centers to espouse the devices of accumulating the electronic information in various forms and the creation of different databases of their own excluding the databases available in Internet will certainly bring a positive accomplishment of the goal and aspiration of the user communities as the e-publishing is more efficient, cost effectiveness, greater educational collision, better reach, providing customization at the student level, improved student exposure, enhancement of research value.

REFERENCES

1. Encyclopedia Britannica. CD. 2001
2. LANCASTER, (F W). Ed. Networked scholarly publishing. *Library Trends.* 43,4; 1995.
3. LANCASTER (F W) and SANDORE (Beth). Technology and Management in Library and Information Services. 1997. Illinois, University of Illinois. P. 150.
4. RAJARAMAN, (V). Fundamentals of Computer. 3rd Edition. 2001. Prentice Hall of India, New Delhi.
5. LANCASTER 9FW0 and SANDORE (Beth), Op. Ci p239-45.
6. SAKSENA (Manesha). Emerging Electronic Information Environment and Its Implication on various types of Libraries. Libraries and Information Services in the Electronic Information Era. 1999. Indian Library Association Papers. 44th All India Library Conference, Hyderabad. 25th -26th February 1999. Sardana, J L. *Ed.*. Indian Library Association, New Delhi. P.152.

28

Measures for Effective Information Services for the Promotion of Distance Mode of Learning

T.P.O. Nasirudheen

Lecturer & Head,
Dept. of Library and Information Science,
Farook College,
Calicut.

Dr. M. Bavakutty

Professor & Head,
Dept. of Library and Information Science and University Librarian,
University of Calicut.

ABSTRACT

Point out the factors contributed towards the emergence of distance education. Define precisely the meaning of Open University. Make out the difference between Open University system and correspondence education. Trace the genesis and development of distance education, which formally started in Europe and U.S.A. in the later half of the 19th century and in India in 1960s only. The authors discuss the impact of emerging information communication technology on higher education, especially through distance mode of learning. Stress the importance of library and information service as one of the important student support services in the distance education system. Highlight the functional role of libraries, especially public libraries in the distance education in U.K., Thailand and other developed countries. Point out the deplorable conditions of library and information infrastructure and service in developing countries like India. Discuss about what sort of role and structure the library and information system should assume in the distance education stream. The distance education system has yet to consider the potential of public library service for its promotion. The effective instrument of public library legislation is still missing in most of the States in India. Suggest that the IGNOU being a premier national Open University and apex body for setting standards and guidance for open and distance education in the country should take a lead in these regard. It should seek for a joint venture the co-operation and collaboration with several agencies and bodies at national and state level. Conclude with a suggestion for forming a consultative study group under the auspicious of Distance Education Council of IGNOU to take suitable steps to improve the present situation. A few suggestions are put forward in this regard by the authors.

INTRODUCTION

The concept of not attending an educational institution in person and yet acquiring education has been identified by a variety of names viz. Correspondence Education, Home Study, Independent Study, External Study, Off Campus Study, Open Learning, Open Education etc. Distance education refers to a mode of education and a system where the interacting learner and the teacher are separated by space and time. Besides this, the planning of education organisation, provision of self-learning materials, wide use of two-way communication media like technical multimedia packages, assignment response and feedback, radio and television broadcasting etc. are some other important characteristics of distance mode of learning process.

However, in spite of differences in phraseology and divergence in views, there is a general consensus on the field of study being defined and certain common elements emerge like communication, distance both in time and space, use of media and technologies, planning and organisation. It is an umbrella concept that covers correspondence courses, radio broadcast teaching, self-learning, open learning, computer assisted instruction etc. It offers interactive and individualised communication opportunities to the learner. It is an open system of education – open to age, formal entry qualifications, place, time, sex, choice of courses, pace of learning and completion time. The major advantage of this system is that it extends educational opportunities to those who can not gain a specialist qualification in a traditional manner.

With the advent of democratisation of education by providing equality of opportunities and demands of equity formed heterogeneous groups in the campus and classroom. To meet the needs of a heterogeneous group who are drawn from various strata of the society i.e., physical, cultural, scholastic environment and to provide individual attention and consideration, the formal education system may not be adequate and up to the mark.

Rapid developments in science and technology and the consequent knowledge explosion, and having knowledge become science based, the updating, upgrading and broadening of knowledge became imperative, but not easy to all through self-study nor could they return to conventional system of education and training. Hence an alternative system transcending the barrier of age resulted.

Those who suffer from early school drop out in conventional system due to economic, social, gender, access handicaps could get relieved, if they were so inclined to further education through open mode of system. Heterogeneity problems like variety of backgrounds, learning of one's own pace etc. demand distance mode of learning to give individual attention.

If the classroom teaching is a craft, the distance mode of instruction is characterised by the application of a host of emerging technologies. While printing technology preceded the classroom teaching, distance mode of learning is preceded by Information Communication Technology (ICT). Distance education will absorb the components of the class room system, modify them, improve upon them so as to reach people at large who remain socially handicapped.

OPEN UNIVERSITIES

An Open University operates with the concept of distance education where instructions are given at a distance through correspondence and modern means of communication. It may also be called a 'University without Walls'. The Open University system is a direct outcome of the failure of the formal system and that of correspondence institutes to deliver the goods. Emphasising the need and importance of an Open University, the New Education Policy (1986) has aptly mentioned that "the Open University has been fully strengthened as an instrument of democratising education"[1].

It may be mentioned that there is no competition between the conventional and open universities. The conventional universities lay stress on regular classroom teaching, while open universities deliver instructional packages through self-instructional print material (SIM) and multimedia mix along with counselling sessions and assignment responses. The open universities meet the demands of social groups such as workers, women, minorities and people in remote areas.

The major difference in the teaching learning through distance mode between open university system and correspondence course institutes are in the mode of delivery of instruction. Print material offered by the correspondence course institutes in most of the cases is not in self-learning format. They are evolving into distance mode of education through the conversion of print material into self-instructional format. But Open University, in addition to print material, uses new technologies – multimedia mix. Correspondence Course Institutes are being encouraged to incorporate these components in their teaching-learning methods.

GENESIS AND DEVELOPMENT OF DISTANCE EDUCATION

The genesis of distance education can be traced to

correspondence education, which has been in existence for over 100 years and still remains the most prevalent form of distance education. The print media and the mail system facilitate the educational transaction. The modern history of correspondence education is traced back to 1840 with Issac Pitman offering short hand courses through correspondence. The formal correspondence education programmes were initiated in Europe and USA in the later half of the 19th century. In Russia, Australia and New Zealand, correspondence education came to be used extensively. In England, a number of private correspondence colleges were established. Since 1858, the University of London has been engaged in awarding degrees to students unable to register for conventional courses of study. The wide spread acceptance of correspondence mode of education generated interest in finding a more suitable term for the system encompassing a broader perspective.

Non-formal education through multimedia had become a part of the development and extension activities of most of the countries. An international forum, the International Council for Correspondence Education (ICCE) had already been formed in 1938 and was audited as a category 'C' international non-government body by the UNESCO in 1967. In 1982, the ICCE was renamed the International Council for Distance Education (ICDE) and promotion and development of research and scholarship on distance education was included as an objective of ICDE. Now it has been recognised as a category 'B' UNESCO organisation. The ICDE is the only world association for open and distance learning and it provides an environment for co-operation between main stream education and single mode distance education institutions.

The establishment of UK Open University (OU) in 1969 acted as a catalyst for the provision of higher education through multimedia system that harnessed educational broadcasting to correspondence teaching and other methods. The establishment of Open University was a landmark in the history of distance education and the period after that has been the most progressive period. Another important landmark in the development of distance education in the commonwealth countries has been the establishment of Commonwealth of Learning (COL) in 1988 at Vancouver in Canada, at the instance of Commonwealth Ministers of Education and Commonwealth Heads of Government. It has contributed considerably in popularising the distance education system and is also emphasising the improvement of the quality of course material, staff development and training and dual mode – a part of the course to be covered by face-to-face teaching and the rest through the distance mode. A select list of important open universities in the world is given in the appendix I.

CORRESPONDENCE EDUCATION IN INDIA

In India the concept of distance education is not very old, it dates back to early 1960s only. The Constitution of India provides for equal educational opportunities for all. But, higher education has got to be selective to provide opportunities on the basis of certain criterion of selection because of the scarce resources at its disposal. There are about 94 per cent of the relevant age group who are outside the system at the tertiary level.

One of the most significant problems faced by higher education has been its rigid and formal structure that renders the system to be selective and difficult to cope with increasing enrolment. The conventional, formal, face-to-face system having become inadequate to meet these growing educational needs of society, alternatives were considered and one of the viable and effective alternatives that the higher education has come up with is Distance Education.

Kothari Commission (1961) made significant recommendations regarding nature, scope and modes of organisation of correspondence courses. This led to the establishment of the Directorate of Correspondence Courses in 1962 by the Delhi University, the first of its kind in India, which was later renamed as the School of Correspondence Courses and Continuing Education. Punjabi University, Patiala in 1963 and other universities followed this. Presently 62 out of 258 conventional universities are offering courses through correspondence[2]. Such universities may be called dual-mode institutions as they offer education through distance modes as well as regular conventional courses.

The number of programmes on offer by Correspondence Courses Institutes (CCI) are approximately 409 at certificate, diploma, graduate, post-graduate and research levels. Out of these, 191 are general programmes, 205 professional/vocational, 12 technical/ vocational and two engineering programmes. The total enrolment of such institutes in the country is approximately 9,00,000.[3]

DEVELOPMENT OF OPEN UNIVERSITIES IN INDIA

Punjabi University, Patiala established a National Council of Correspondence Education in 1976. However, a lead to establish an open university was taken up by Andhra Pradesh and it established in 1982 an open university named as Andhra Pradesh Open University (APOU). This was renamed as Dr. B. R. Ambedkar Open University in 1991. This university was the first of its kind in the country. Since then the idea of Open University seems to have caught on and today we have nine state open universities, one national open university and two open school systems. The Indira Gandhi National Open University (IGNOU) was established by an Act of Parliament in 1985. It is the largest open university in the Commonwealth. It is the apex body in India for setting and maintaining standards in distance education. A list of open universities in India is given in the appendix- II.

The open universities, though a few in number, have created an impact on higher education system in India by extending access to higher education to a large number of learners offering diversity of programmes. The open universities together are offering 288 programmes and 1920 courses of conventional and non-conventional types at different levels in general, professional, technical/vocational areas.[4] The open universities negated the popular belief that only liberal education programmes can be offered through distance mode. Today the distance mode of education is complementing formal education and also providing an alternative channel for widening access to the people and giving them quality education which is equivalent, if not higher in standards of formal education.

The annual student enrolment of these universities is 6,18,295 with a cumulative enrolment of 17,84,964 in 2000-2001. These universities have established a wide network of Regional and Study Centres for providing student support services and effective delivery of programmes. More than 38 thousand academic counsellors are engaged by the open universities to provide tutorial and counselling services to the learners. The counsellors are mostly full-time academics of the conventional education system, and take up this assignment on part-time basis. The open universities are employing full-time academics, professionals, and administrative and technical staff to manage the system. The total staff engaged by these universities on full-time basis is 3029 of which 631 are academics.[5]

EMERGING TECHNOLOGIES IN DISTANCE EDUCATION

The open learning methodology is vastly different from the correspondence mode. As in the correspondence system, the teacher is absent but he is very much inbuilt in the instructional material. The methodology has undergone several stages of evolution and the first stage happens to be the self-instructional printed materials (SIM).

Information Technology (IT) refers to the hardware, software, networking, logistics, while Information Communication Technology (ICT) is more concerned with the ways in which these technologies can enhance the teaching and learning process. ICT forms part of the essential requirements of the infrastructural facilities for both formal and distance education. The working document on higher education in the 21st century – vision and action, prepared by the UNESCO (1998) reiterates that the quality of higher education in future will depend on the attention paid to the development of the new ICT, distance learning and virtual university. IT in general and ICT in particular have radically altered the procedure of formal education and opened up new avenues or vistas in non-formal and distance education systems.

Distance education has been a major beneficiary of the developments in information communication technology. Early innovations of ICT products like audio and video cassettes facilitated the dissemination of information and delivery of guidance and instructions. The subsequent introduction of the interactive video-communication systems such as the two-way telephone, interactive television, teleconferencing and the latest on-line discussions on internet facilitate distance learning for groups at off-campus locations and give rise to the distributed classroom model.

The advanced communication technology especially the satellite based teleconference, have made it possible to use distance education for training in skills in virtual classroom. The interactive television as it allows two-way audio and one-way video interaction between the experts and learners is ideal for distance education.

The other live interaction modes include two-way radio, audio-graphic teleconferencing, interactive television systems (ITV), computer conference etc. Now-a-days the credibility enjoyed by the distance mode of learning is mainly due to adoption of multimedia approach of ICT. Communication media eliminates the problems of distance education and brings education to the doorsteps of the learners. In the 21st century the use of digital multimedia computers, telecommunication networks and the internet will considerably enhance the user's efficiency, productivity and knowledge base by providing the capability to access, retrieve, use and exchange information from a variety of national and international databases available on internet and CD-ROMs.

Open universities adopt new information communication technology (ICT) such as audio-video cassettes, computers, telecommunication systems like telephone, fax etc. Open universities deliver the instructional packages through a host of services such as radio broadcast, satellite based countrywide classroom programme, computer and satellite based audio/video teleconference, internet etc. The internet tools include e-mail, telnet, File Transfer Protocol (FTP), archive, gopher, Wide Area Information Services (WAIS), and the most popular World Wide Web (www).

LIBRARIES IN DISTANCE EDUCATION

The role of a library within an academic institution can be realised only in the context of the institution's philosophy of education. This is true of most of the libraries of the academic institutions in the world at large and the libraries of open universities in particular.

Education in open universities is characterised by independent learning supported by self-instructional material, contact-cum-counselling sessions, audio-video replays and library facilities. In the absence of conventional class room teaching, the 'quality' aspect is infused into the system by providing carefully designed self-instructional printed course material and making available other student support services. Library and information services form an essential part of the student support services.

The library system caters to the on-campus teaching community as well as to learners residing in remote areas with different economic, social and educational background. Library has to acquire, organise and disseminate information in the form of print as well as non-print materials. The library assumes new dimensions in operations and functions in the context of emerging Information Communication Technology (ICT) being adopted in the distance mode of learning. While explaining the importance of multimedia approach of ICT, Taylor observed that "A second major impact on libraries will result from the broadening of the communication spectrum from print to sound to image......[6] The capability to transmit non-print forms by video or audio channels opens up, for libraries, a whole new spectrum of services, systems and functions.

The library of an open university has to serve two types of clientele. It has to cater to the needs of the resource persons as well as to the learners who are geographically scattered.

Most of the open universities operate either through three-tier system consisting of the main university, regional centres and study centres like Indira Gandhi National Open University (IGNOU) and U.K. Open University or through two-tier system having the university headquarters and study centres like Dr. B.R. Ambedkar Open University (BRAOU), formerly known as Andhra Pradesh Open University, the first of its kind in India and Sukhothai Thammathirat Open University, Thailand. The National Open University and other state open universities in India have a network of libraries comprising two distinct categories:

1. Central Library as the apex at the university headquarters.
2. Libraries at the regional and study centres as the branch libraries.

The central library at the headquarters is mainly meant for the faculty and experts to support them in planning and designing the curriculum of academic programmes launched by the university and in the preparation of course material. The branch libraries of regional centres of IGNOU are resource centres to cater to the needs of academic counsellors and research scholars of various academic institutions and also of distance learners of some major programmes. The study centres of all these open universities serve as student support centres for lending books for home study and reference, and helping them in preparing assignment responses. The regional and study centre libraries also collect and organise the audio-video cassettes and arrange teleconference programmes for learners. Regional centre libraries deliver the instructional packages and counselling through a host of telecommunication and information technologies like telephone, fax, e-mail, videotex, interactive television programme and summer courses for both faculty and distance learners.

The central library combines the features and functions of both academic and special libraries. This dual characteristic increases the complexity of library policies regarding the development of collection and provision of library and information services. Acquisition management being a centralised process, the central library has the responsibility of acquisition management and collection development for the main as well as branch libraries to cater to the needs of various categories of clientele. The selection of library materials is the joint responsibility of the librarian and the academic staff. Print and non-print materials such as books, periodicals, reports, recordings, films, slides, microforms, computer floppies, globes, models, dioramas, kits etc. are acquired to facilitate the production of multimedia packages of course material. The central library cater to the requirements of academic and media consultants, professional, technical and administrative staff involved in the course development i.e., planning, designing, creating, producing and distributing of multimedia package. The central library has not only to acquire, process, despatch and monitor the receipt of books and non-print materials sent to the centres but also to take policy decisions regarding the management of the branch libraries as well as providing the maximum services safeguarding the resources.

LIBRARY AND INFORMATION SERVICES TO DISTANCE LEARNERS

Library policies of different distance teaching universities in India and abroad vary from zero provision of books to exhaustive library services. In India the library services in the universities offering correspondence education are negligible, whereas the distance teaching universities abroad give high priority to the provision of library services to both their on-campus and off-campus students. They have the same system of central library and study centre libraries as we have in Indian Open Universities, but their library services are much more functional. The public library system is well organised in these countries and they have attained great popularity by promoting distance education and by providing library and information services to adult learners.

INTERNATIONAL SCENARIO

The emerging Information Communication Technologies (ICT) are widely applied in North American and European countries for the distance mode of learning. Internet infrastructure is reasonably developed in some of the eastern countries like Japan, Korea, Singapore and Hong Kong where pressure is increasing to use the internet in education because of growing number of foreign universities offering virtual courses. In the field of information communication technology based education, South Korea has definitely taken the lead, at all levels.

Distance education is characterised by provision of instructional delivery through multimedia mix along with counselling and self-instructional reading materials. Vigorous exercise of assignment responses along with practical and project works are also some other significant features of the system. But the emphasis is on the wide application of information and telecommunication technologies for the instructional strategy and delivery. This mode of delivery makes the system different from the conventional system of education where classroom teaching is predominant.

INDIAN SCENARIO

India being a developing country with half of the population functionally illiterate confronts with many socio-economic problems. Though the country has much advanced in science and telecommunication, it is struggling hard to put these benefits in the education and human resources development areas. Distance and open education is not an exception in this regard.

In developing countries like India where modern sophisticated gadgets like TV, VCR, tape recorder, radio, telephone, computer etc. are not equally and adequately accessible to all the distance learners, library facilities have to remain one of the basic student support services to learners. Thus libraries have to play a significant role to provide student support services to the distance learners. But in Indian context this tremendous task of providing library facilities to masses scattered throughout the country can not be accomplished by the distance teaching universities alone. They have to meet with the demands of the diverse learners by co-operating with all types of libraries, viz. academic, special and public to extend appropriate library service to the learners. This can be made possible by the joint efforts of all the existing libraries and utilising their infrastructural facilities and library resources for longer hours which otherwise remain idle on the holidays and evenings, to cater to the needs of the distance learners without the imposition of additional financial burden.

ROLE OF PUBLIC LIBRARIES IN DISTANCE EDUCATION

Among the various types of libraries, public libraries have got a prominent role to play as they are the libraries to which every citizen has access as a matter of right. In Britain, which gave the lead in open and distance education concept, there is a strong public library base which unlike the common concept of a public library as a centre for recreational reading, collects and makes available books for academic and research purposes. In Thailand the learners of the Sukothai Thammathirat Open University do not have libraries at their study centres. They usually avail of library services at the nearby public libraries. The public libraries are well organised in these countries and they have attained great popularity by promoting distance education and by providing library and information services to adult learners.

Public library system in India has left much to be desired. Public library legislation is an effective measure to establish public library system in a State. India as a country lacks a federal law of public libraries. Even after fifty years of independence more than half the number of States in India are without public library legislation. Only ten States have so far enacted public library law in India. A list of the States with public library law is given in appendix-III. Even in these States, because of financial constraints the public library service cannot be regarded as satisfactory. A casual perusal of the State Public Library Acts in force in India shows that no Act except Kerala Public Libraries Act (1989) has even mentioned the promotion of distance education in the enlisted functions of the library authorities in the State. The Kerala Public Libraries Act has authorised the State Library Council, the apex body in the State for the matter connected with public library organisation and activities, among the functions to be discharged, to organise activities for promoting distance education and adult education. Though more than 10 years have passed after the Act came into being, no attempt has been seen made by the government and the concerned authorities to bring provisions for establishing a public library system with adequate provision for sharing library resources and a modern library and information network. No attempt was seen made to establish and develop well organised libraries even at district and taluk headquarters except for district libraries at Kottayam, Quilon, Ernakulam and Trichur which were developed even before the Act came into existence.

DISTANCE EDUCATION LIBRARIES IN KERALA

More than one lakh students have got enrolled in the State for the various academic and professional programmes of IGNOU under the regional centre at Cochin. The counselling, guidance for assignment responses, practical and project works and other necessary information and services are provided through 35 study centres scattered throughout the State. A list of study centres of IGNOU in Kerala is given in appendix IV. Most of these study centres are working in colleges and other academic, management and research institutes and making use of their infrastructural facilities. But sorry to note that none of these centres has got a well-organised library with adequate collection covering all the subjects/areas of programmes delivered through these study centres. The national open university has not yet given serious thought and attention to improve the library and information services to the distant learners through these study centres. The university has not made any attempt to explore the possibility of using the library and other infrastructural facilities of these organisations and institutions for the benefit of distance learners through some joint ventures in collaboration with them. The university could better utilise the resources and facilities of the existing well-organised resourceful public libraries at the district headquarters like Trivandrum, Kottayam, Quilon, Ernakulam and Trichur. The promotion of distance education being one of the main functions of the State Library Council in Kerala, the university should make some provisions for a joint venture in collaboration with the Council and other bodies like Raja Rammohun Roy Library Foundation (RRRLF) in the State for enriching the resources of these public libraries and establishing new libraries at district headquarters and gradually bring to the taluk level.

Such attempts can also be made to join in hands with the state universities and other management and research institutions. Being an apex body in co-ordination and management of distance and open education in India, IGNOU should initiate joint ventures and take the responsibility of improving library and information resources and services in the different types of libraries especially university and public libraries. Some premier colleges and professional institutions could also be identified for this.

Besides the national open university, the Kerala and Calicut universities are providing distance education through their Correspondence Courses Institutes/ Schools of Distance Education. About 25000 students (2000 admission) have got enrolled in the School of Distance Education of Calicut University for the various academic courses. A little more than this figure has also got registered in the Institute of Correspondence Education of Kerala University. Mahatma Gandhi University, Kottayam has recently launched off-campus programmes for management studies. But none of these universities has given proper attention to provide adequate library and information services to the distance learners. They are satisfied with the delivery of print materials, that also not in self-instructional material format as in the case of open universities, just before the commencement of terminal examination. This is to be noted with grave concern when the learners pay heavily for the delivery of the programmes to these universities. All the education commissions have laid stress on the provision of proper and adequate library and information services in higher education. It is an indispensable component of an education process. It becomes more relevant when it is the case of distance mode of learning where institutional support is missing with no regular classroom teaching and the teacher being absents in person. The entire responsibility of student support services rests on the library.

SUGGESTIONS

Public library service in general and in distance education in particular is far from satisfactory. It may be noted that an effective well-organised public library system has not been established in most of the States in India. The effective instrument of public library legislation is missing in these States. The library infrastructure and service even in those States with library law are not satisfactory. A well-organised network of resourceful libraries is an essential component to support the distance education delivered through the study centres. All the States that have not yet passed public library legislation should enact the law as early as possible. The States with public library law should incorporate in their Acts such legislative measures as to promote distance education in the State. The state library authorities should be empowered to initiate joint ventures with national and state open universities to enrich the resources of public libraries and to establish a public library system in the State.

The Distance Education Council (DEC) of IGNOU being the apex body for the co-ordination and guidance of distance and open education in India can do a lot in this regard. The DEC should set up a consultative group of library and information science experts and distinguished library professionals to conduct a study and to suggest suitable steps to improve the present situation. The following are the few suggestions in this regard:

1. To set up a national network of distance education libraries and information centres catering to the academic needs of distance learners of national and state open universities.
2. To explore how the distance educational institutions in India can better utilise the resources and services of the existing university and other academic libraries in the country.
3. To derive a mechanism for this purpose in consultation and collaboration with the national higher education bodies like University Grants Commission (UGC), National Council for Teacher Education (NCTE), All India Council for Technical Education (AICTE), Medical Council of India (MCI), INFLIBNET, etc.

4. To initiate joint efforts in collaboration with Raja Rammohun Roy Library Foundation (RRRLF), National Library of India (Culcutta), Task Force for Information Technology, etc. for better utilisation of public library facilities and infrastructure in the country by the distance learners, and
5. To provide finance and expertise to the state library authorities and state central libraries to enrich their resources and to modernise the services rendered by the public libraries in the State with a view to catering to the diverse needs of the distance learners.

REFERENCES

1. India, Ministry of Human Resources Development. National Policy on Education 1986. New Delhi, Govt. of India, 1986.
2. Rausaria, R.R. and Bharat Bhusan. Institutional Models for Distance Learning in India. *University News*. 39(27), July 2-8, 2001. P. 10.
3. Rausaria, R.R. and Bharat Bhusan. Ibid. P. 10.
4. Rausaria, R.R. and Bharat Bhusan. Ibid. P. 9.
5. Rausaria, R.R. and Bharat Bhusan. Ibid. P. 10.
6. Taylor, Robert S. Technologies and Libraries. *Educom*. 5(5). Quoted in G. Sujatha. Internet Based Library Services for Distance Learners. *CLIS Observer*. 18(3-4). P. 80.

BIBLIOGRAPHY

1. Amudhavalli, A. Libraries in Distance education. In: Libraries in Distance educatoin, ed. K.A. Issac and G. Devarajan. New Delhi, Ess Ess Pub. P. 74-80.
2. Arora, Asha. Distance education. *University News*. Vol. 32, No. 21. May 23, 1994. P. 1-13.
3. Baburajan, A. Distance education and libraries. In: Libraries in Distance educatoin, ed. K.A. Issac and G. Devarajan. New Delhi, Ess Ess Pub. P. 81-9.
4. Bavakutty, M. Role of university libraries in distance education. In: Libraries in Distance educatoin, ed. K.A. Issac and G. Devarajan. New Delhi, Ess Ess Pub. P. 171-5.

5. Chaudhari, Umrao Singh. Distance education and print media: Some instructional strategies. *University News*. Vol. 38, No. 43. Oct. 23, 2000. P. 7-8.

6. Haider, Qaseemuddin. Use of multimedia in distance education. *University News*. Vol. 36, No. 11. Mar. 16, 1998. P. 2-4.

7. Issac, K.A. Distance education and libraries. In: Libraries in Distance educatoin, ed. K.A. Issac and G. Devarajan. New Delhi, Ess Ess Pub. P. 3-8.

8. Kulandai Swamy, V.C. Distance Education: Status and Prospects. In: Higher Education in India: Retrospect and Prospect, ed. by Moonis Raza. New Delhi, AIU, 1991. P. 109-30.

9. Madhavan, K. and Manoj Roy. Distance education: A social catalyst for third world countries. *University News*. Vol. 36, No. 43. Oct. 26, 1998. P. 12-4.

10. Neela Jagannathan. Libraries in Distance Education. In: Literacy Campaign and Libraries, ed. Velaga Venkatappaiah. New Delhi, Ess Ess Pub., 1996. P. 71-80.

11. Pulist, S.K. Reaching the disadvantaged through open and distance education. *University News*. Vol. 38, No. 42. Oct. 16, 2000. P. 4-10.

12. Ransaria, R.R. and Bharat Bhushan. Institutional Models for distance learning in India. *University News*. Vol. 39, No. 27. July 2-8, 2001. P. 9-12.

13. Shastree, Nalin K. Distance education: The third wave in higher education. *University News*. Vol. 40, No. 4. Jan. 28-Feb. 3, 2002. P. 3-12.

14. Sinha, Manoj Kumar, et.al. Emerging trends in Information Communication Technology and their impact on higher education system in India. *KELPRO Bulletin*. Vol. 3, No. 1. June 1991. P. 3-21.

15. Swarnalatha Das and Gautham Das. Role effectiveness of

an open university centre: A micro approach. *University News*. Vol. 33, No. 51. Dec. 18, 1995. P. 9-12.

APPENDIX – I

A select list of important open universities in the world with their addresses and year of establishment.

1. The Open University, Walton Hall, Milton Keynes, MK 7 6 AA, United Kingdom (1969).
2. Universidad Nacional De Education a Distencia (UNED), Madrid, Spain (1972).
3. Allama Iqbal Open University, Islamabad, Pakistan (1974).
4. Everyman's University, Israel (1974).
5. Fern Universitat, Fleyer Strasse 204, D 5800, Hagen, West Germany (1974).
6. Athabasca University, Box 10,10,000, Athabasca, Alberta, Canada, TOG 2 RO (1975).
7. Universidad Nacional Abierta (UNA),Venezuela (1977).
8. Universidad Estatal a Distancia (UNED), Cost Rica (1977).
9. Central Radio and Television University, Beijing, China (1978).
10. Korea Air and Correspondence University, 169, Dongsuog-Dong, Chongro-ku, Seoul - 110, Korea (1982).
11. The University of Air, Wakaba, 2-Chome, Chiba, 260, Japan (1983).
12. Universitas Terbuka, Pondok Cabe, Ciputat Tangerang 15418, POB 6666, Jakarta - 10001, Indonesia (1984).
13. Indira Gandhi National Open University, Maidan Garhi, New Delhi – 110 068, India (1985).
14. Sukhotai Thammathirat Open University, 9/9 M009 Tambo Bangpood, Nonthaburi – 11120, Bangkong, Thailand (1978).
15. Open University of Sri Lanka, PO Box 21, Nawala, Nugegoda, Sri Lanka (1981).

16. Korea National Open University (1972)
17. African Virtual University established by World Bank (1997).
18. The Dutch Open University, Netherlands.
19. National Open University of Republic of China.
20. British Columbia Open University.
21. National Open University, Taiwan.
22. Open University, Russia.
23. Open University of Slovac Republic.
24. University of South Africa.
25. University of Manitoba, Canada.
26. University of New England, New South Wales, Australia.
27. Deakin University, Victoria, Australia.
28. University of South Pacific, Suva, Fuji.

APPENDIX II

Sl. No.	Name of the University	Year of establishment	Students Registered	Progra-mmes on Offer	No. of Study Centres
1.	Indira Gandhi National Open University, New Delhi.	1985	1,72,543	48	450
2.	Dr. B.R. Ambedkar Open University, Hyderabad.	1982	93,570	21	130
3.	Kota Open University, Kota, Rajasthan.	1987	8,141	21	36
4.	Nalanda Open University, Patna.	1987	641	9	4
5.	Yashwantrao Chavan Maharashtra Open University, Nashik.	1989	1,04,551	54	1,399
6.	Madhyapradesh Bhoj Open University, Bhopal.	1992	56,123	29	670
7.	Dr. Babasaheb Ambedkar Open University, Ahmedabad.	1994	5,556	9	70
8.	Karnataka State Open University, Mysore.	1996	27,231	23	218
9.	Netaji Subhas Open University, Calcutta.	1997	434	3	36
10.	UP Rajarshi Tandon Open University, Allahabad.	1999	3,307	18	18

A list of National and State Open Universities in India with their addresses.

1. Indira Gandhi National Open University, Maidan Garhi, New Delhi – 110 068.
2. Dr. B.R. Ambedkar Open University, Road No. 46, Jubilee Hills, Hyderabad - 500 033.
3. Kota Open University, Akelgarh, Rawat Bhata Road, Kota – 324 010, Rajasthan.
4. Nalanda Open University, 9, Adarsh Colony, Kidwaipuri, Patna – 800 001, Bihar.
5. Yashwantrao Chavan Maharashtra Open University, Dnyangangotri, Near Gangapur Dam, Goverdhan Nashik - 422 222, Maharashtra.
6. Madhya Pradesh Bhoj (Open) University, Red Cross Bhawan, Shivaji Nagar, Bhopal – 462 016.
7. Dr. Babasaheb Ambedkar Open University, Government Bungalow No. 9, Near Dafnala, Shahibang, Ahmedabad – 380 003, Gujarat.
8. Karnataka State Open University, Manasagangotri, Mysore, 570 006.
9. Netaji Subhas Open University, 1, Woodburn Park, Calcutta – 700 020.
10. UP Rajarshi Tandon Open University, 17, Maharshi Dayanand Marg, Thornhill Road, Allahabad – 211 001.

APPENDIX III

A list of States in India with public library legislation with the year of enactment.

Sl.No.	Name of the State	Year of enactment
1.	Tamil Nadu	1948
2.	Andhra Pradesh	1960
3.	Karnataka	1965
4.	Maharashtra	1967
5.	West Bengal	1979
6.	Manipur	1988
7.	Kerala	1989
8.	Haryana	1989
9.	Mizoram	1993
10.	Goa	1995

APPENDIX IV

A list of study centres of IGNOU in Kerala.

Sl. No.	Centre Code	Study Centre Address
1.	1401	Institute of Management, Vikas Bhawan, Trivandrum.
2.	1402	Sacred Heart College, Thevara, Kochi – 682 013.
3.	1403	JDT Islam, Mari Kunnu P.O., Calicut – 673 012.
4.	1404	Catholicate College, PO Box No. 102, Pathanamthitta – 686 645.
5.	1405	Shri. Narayana College, Kannur – 670 007
6.	1406	CMS College, Kottayam – 686 001.
7.	1407	Sree Kerala Varma College, Trichur – 680 001.
8.	1408	Newman College, Mallapuram, Thodupuzha – 685 585.
9.	1409	PSMO College, Tirurangadi – 676 306.
10.	1412	St. Albert's College, Ernakulam – 682 018.
11.	1413	Sree Narayana College, Kollam – 691 001.
12.	1414(P)	College of Nursing, Thiruvananthapuram – 695 011.
13.	1415(P)	T.K.M. College of Engineering, Kollam – 691 005.
14.	1416(P)	Tandem Institute of Computer Tech., Training Institute, Thiruvananthapuram – 695 010.

Sl. No.	Centre Code	Study Centre Address
15.	1417(P)	IRS Computers Communication Pvt. Ltd., Naduvilal, Trichur – 680 002.
16.	1418(P)	National Institute of Computer Technology Training Instt. Thiruvananthapuram – 691 001.
17.	1419(P)	Data Point, via Anand, Sulthan Bathery – 673 592.
18.	1420(P)	Rajagiri College of Social Sciences, Kalamassery, Cochin – 683 104.
19.	1421(P)	Govt. Medical College, Thiruvananthapuram – 695 001.
20.	1422(P)	Mar Ivanios College, Nethary Hills, Nalanchira, Thiruvananthapuram – 695 015.
21.	1423(P)	Chips Software Systems (P) Ltd., Sahitya Parishad Building, Hospital Road, Cochin – 682 011.
22.	1424(P)	International Institute of Information Technology, Municipal Shopping Complex, T.B. Road, Kottayam – 686 001.
23.	1425(P)	Kuttakaran Institute for HRD, San Juan Towers, P.B. No. 3015, Old Rly Station, Cochin – 682 018.
24.	1426(P)	N.S.S. Training College, Ottapalam, Palakkad – 679 101.
25.	1427(P)	N.S.S. Training College, Changanachery – 686 102.
26.	1428(P)	Centre for Development Studies, Prasant Nagar, Ullor, Trivandrum – 695 011.

Sl. No.	Centre Code	Study Centre Address
27.	1429(P)	Govt. Engg. College, Trichur – 680 009.
28.	1430	St. Mary College, Sultan Bathery, P.O. Kuppadi, Wayanad Dist. – 673 592.
29.	1431	Centre for Development of Imaging Technology (C-DIT), Chitranjali Studio Complex, Thiruvallam P.O., Trivandrum – 695 027.
30.	1432(P)	Al-Farook Educational Centre, Farook College, P.O. Feroke, Calicut – 673 632.
31.	1433(P)	Regional Computer College, I & II Floor, Statue Junction, Trivandrum – 695 001.
32.	1434(D)	Kerala Vocational Training Centre, West Nada, Kodungallur, Trichur – 680 664.
33.	1435(D)	Imperial College, Michel Junction, Mavelikkara, Aleppey.
34.	1436(D)	Mahatma Gandhi Trust, Maniamcott Buildings, KP Vallon Road, Kadavanthra Jn., Cochin – 682 020.
35.	3001	Jawaharlal Nehru College, Kavarati, Lakshwadeep – 682 555.

29

Implications of Information and Communication Technology on Distance Education

M. Natarajan
Scientist,
INSDOC Regional Centre,
CSIR Madras Complex
Taramani,
Chennai.

ABSTRACT

There is rush to distance learning, which is being fueled by three major events. One of the major events is the convergence of the communication and computing technologies. A second major reason is that the Information Age requires workers in all sectors of the economy to be knowledgeable and highly skilled - without interrupting work service for extended periods of time and the third major reason for the renewed interest in distance learning is the cost factor. This article defines the distance learning and the access provided to higher learning is discussed. Technologies adopted for distance learning and the advantages are mentioned. Limitations of the exiting teaching methods and the curriculum issues are discussed.

INTRODUCTION

Society is rapidly moving towards a position where its primary role material is human capital. In this context, education assumes increasing importance and becomes the key to success. Therefore, education is repositioned, which is seen. To be successful in knowledge society, individual needs more education. Distance learning in higher education evolved to provide access. It is not a recent development in education. The correspondence course, considered the earliest form of structured distance education, began in the mid - late 19th century. Today, courses are delivered through a variety of media including audio transmission and CD-ROM as well as through correspondence. Before going further, it is important to differentiate distance learning from other types of learning.

DEFINITION

The definition used by the U.S. Congress in a 1992 Office of Technology Assessment report, as

"Distance education can be broadly defined as the transmission of education or instructional programming to geographically dispersed individuals or groups".

More recently, radio and instructional television were much-touted distance learning delivery models in the 1950's and 1960s. However, instructional television, together with earlier technologies, fell short of expectations. But today's telecourses - designed as a content resources and combined with interaction and communication with the faculty member and other students via the Internet - can become a more powerful delivery model and meet more of the great expectations.

ROLE OF TECHNOLOGY

It is important to explore the role of technology in distance education. "*At its most basic level, distance education takes place when a teacher and student(s) are separated by physical distance, and technology, that is, voice, video, data, and print, is used to bridge the instructional gap*".

Even though it is technology that is opening the doors to so many new distance learning models, the use of technology in distance education should remain transparent and user-friendly, allowing the instructor and students to concentrate on the processes of teaching and learning. Some of the major questions facing us today in defining the new generation of distance learning programs are:

- How do we design effective learning systems for a virtual teaching and learning environment - when faculty and students are not physically together and we have a complex set of media at our disposal?
- How do we structure information content and provide content access to meet the curricula demands of the Information-Age learners, given the additional power and flexibility of the new technologies?
- What is a good balance of independent study and interaction with other students?
- How do we balance the costs of the new media with their needed benefits?

Designer and planners of the new generation of distance learning programs will need to address these questions. Before discussing the generations of distance learning in more depth, let's review the role that distance learning has played in learning systems in the past.

RUSH TO DISTANCE LEARNING

The rush to distance learning is being fueled by three major events. One of the major events is the convergence of the communication and computing technologies. This convergence is producing a plethora of hybrid technology products and services. These new products and services will soon permit widespread availability of diverse forms of information, education, services, and entertainment. Some of these products might be able to address persistent and difficult educational problems. Multiple, and occasionally seamless, communication links now exist between homes, offices, schools and workplaces. The Information Age has definitely arrived.

A second major reason is that the Information Age requires workers in all sectors of the economy to be knowledgeable and highly skilled - without interrupting work service for extended periods of time. Workers also need to be able to solve many more problems and more complex problems on their own. And workers must stay up-to-date and knowledgeable in fields that are dynamic and constantly changing. So learning should be continuous and available wherever the people are; learning needs to be just in time; learning must be concurrent with work. The widespread availability of information tools promises at least some partial solutions to all these needs. The amount of learning required by every Information-Age worker is steadily increasing. Thus education across all segments of the higher education markets - undergraduate, graduate, professional, certification, and lifelong learning - is a growth market. To meet these needs and take advantage of the opportunities one must fund, design and implement new flexible learning programs. The needs are great; and our traditional models are no longer appropriate.

Another major reason for the renewed interest in distance learning is the cost factor. Our current models of higher education are very resource-intensive, in terms of people, space, content development, and time for learners. The budget will not be expanding sufficiently to meet the knowledge requirements of the future using our current models. The technologies help for the distance learning by reducing the cost of teaching and learning. There is a widespread perception that distance learning models can reduce the cost of teaching and learning in the higher education and professional markets. There can be real cost savings in certain areas.

Programs should be planned and designed well in advance. Also, quality distance learning programs still provide a certain amount of interaction and mentoring with faculty and tutors on-line or in person. So, while there will be some savings in the long term, significant investments are generally required upfront.

ACCESS TO HIGHER EDUCATION

Distance learning in higher education evolved to provide access. Programs have often been structured for use in homes or small geographically distributed study centers, reducing the need for travel and also reducing the dependency on specific spaces and times. The early generational models of distance learning have traditionally been perceived as less costly - for students, faculty and institutions, and, in many cases, they have been. The great need for the benefits of increased access and lower costs per student are some of the reasons driving this rebirth of interest in distance learning.

Also provided options for individuals who desire to combine work and learning experiences, and for those individuals who decide to return to school later in life. Many of these individuals may have demanding job and family responsibilities and find that the only way they can complete higher education degree programs is through distance learning programs. Students use distance education, not necessarily because they want to or because they believe it is a preferred alternative to on-campus instruction.

EFFECTIVENESS OF DISTANCE LEARNING

Distance learning experiences are often considered "less than" and "not as good as" on-campus programs at producing quality educational outcomes. Thus, degrees from institutions that are highly dependent on distance learning technologies and where much of the education occurs off-campus and off-hours are sometimes viewed with suspicion and skepticism. This is a perception by many, despite a wealth of studies documenting that students at a distance learn as much or more as on-campus students, and do as well or better in specified learning outcomes. So there is a feeling that something must be missing from distance learning experiences.

Much peripheral learning of a person happens during the course of on-campus experiences that are not part of the explicit course activities, goals and objectives. Even though these components of the learning experiences have never been explicitly defined, it is judged that off-campus students who do not participate in informal discussions and activities are less likely to incorporate the values, and the perspectives that often are part of the osmosis or environment of learning. Do the new technologies possibly offer an effective response to this need and this perception - at long last?

Let's take a look at the technologies that are now available for distance learning and consider what impact the substantial leap in power of these technologies may have for distance learning.

DEVELOPMENTS IN INFORMATION AND COMMUNICATION TECHNOLOGIES

With the inception of computer technology and developments in communications technology, the potential for improving the quality and effectiveness of distance learning has grown. This has resulted in the development of a variety of learning technologies and the incorporation of a number of new elements into distance learning: video films, multimedia courseware, and live lessons delivered to remote classrooms. Until the mid 1990s, the integration of such educational technologies was only partly successful, for methodological reasons, and due to considerations of cost and accessibility.

Today, Internet has become an essential communications platform; private Intra-net networks are providing specific organizations and populations with higher levels of Internet service; technological learning environments are being developed; a wide range of improved graphic means of presentation are available; and simple, user-friendly means of desktop production are providing solutions which, until recently, required large, expensive facilities. Continuous improvement in Internet capabilities - both in terms of applications and transmission rates – is transforming it into a vehicle for the delivery of an ultimate learning environment for distance learning in the 21st century.

Technological advances have made synchronous (same time) distance learning both viable and effective, primarily through video-conferencing and satellite systems. Combining this with asynchronous

Internet-based delivery makes it possible to provide first-class teaching by excellent instructors to distant students while maintaining interaction between instructor, students and peers. The technology allows the same experts who prepared the learning materials also to take command of and guide the learning process (unlike traditional distance teaching, where they were usually not involved in the actual teaching). As a result, there is a growing trend to utilize various means for distance education (correspondence, extended classrooms, and recently, web-based online courses).

Technological developments (e.g., WWW, digital satellite technology, and innovative applications of virtual reality) are having dramatic effects on learning environments at all levels. New teaching and learning styles are being developed: learning based on prepared electronic materials; on-going interaction between partners in the learning process; learning by doing; and collaborative learning. There is a shift from lecturing and telling ("sage on the stage") to facilitating and guiding ("guide on the side").

Most of the universities are in the process of integrating advanced technologies into their regular on-campus teaching methods. These are usually asynchronous modes (that allow for any-time, any-place, any-pace learning and are generally delivered via the Internet) that are intended to supplement traditional (synchronous) on-campus teaching. The successful implementation of technologies in leading universities has increased the status of distance learning and is beginning to blur the distinction between on-campus and distance learners. Developing effective learning solutions that combine advanced technologies with methodology and pedagogy has led to collaborations with relevant business partners.

THE TECHNOLOGIES OF DISTANCE LEARNING

The technologies used in distance learning have paralleled the technologies used for communication, news and entertainment. This is an obvious cost-effective strategy, as the infrastructure for the technologies can be constructed and paid for by the other public-private institutions, and then directed as appropriate to educational needs and opportunities. This has been the case with mail, radio, television and audio and videotaping technologies. The same may hold true for the infrastructure essential for the new generation of technologies characterizing the Information Age.

The next five years will see the rapid development of new categories of computing and communication products - or network appliances - that may serve the educational needs. Some of these types of products are already being licensed and marketed. For example, Oracle and Apple Computer are each developing and licensing new environments that serve the specific purpose of accessing and communicating via the World Wide Web. This may well be the key to enable the shift to a web-centric teaching and learning paradigm. Such a new home appliance combined with telecourse material may support the evolution of a much more highly interactive model for distance learning.

The generations of distance learning technologies according to five characteristics are:

1. The media and the technologies
2. Communication features
3. Student characteristics and goals
4. Educational philosophy and curriculum design and
5. Infrastructure.

Let's briefly consider how each of these characteristics may impact the evolving interactive distance learning models.

THE MEDIA AND THE TECHNOLOGIES

One of the key differentiating characteristics of the communication technologies is whether the technologies provide one-way, two-way, or multiple way communication, and whether the "ways" are broadband or narrowband, and whether the return rate is fast or slow. The technologies predominately used in distance learning in the early and mid 20th century such as print, radio and television have been primarily broadband in one direction - fitting the educational model of education as an information transfer or "dump" between faculty and student. Time and expertise was and is needed to prepare materials for delivery in this stand-alone mode.

Lack of a two-way audio-video broadband communication with the television or print media restricted the dynamic interchange between the faculty member and the students. This constraint also restricted the type of instruction that could be delivered, as the students could not effectively collaborate with each other across distances. Students can now tape programs and view it at other more convenient times. These new technologies also meant that distance learning programs could be developed with a variety of prepackaged media, such as print, audio, and video components. Students then would have full flexibility in when and where to take the course.

Thus, a major constraint of the broadband one-way technologies is that it is difficult to create a meaningful relationship between a faculty member and isolated students, or to develop a community of learners among the faculty and the possible cohort of students. The technologies of the third and fourth generation - the electronic mail, chat rooms, bulletin boards and desktop videoconferencing - now make possible the development of learning communities across time and distance.

Communications Features

The primary differentiating feature among the distance learning technologies today versus previous generations is the ability for timely and personal interaction, the basis of most satisfying relationships. The technologies now provide choices that enable the delivery of distance learning programs almost anytime, anywhere. The next generation of technologies that will extend the communication features beyond today's capabilities will include wireless technologies. Today's technologies enable synchronous communications across long distances and with large groups - providing the perception of "almost being there" no matter where one is.

Today's technologies enable rapid response asynchronous

communications - very different from the mail. A student can post a question for a faculty member or for other students and receive a reply in hours, and sometimes minutes. This capability also creates new communication patterns and expectations. A faculty member can manage a course using a variety of social and intellectual spaces on the net. These new technologies also enable faculty, students, and support staff to handle all recruiting, admission, registration and fees, and student life on-line.

Student Characteristics and Goals

Students who successfully complete distance learning programs are generally very motivated, highly disciplined, and with a clear vision of the goals that they want to accomplish. Successful distance learning students also generally have the skills to be independent learners, and are comfortable in the realm of textual materials. Most students with this set of characteristics also tend to be mature adult students.

Student characteristics will always be important indicators of success in learning, but they will be less important in the future. The new distance learning technologies enable faculty to hold meetings, stay in touch, provide structure, and provide frequent response and interaction. It enables faculty or support staff - with time - to provide much needed guidance, encouragement, etc. with students who need such assistance. However, particularly younger students, for whom distance learning programs are not a good match for their learning needs and levels of learning skills.

Educational Philosophy and Curriculum Design

The view of the student and the design principles of curriculum development is an important factor. In the early 1900s the student was viewed as an empty vessel into which the faculty member "poured" knowledge. In this model, the faculty member was the "one who knew all" and students came to the faculty member with a yearning to know what the faculty member knew. With this philosophy the goal of distance learning was to "get the knowledge content" out to the student. So the curriculum designers analyzed the knowledge content, divided it into appropriate size chunks, and structured readings, and video, to teach the knowledge objectives in the chunks. This sounds like a reasonable approach.

Our view of the student is now quite different, and it is reasonable also to say that students are qualitatively different as well. Our understanding of the teaching and learning process is more advanced; and that the students need to be actively processing and integrating information for learning to occur. The focus is changing for the curriculum designers as well. Designers still must analyze the knowledge content, and determine appropriate-size chunks; but designers must also analyze the skills to be developed and incorporate complex real-world problems into the content materials. Seldom will the problems that are at the end of the chapter have easy answers or even any answers at all. Additionally, students may bring applied knowledge to the teaching and learning event that is new to the faculty member. In these cases, the role of the faculty member changes from the font of all knowledge to the mentor who helps to interpret information in the light of the discipline and his/her more comprehensive perspective. For effective learning today, designers must plan for interactive collaborative events among faculty, students, and other resources. The pace of knowledge development may require input from students as well as from the faculty member - especially in the applied fields.

Infrastructure

One possible definition of infrastructure is that it is the set of technologies in an environment that supports the mission of an institution. In the early generations of distance learning the infrastructure requirements for student support consisted of what we now view as fairly straightforward technologies - the postal service, radio, television, and audiocassettes. The list of infrastructure requirements for distance learning programs based on computers, computer networking, databases of digital information, the Internet is daunting. EDUCOM, a consortium of universities and companies formed to support the building of a networking infrastructure for research and learning, launched a new initiative in 1993 called the National Learning Infrastructure Initiative. This organization has a new goal of defining the components needed for a comprehensive teaching and learning infrastructure, and to form alliances and coalitions to support the development of the components of such an infrastructure.

Curriculum designers must know what resources students will have access to, while designing programs. While designers cannot assume access today for all populations of students, many distance learning programs are moving forward by stating computer and computer network access as a requirement for participating in certain distance learning programs.

CURRICULUM ISSUES

In the light of the changing information environment and consequent changes, one has to think of the issues related to the curriculum as an alteration of syllabuses. However, such change was felt to be relatively slow compared to the changes that would be necessary in a context of greatly increased availability of information and level of global interconnectedness. The issues, which needed to be addressed, were:

- What content is essential? Is content to become more skills-based?
- Is content still based on subject disciplines?
- How can essential content be packaged so students can access knowledge and information in different ways?
- To what extent should syllabus documents specify pedagogy?
- Who decides what content is relevant in syllabuses? Who decides on a day-to-day basis in schools?
- What is the place of Information and Communication Technologies in the curriculum?

These issues would need to be the subject of considerable

research and discussion in order to best inform the decisions of curriculum and other authorities.

CURRICULUM CONTENT

Debate around the extent and nature of essential content to be included in the curriculum was seen as ongoing and subject to a wide range of social, community, political and other pressures, as well as changes in the information and communications environment. It was also noted that there had been a general move in syllabus documents toward an outcomes-based approach. Within this approach, the focus of the syllabuses moves towards required student outcomes rather than the coverage of specific content. A number of student skills were identified, such as the ability to access, analyse and use information and the skills of critical awareness and evaluation of evidence from many sources.

SUBJECT DISCIPLINES

A number of points regarding the future of a curriculum structure and the views expressed included:

- educators tend to be captured by the current discipline boundaries and traditions in which they operate
- cross-disciplinary courses may have lower status and find it hard to justify their place in curriculum
- there are some instances of a breaking down of subject boundaries because the structure of disciplines don't meet student needs
- the structure of information and knowledge and the way in which it is recorded tends to vary across disciplines and thus, different skills and knowledge may be necessary to access this information in different disciplines
- to start with the developmental stages then move to subject outcomes that illustrate each developmental stage. This may lead to more widespread adoption of integrated or other types of approaches.

DELIVERY OF CURRICULUM

Technology can instantly provide information out of context to enable students to make all kinds of comparisons of a kind that in the past weren't possible. However, while computers free up the sequencing of content, the process of learning may have a sequence and some content is a prerequisite to further or higher levels of content. It was felt that material on the conditions that are best for learning in a subject area needed to be to be in syllabus documents for that subject. However, the view was also expressed that the distinction between pedagogy and curriculum must be sustained or else the implication arises that there are designated ways of learning as well as designated things that must be learned. There was also a strong view that curriculum documents must be congruent with the flexibility of learning approaches that the new technologies engendered.

ADVANTAGES OF DISTANCE LEARNING

Students can read from remote place at their convenient time E-mail acts as a communication medium between staff and students Online access to course materials Assignments can be submitted with multimedia capabilities Easily select the relevant portions for reading from the voluminous course material supplied by electronic means Can be edited, modified and sent to others / friends / for own use.

DISADVANTAGES

Students should have Internet / Computer facility for reading at home, when material is received in e-format.

The problems of availability of remote server, when the content is ported on it and the accessibility, cost of learning.

Not possible to have immediate interaction with the teachers for any clarifications.

One has to check regularly e-mail or other communication media for the subject coverage, clarifications, etc.

Availability of full course material at the same time.

CONCLUSION

Traditional distance learning methods mainly use textbooks and other written materials (which replace lecturers), and supply students with varying degrees of individual support (academic and administrative). Under this model, distance learning is essentially self-learning, and requires great will power and self-discipline on the part of the student as well as suitable learning skills. Such studies often suffer from an inferior public image and/or low popularity compared to studies conducted at traditional universities, either due to low-quality academic materials and poor academic control, or because of the difficulty of dealing alone with complex learning materials. With vision one can make wise decisions in terms of technology and in personnel - and in our buildings and program offerings. Each institution has its strengths and its weaknesses and each institution will target future opportunities based on people's visions and energies and opportunities. The needs are great.

REFERENCES

1. Atkins, M.J. – Theories of learning and multimedia applications: an overview. Research papers in Education 1993; V 28 (11), p.13 – 6.
2. Belleer, Michal and Or, Ehud. – The croosroads between lifelong learning and Information Technology: A challenge facing leading Universities. JCMC 1998; V 4 (2).
3. Boettcher, Judith V. – Distance Learning: Looking into the Crystal ball. July 1996.
4. Goodyer, Andrew – Workshop on Information and Communication Technologies and the Curriculum. July 1999, Board of Studies NSW.
5. Hamilton, Mary – Distance Learning: A new spin on traditional library services. University of Southern Mississippi.

30

The Broadband Services :The Emerging Convergence Trend in IT

Y. Venkatesh,

Lecturer,
Department of Studies in Library and Information Science,
University of Mysore,
Manasagangotri,
Mysore.

C.P. Ramasesh

Course Co-ordinator, IT Programmes,
Centre for Information Science & Technology,
Rajiv Gandhi Convention Centre (Senate Bhavan),
Manasagangotri, Mysore.

ABSTRACT

Broadband access is the most sought after by the successful enterprises including educational and R & D sectors across the country. The transmission of voice, images and text will be superfast. A single strand of optic fibre can carry 320 gigabytes of text in a second and the bandwidth is enough to support 60 lakhs of PCs with 56 K Modems, simultaneously hooked to the Web. Competing with the local data circuits of BSNL, the Reliance Infocom have advanced with the project of building a world class digital telecommunications network comparable to the best in the world. The ultimate aim is to create facilities and services for the next generation communication network with terabyte bandwidth capability to match with the needs of emerging technology. Paper explains various aspects of cable network for broadband facilities going to be initiated by Reliance Infocom Ltd., and Zee, a media company, reaching 280 million viewers. Zee has now taken up the task of providing fibre optic network in 26 cities in India. Also launched is the internet access in major cities through coaxial cable network without blocking the existing telephone line, as well as the T.V. channel at home, and at unmatched cost benefit. Broadband services is also being offered through many cable operators.

INTRODUCTION

Reliance Infocom and Zee, leading networking establishments have taken-up the project of building a world-class digital telecommunication network comparable to the best in the world. The main vision is to create facilities and services for the next generation communication network with terabit bandwidth capacity to cater to the needs of the emerging digital economy. This will involve rolling-out a world-class, all optic internet protocol based broadband network.

To overcome the main barriers of internet and telecommunication service providers i.e. 'Last Mile Connectivity' problems and "low bandwidth" bottlenecks, which limits the service offering and reliability of the service provides, Reliance Infocom Ltd., Zee and many other renowned, successful private sector enterprises have come up to offer competitive services for broadband telecommunication network.

Reliance Infocom is in the process of wiring-up of all major commercial, educational, research, industrial and residential buildings to offer the best telecom services. To start with, in the first phase 115 cities of the country will be connected with Fible Optic Network, which will create an information super-highway to the tune of 67,000kms, at the estimated cost of Rs.25,000 crores.

Broadband cabling facilitates communication of voice, images, video, data, textual matter at the rate of 326 Gbps (Gigabytes Per Second). The facilities that can be obtained will be enormous -

Reliable telephone service, High Speed Point-to-Point Connectivity, Internet Data Circuits, Asynchronous Transmission Mode (ATM), Desk Top Video conferencing and many more in this direction.

The Services From Reliance Infocom

Switched Access	Non-Switched Access	Managed Modem
Voice PT	Point-to-Point Private Line	Managed Modem
PBX Interface	Local Area Network & wide Are Network Interconnect	Co-location
Operation & Directory Assistance	Leased line	Managed Networks
Voice Mail	Code Division Multiple Access	
Audio Conferencing		
Toll Free Calling		
CENTREX		
ISDN		
Asynchronous Transmission Mode (ATM)		

By Broadband Telecommunication facility our way of life, work, accomplishments and entertainment is going to be transformed. It is said that the broadband access is most sought after by the successful enterprises/industries and research sector across the country. Needless to say, values of "connected" properties will appreciate. Reliance, Zee Next and such other companies are in the picture and forefront to place your building on the global information superhighway effortlessly. They are competing with each other to bring the future to our door. We have to look forward taking into consideration that we are in the era of "information revolution". They ensure complete control over the quality of services.

One of the important point that we have to bear in mind is that the fibre optic cable has a much larger capacity to carry voice, data and images as compared to the earlier conventional copper telephone cable. A single (light core cable) fibre optic strand can carry 320 gigabytes of text/data in a second, and enough bandwidth to support 60 lakhs of PCs with 56K Modems, simultaneously hooked to the web. Further, the transmission of data / text or for that matter the voice and images will be crystal clear and super fast. The video conferencing and streaming video or audio conferencing and multimedia applications, thus organized on broadband will be distortion-free and the access will be astonishingly expeditious.

Broadband is changing the way we think, act and take decisions. The technology is fast encompassing every city from New York to Tokyo. The requirement at our premises is a space of 100 Sq. Ft. to install the necessary equipment for fibre optic termination and the cost of the OFC. Reliance has offered the cable network facilities to many of the educational and research institutions free of charge, without any legal binding. In case of OFC being provided by the customer, the cost of equipment and installation will be borne by the company. The technical work of installation and the lying of the OFC will be attended to by the professional staff without distorting or causing damage to the already existing cables, wires, if any. Further, there will be no obligation on the part of the customer to subscribe to the services of the company for having provided cable network facilities for broadband services. However, in case the customer desires to avail the services through broadband, then the subscription will come to the picture. It is assured that the prices/charges will be competitive and comparatively low. (compared to the charges of Government organization) (For details see the table in the next page).

ZEE NEXT BROADBAND SERVICES ON COAXIAL CABLE NETWORK

With the convergence of technology, a single network is capable of providing a subscriber multiple services. As of today, Zee reaches 150 million Indians apart from 100 million viewers across 80 countries. Zee Group is now integrated across media value chain, with a major presence in TV programming, films, music, print, broadcasting, internet portals, ISP, cable distribution and many others.

BROADBAND SERVICES

Voice Services	Video Services	Data Services	Management Services
Telephony	Streaming Video	Broadband Internet Bandwidth	End-to-end Network services
ISDN	Video Conferencing	Virtual Private Networks	Back up & Storage Services
National Long Distance	Enhanced Services	Web Hosting & Co-location	Managed Customer
Calling Cards		Application service Provider	Premise Equipment
CENTREX		Messaging	Security services
Integrated Network Services			Load Balancing
Audio Conferencing			

Zee is now in the forefront, transforming itself from mega media player into an integrated, interactive convergence conglomerate, by networking 26 Indian cities with optic fibre. This will allow Zee and its group of companies, Siti Cable and Zee Interactive Multimedia Ltd., to optimize the business potential of network capabilities, offering video, data and eventually voice services to subscribers at low costs, as a full service convergent network.

Zee Interactive Multimedia Ltd., has launched the cable internet access in Bangalore and Delhi, extending it to other cities as well. One can get Internet access, high speed, without blocking the existing telephone line at home. The most important advantage is that the internet access through cable is unmatched cost benefit for those who use internet heavily. Broadband services do not require through and lengthy connection process. Instead, they offer a continuous / persistent connection to the Internet. Sometimes referred to as "always on", that is to say, you are connected to the web whenever your computer is switched on. The only requirement is the connectivity to the local Internet Service Provider (ISP) through any transmission media like cable, ISPN, leased Line etc. The company also gives Virtual Private Network at various layers like physical, data and network layer on the equipment located at the user's premises.

Zee Next service is high speed Internet service that one can get for home on coaxial, cable instead of a phone line. Since coaxial cable is used, one need not bother about his phone line being engaged. Zee Next supports windows '95, windows '98, windows NT 4.0, windows 2000 professional or any operating system on the PC, provided the PC must have an Ethernet card. A cable modem and the necessary components to connect it is essential. Instead of getting Internet connection through telephone line, you have to get a connection through the cable network (cable TV connection). This cable Modem translate radio frequency signals into Internet protocol. What you have to pay is for coaxial cable and cable modem installation. One can turn on TV, as well as access internet - neither the TV nor data signals are affected by simultaneous use.

Broad band services are also being offered by quite a number of commercial firms in many cities. In Mysore City, as of today, there are six private establishments;

Mysore One

Avina Communications

Lan Net

Lamda Communications

V9 Technology Consultants

Intech Pvt. Ltd.,

The effectiveness of the services are comparable both qualitatively and cost wise. The major services that are said to be provided by these firms are;

Internet

E. Commerce

Interactive Games

VOIP

Virtual Private Network

Application Service

CD-ROM based Education Services

Audio Streaming

What is crucial is that the broad band connectivity augments communication of voice, video, data and sound at a high speed.

The table in the next page give the technical details or the descriptors that are commonly used during the installation and service. The different Internet Service Providers are selected for the purpose. VSNL gives internet access an terrestrial data transmitting cable network. Secondly, the software technological parks of India (a Society under Government of India) provides access through Radio frequency waves. Finally, the broad band connectivity being offered

Comparison of Internet Connectivity on Technical Aspects

Sl.No.	Internet Service Providers	Type of Connectivity	Installation Mode	Service Charge Pattern
1	VSNL	Terrestrial Link	BSNL Local Data Circuit	Quarterly rental
2	STPI	Radio Link	Antenna mast & R.F. cable	Quarterly port access and loop maintenance charges
3	Mysore One	Broadband	Coaxial cable & Modem	Quarterly band width charges

from a commercial agency in Mysore namely M/s Mysore One extends Internet access on Coaxial cable network.

Cost-wise Comparison of Internet Service Providers

Sl.No.	ISP	Bandwidth	Registration	Installation	Annual Rent
1.	VSNL	128 k	Rs.20000/-	Rs.100000/-	Rs.760000/-
2.	STPI	128 k	Rs.20000/-	Rs.20000/-	Rs.560000/-
3.	Mysore One	128 k		Rs.25000/-	Rs.135000/-

The first two, VSNL and STPI are Govt. of India establishments. Hence the subscription charges are almost equal. On the other hand, Mysore one, a commercial company which extends broad band service is far cheaper, but the transmission speed at times will be slow and there is no systematic monitoring mechanism. Further, the down time will be more as they have to identify the flaw and rectify it with the assistance of the technical staff.

CONCLUSION

Availing broadband services on voice, data and video definitely transform our lives and the way we take decisions for development. The proposal of Reliance Infocom and Zee Next will definitely be beneficial and will add to the already existing IT infrastructure in any academic and research organizations. In fact, it will strengthen and widen the scope and reliability of the information and communication services. For some of the government and autonomous institutions, Reliance is offering OFC cabling network free of charge, without legal binding. It is certain that many of the academic institutions, including industrial and commercial enterprises can leap forward to seize the opportunity to extend up-to-date and value added services to the public, as well as members of their own organizations. The investment on infrastructure will be high in case of broadband services on OFC networks. However, such of those institutions can depend on local cable operators who extend services on coaxial cables.

REFERENCES

1. Barkely, Scott, Broadband man. New Zealand PC World, Issue No.145, Dec.2001/Jan 2002, pp. 83-88.
2. Balasubramanian, A and Talawar, V.G. : Problems and prospects of internet in newmillennium. *In* : First ASSIST Seminar, Ibid : 290-299.
3. Reaching new heights with backbone connectivity. Bangalore. STPI (Guide).
4. Videsh Sanchar Nigam Ltd., URL :http://www.vsnl.net.in
5. Software Technology Parks of India URL: http://www.soft.net
6. Mysore Libraries Network URL :http://www.mylibnet.org
7. Internet Library for Librarians URL ***http://www.itcompany.com/infortriver***

31

Importance of Search and Retrieval in CD-ROM Full Text Publishing: Experiments using PDF Documents and 'Nitya' Archival System

K.H. Hussain,
Documentation Officer,
Kerala Forest Research Institute,
Peechi.

R. Raman Nair,
Former Librarian,
Kerala Agricultural University.

K. Raveendran Asari,
Head,
Department of Medical Documentation,
Mahatma Gandhi University,
Kottayam.

ABSTRACT

CD-ROM has indispensable role to play in the dissemination of electronic information. Full Text archiving and publishing in CD-ROM have already found a special place in the rapidly growing digital libraries. Many of full text CD-ROM titles are coming with thousands of document files, but without efficient retrieval facilities. Paper discusses the growing importance of CD-ROM publishing and the necessity of providing efficient search mechanism in full text CDs. 'Nitya' is a program for digital archiving giving prime importance to search and retrieval. It is highly suited for CD-ROM full text publishing.

As information technologies associated with CD, Web and Multi-media are making rapid advances, Electronic Publishing opens hitherto unknown areas in presenting, expressing and propagating ideas. Digital libraries are becoming a reality faster than librarians have dreamed or dreaded. No live library system can disregard these developments.

CD-ROMS IN DIGITAL LIBRARIES

Few years back CD-ROM had been looked as a 'transient technology', in the hope that web technology would ultimately take over CD-ROMs. However, rise in number of commercial and technical CD-ROM titles shows that it has a big future. CD-ROM collections in the libraries are getting thicker day by day. Concept of 'paperless library' is now equated with CD-ROM Library. Its role in digital library will become more prominent with the spread of DVDs in coming years.

CD-ROM titles can be mainly categorized in to three:

1. Multimedia presentations: Audio and video CDs are produced in millions and becoming the most popular products of entertainments.
2. Indexing and abstracting services. e.g. 'Tree-CD' by Commonwealth Agricultural Bureau (CAB), AGRIS by FAO, etc.
3. Full text CDs: Though more and more digital libraries are created and made available through Internet, CD-ROM full text publishing is also flourishing. CD-ROMs are ideal for publishing reference works. Encyclopedia Britannica is now available in three CDs. Full texts of research reports and scientific papers on topics of academic interest are now a days collected and published in CDs. e.g. 'Solid Waste Management' by Environmental Protection Agency (EPA, USA)..

Now a days any thing that is electronic / digital are put in

CD, calling them 'Electronic Publishing'. Standards are yet to be evolved for electronic publishing, especially for CD-ROM publishing. Indexing and Abstracting services in CD are published with excellent search engines. 'WinSpirs', a retrieval package developed by SilverPlatter is considered to be one of the finest search engines. It is used to produce important abstracting databases in CDs, such as CAB Abstratcs, AGRICOLA, AGRIS, etc.

FULL TEXT CDS

Since CDs hold huge store of information, full text CDs resemble collections in special libraries. Strong similarities exist in between collection inside a library and a CD. While even a few hundred books are shelved in a library applying cataloguing and classification, thousands of document files are put in CD without applying proper documentation methods. Most of the CDs with full text are mere stack of thousands of files. This makes many full text CDs some thing like black- holes, where enormous quantity of information is roaming around inside with out finding a way to the out side world of information seekers.

Most of Full Text CDs are coming with a hypertext file, in which hundreds of titles are loosely classified under some categories. These titles are hyper linked with the original full text file, clicking upon which the full text is opened. In-depth free text search is impossible and users should be content with the categories provided. One has to browse all the titles under a category to get the needed one. If the title is inter-disciplinary, it may not be there in the category he is looking under. In some CDs of conference proceedings, thousands of papers are scattered under different sections. Looking for a particular title often becomes a formidable task.

In some CDs an index made of title words / key words are provided and hyper linked with the full text file. Here in-depth search is possible. However, the static nature of the index limits the search, since free combination of key words cannot be tried for retrieval.

Above cases underlines the need for alternate retrieval

mechanisms in CD-ROM full text publishing. The dynamism of electronic media should fully be utilized in bringing out usable digital collections in CD by providing efficient free text search facilities. Such full text CDs are mass-produced by first developing a digital archive of document collections and creating a master CD.

DIGITAL ARCHIVING

Digital archiving constitutes one of the main components of digital libraries. It adds value and saves time while extending the hours of access. It reduces the need for proximity to information resources, but still emphasizes the quality of those resources. It is a library that can be individually customized and, ultimately, will be easy to use.

When Johannes Gutenberg of Germany invented the art of printing during the 1440s, the trend was to convert every manuscript into printed form. Microfilming technique helped to convert at least archival materials like old books, library catalogues, journals and newspapers into microform. What is prevalent at present is conversion of printed documents into digital form.

One can now easily scan thousands of printed pages and put in hard disk/CDs. More than thirty thousand word-processed pages can be stored in one CD. Although, several packages are in vogue for materializing digital archives, they lack efficient search mechanism. Devoid of a search mechanism, digital storage mediums will remain as dump places of information, just the same way as documents converted into microform. The full potential of digital archiving can be exploited only if selective access is made possible. 'Nitya' succeeds in achieving this goal.

NITYA ARCHIVES

Nitya is an interface between CDS/ISIS by UNESCO and Adobe Acrobat. Nitya combines high-level text compaction technique and highly sophisticated free text search. The most outstanding aspect of Nitya is that any piece of information can be retrieved from a huge store of information within seconds.

Main objectives of Nitya are:

* It is meant for fast search and retrieval of digitized documents
* It is for creating stand alone Digital Archives.
* It is ideal for CD-ROM Full Text publishing.

Nitya has got two components. One is a collection of PDF documents created by Adobe Acrobat. Second is a database describing document elements using CDS/ISIS

ADOBE ACROBAT

Acrobat is a brilliant e-Paper solution that converts scanned pages to PDF (Portable Document Format) documents. Conversion keeps all the page lay out features intact and compresses the file sizes to minimum. PDF files can be subjected to OCR.

Adobe Acrobat provides many hypertext facilities to make the documents 'navigatable'. 'Book marking' is the most out standing one, which is made by headings of chapters and sections. This functions as a Table of Contents and clicking the bookmarks will open pages of respective chapters/ sections.

PDF documents have got many advantages over word-processed and scanned pages:

* Acrobat Reader is freely available and can be freely distributed to view PDF documents. Different 'pages views' are available and any part of the text/image can be magnified up to 1600 percentage.
* Different kinds of hyper links can be constructed easily.
* Acrobat retains lay out features of original pages and keeps the historicity of the document.

FEATURES OF NITYA

Nitya offers full functionality of windows. It only takes a few seconds to install. When it is opened it shows distinct areas for Dictionary, Query and Bibliographic exhibits. Dictionary contains searchable terms arranged under different categories such as subject, author, general topics, etc. Number of categories depends on the type and characteristics of the collection. (For example, categories of an archive of palm leaf manuscripts may be author, title, leaf no., first line, subject, etc, where as categories of an archive of theses may be the researcher, guide, departments, university, subject, etc). Search terms from the dictionary can be selected by a fewalphabetical strokes. Clicking in the dictionary, terms are transferred to 'Query' area. Queries are formulated using Boolean/ proximity operators (OR, AND, NOT, *, NEAR). Queries are submitted to search and results are first exhibited in minimum details and then in full bibliographic details. When the 'Full Text' button is clicked, the full text is opened in Acrobat Reader and there after the document is navigated using book marks and other hyperlinks.

CONCLUSION

Unlimited number of documents can be digitized, stored and retrieved using Nitya Archives. Old books, manuscripts in palm leaves, research reports, conference proceedings, parliament/ legislative proceedings, theses/dissertations, government orders, journals, newspaper clippings, etc can be made in to digital archives and published in CD ROMs. Retrieval of a document is accomplished in seconds and thus Nitya solves many of the problems information access in CD-ROM Full Text Publishing.

Consultancy and training of 'Nitya' is undertaken by CIRD (Center for Informatics Research and Development, Thiruvananthapuram). CIRD is a group of professional librarians engaged in developing techniques for library automations. It aims transfer of technology to professional librarians, archivists and electronic publishers for digital archiving and CD-ROM publishing.

(For further details on Nitya and CIRD consultancy please visit the web site: cirdindia.org)

REFERENCES

1. Breeding, M. Does the web spell doom for CD and DVD? Computers in Libraries. 19(10) 1999: 70-77.

2. Gopinath, M.A. CD-ROM technology and its impact on Library and information science. *In*: Devarajan, G. (ed.). Progress in information technology. New Delhi. Ess Ess Publications, 1996: 115-128.

3. Hasan, M; Muktiar Sing; Sharma, A.R. CD-ROM: A powerful media for information packing, retrieval and dissemination. *In:* Parthan, S. (ed.). Proceedings of the National Conference on Information Management in e-Libraries, 26-27 February 2002, IIT, Kharagpur. Allied Publishers Limited, New Delhi: 67-73.

4. Mishra, R. CD_ROM: A medium of electronic publishing. *In:* Sardan, J.L. (ed.) Library vision 2010: Indian libraries and librarianship in retrospect and prospect. Seminar papers, 45th All India Library Conference, 23-26 December 1999, Hisar, CCS Haryana Agricultural Library: 316-320.

5. Neena Sing. CD Technologies and libraries. *In:* Vyas, S.D. (ed.). Excellence in Information Technology. Dr. S.P. Sood Festschriff. Raj Publishing House, 2000: 124-131.

6. Ravindran Asari, K.; Hussain, K.H. and Raman Nair, P. Nitya archives: Innovative blending of Techniques for selective Access to Information from Digitally Organised Text (SAIDOT) *In:* Parthan, S. (ed.). Proceedings of the National Conference on Information Management in e-Libraries, 26-27 February 2002, IIT, Kharagpur. Allied Publishers Limited, New Delhi : 275-285.

7. Vijayakumar, J.K; Manju Das. CD-ROM to DVD-ROM: A new era in electronic publishing of databases and multimedia reference source. IASLIC Bulletin 45(2) 2000:49-54.

Index